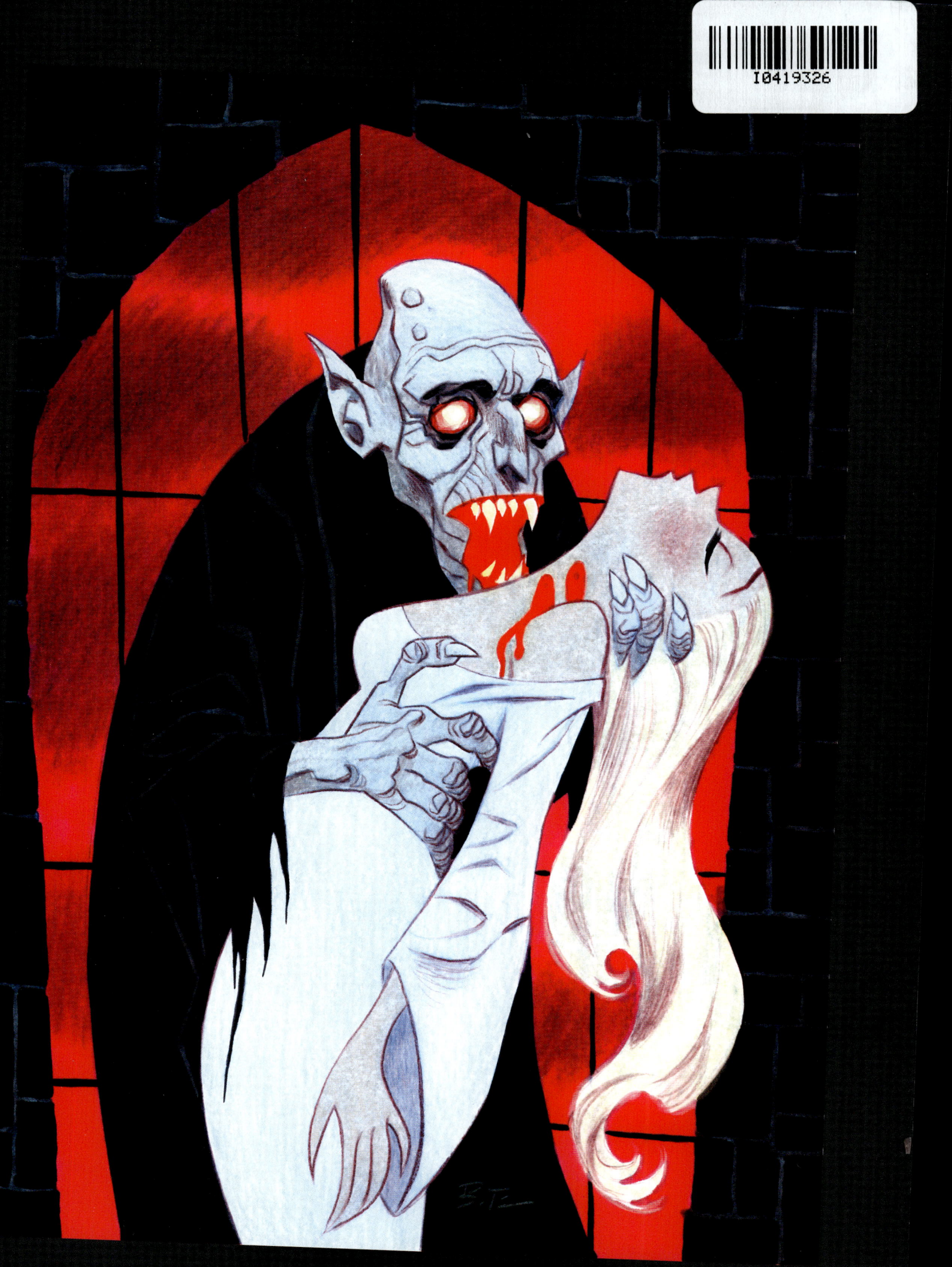

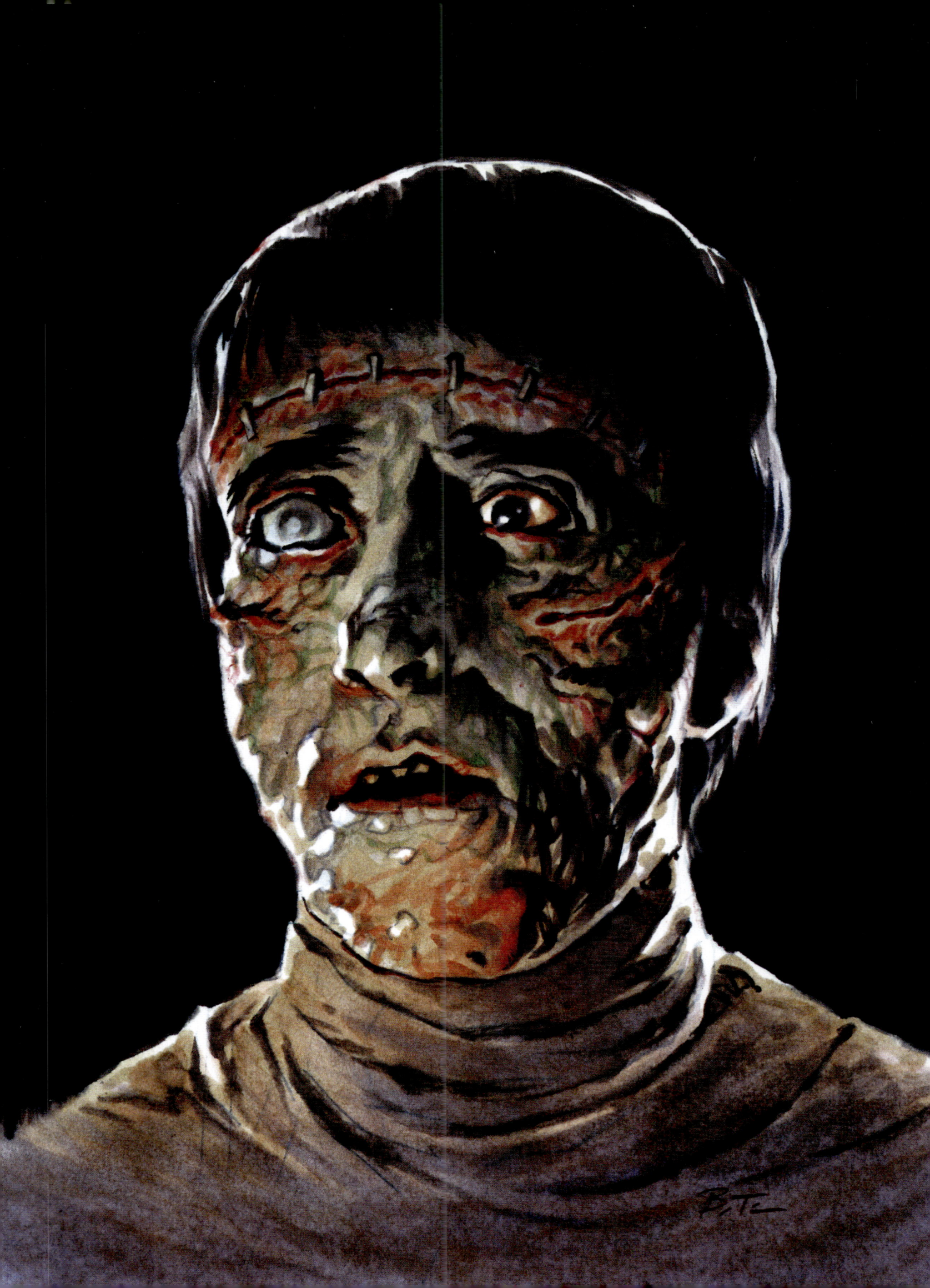

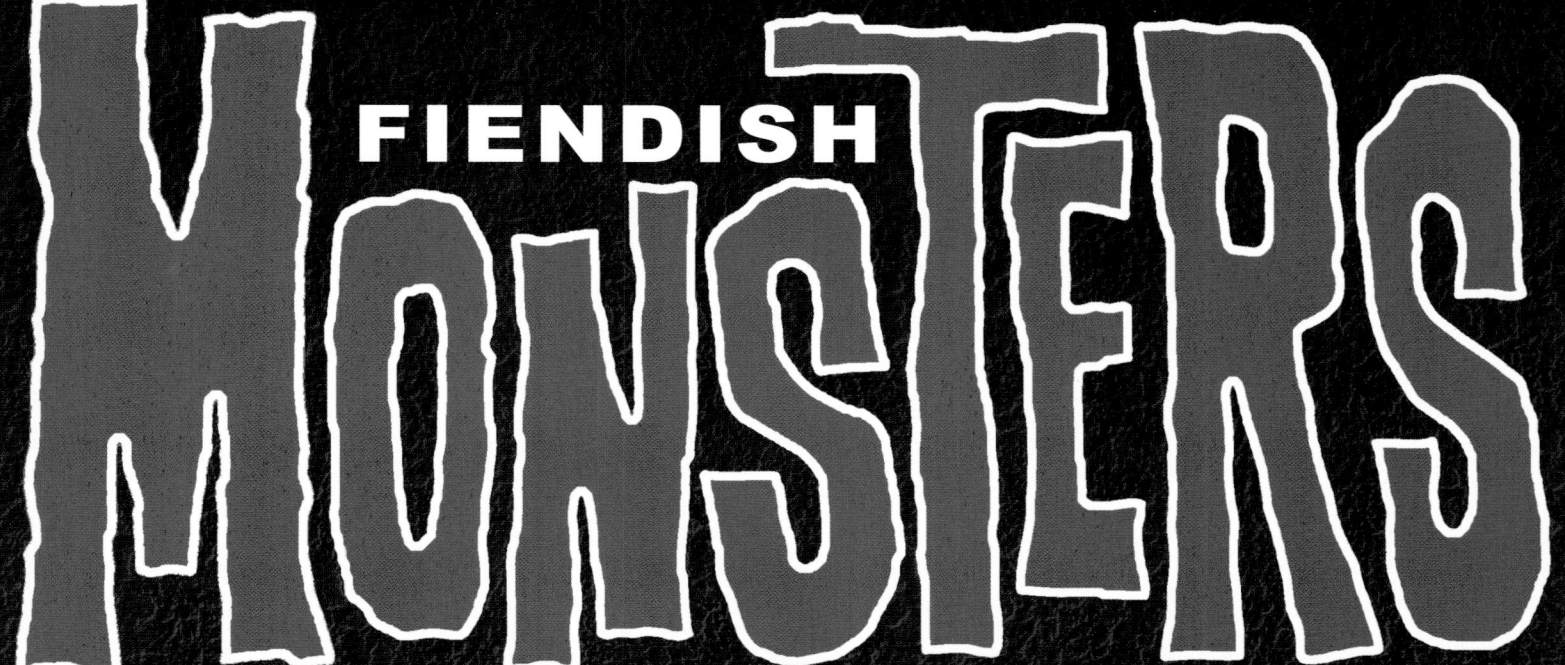

FIENDISH MONSTERS

THE HORROR ART OF BRUCE TIMM

FLESK

SPINE-TINGLERS

Monster Kids of a certain age relish the memory of being scared silly by Dan Curtis' *Trilogy of Terror* on ABC's *Movie of the Week* back in 1975, especially the sequence where Karen Black gets chased around her apartment by a knife-wielding Zuni fetish doll. At one point, my pal Dick Klemensen was planning to do a special issue of his magazine *Little Shoppe of Horrors* focused on the various Richard Matheson/Dan Curtis TV movies (*Trilogy of Terror*, *The Night Stalker*, etc), but for some reason or other it didn't happen. I did the piece on the opposite page before his plans changed and had fun drawing it anyway.

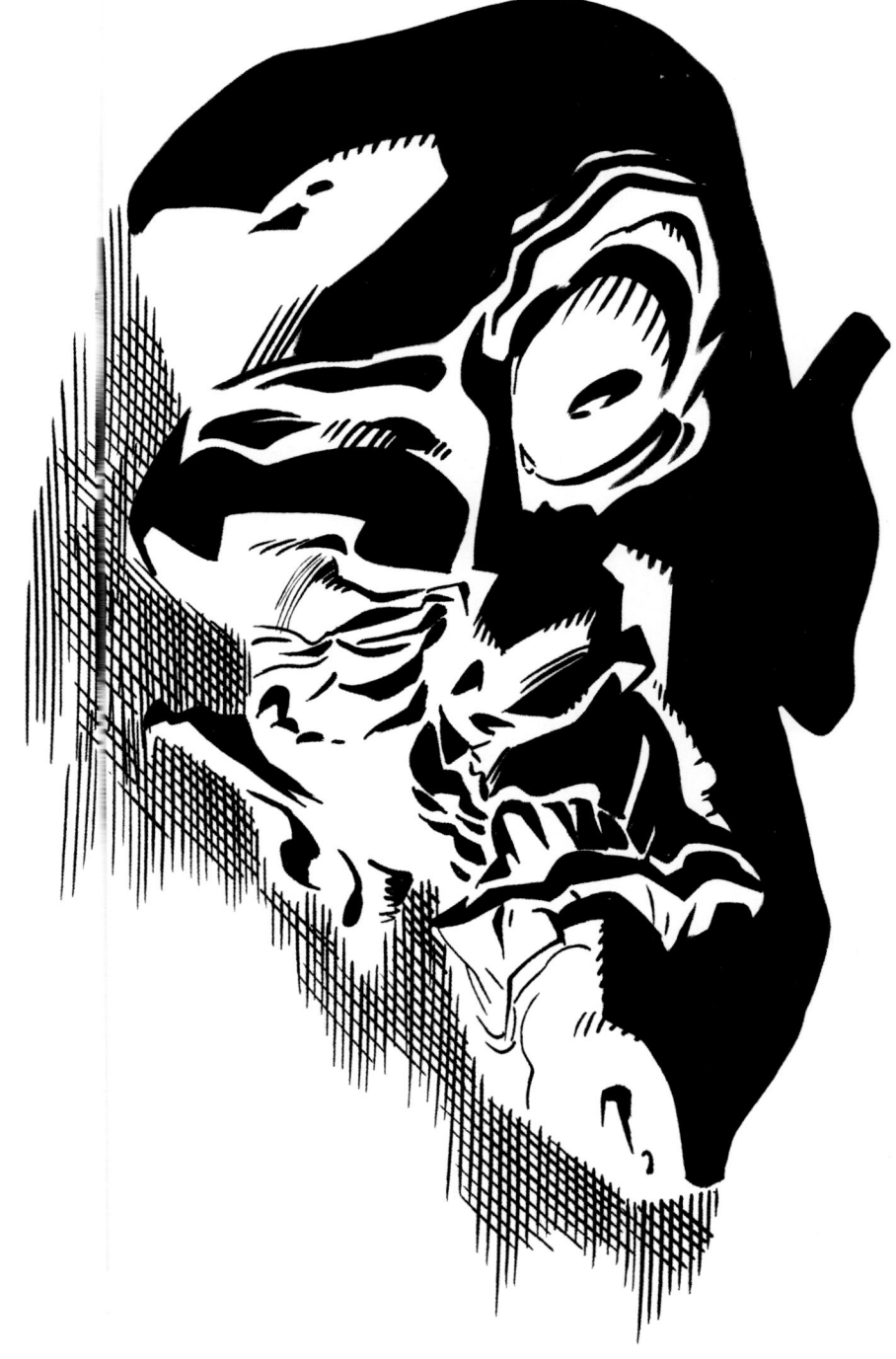

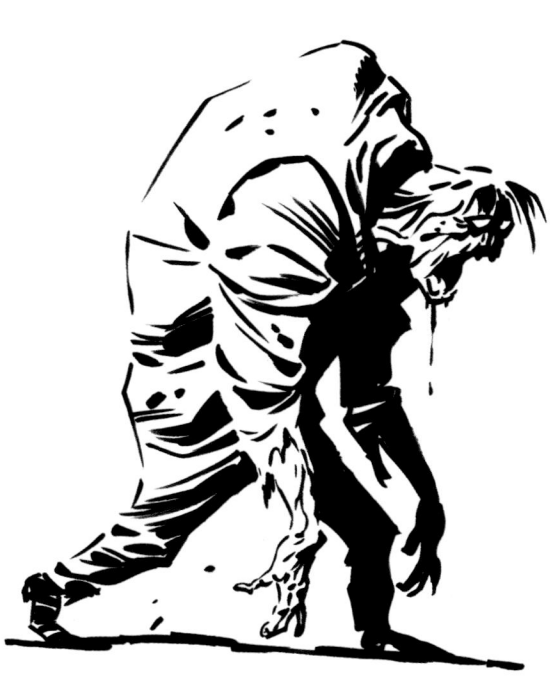

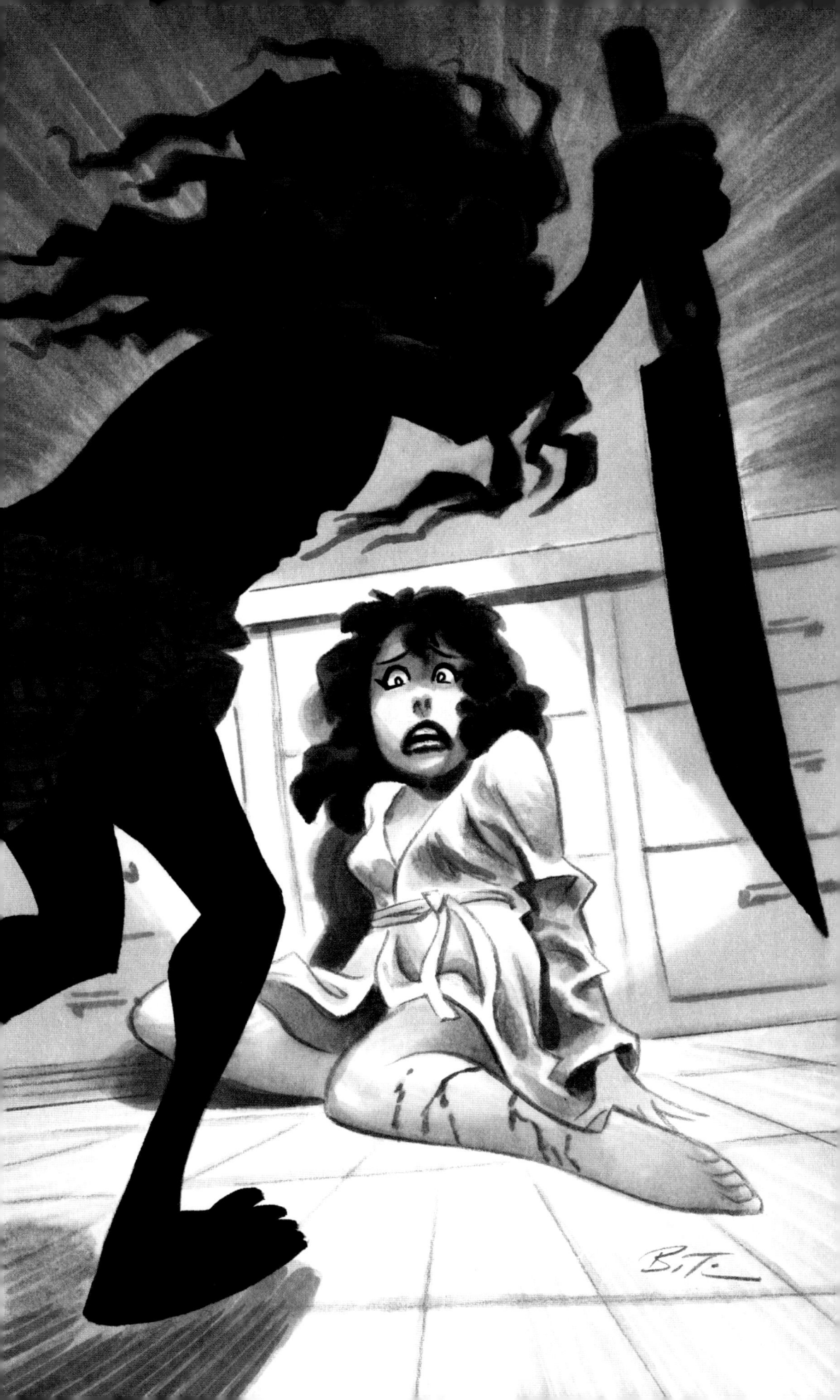

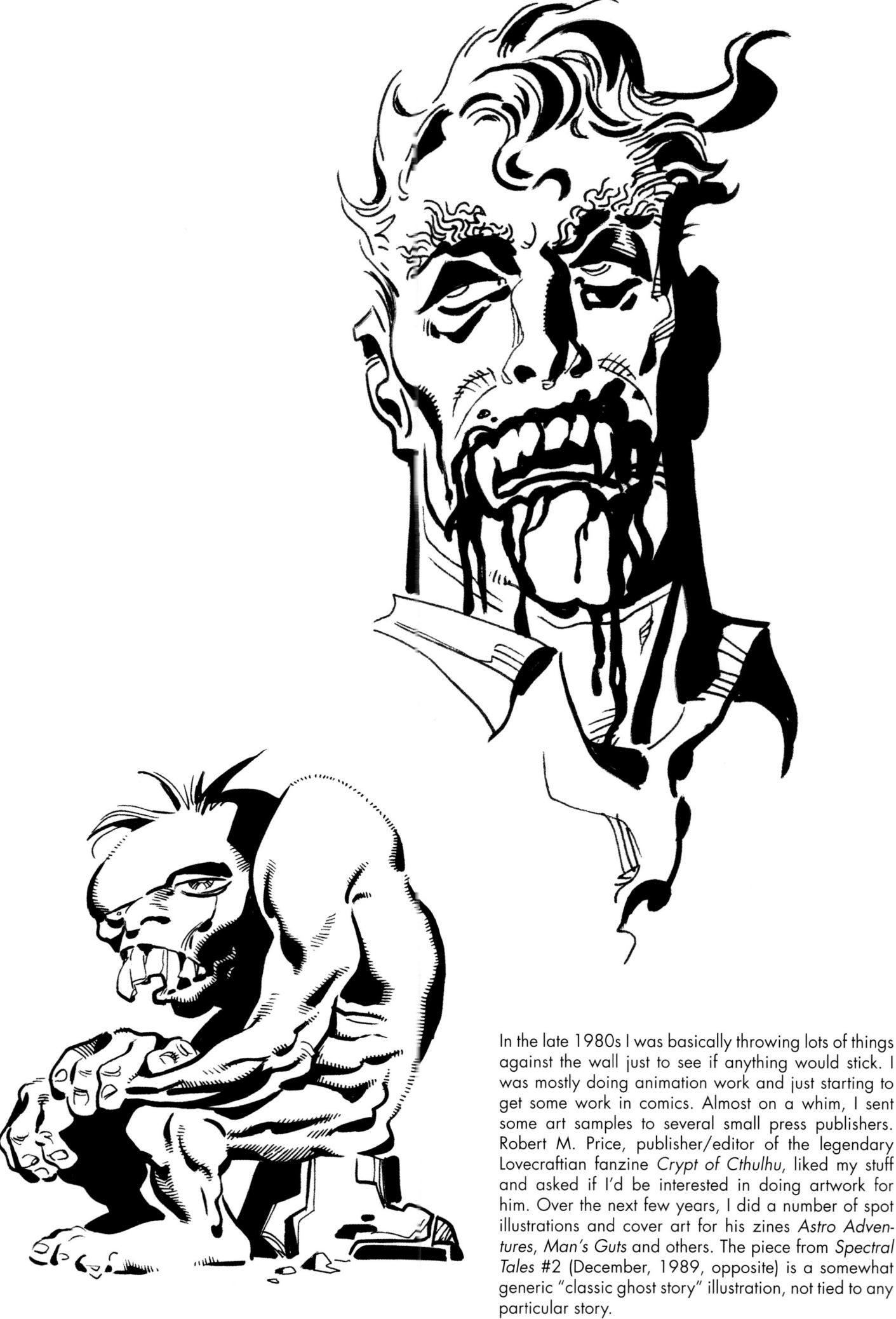

In the late 1980s I was basically throwing lots of things against the wall just to see if anything would stick. I was mostly doing animation work and just starting to get some work in comics. Almost on a whim, I sent some art samples to several small press publishers. Robert M. Price, publisher/editor of the legendary Lovecraftian fanzine *Crypt of Cthulhu*, liked my stuff and asked if I'd be interested in doing artwork for him. Over the next few years, I did a number of spot illustrations and cover art for his zines *Astro Adventures*, *Man's Guts* and others. The piece from *Spectral Tales* #2 (December, 1989, opposite) is a somewhat generic "classic ghost story" illustration, not tied to any particular story.

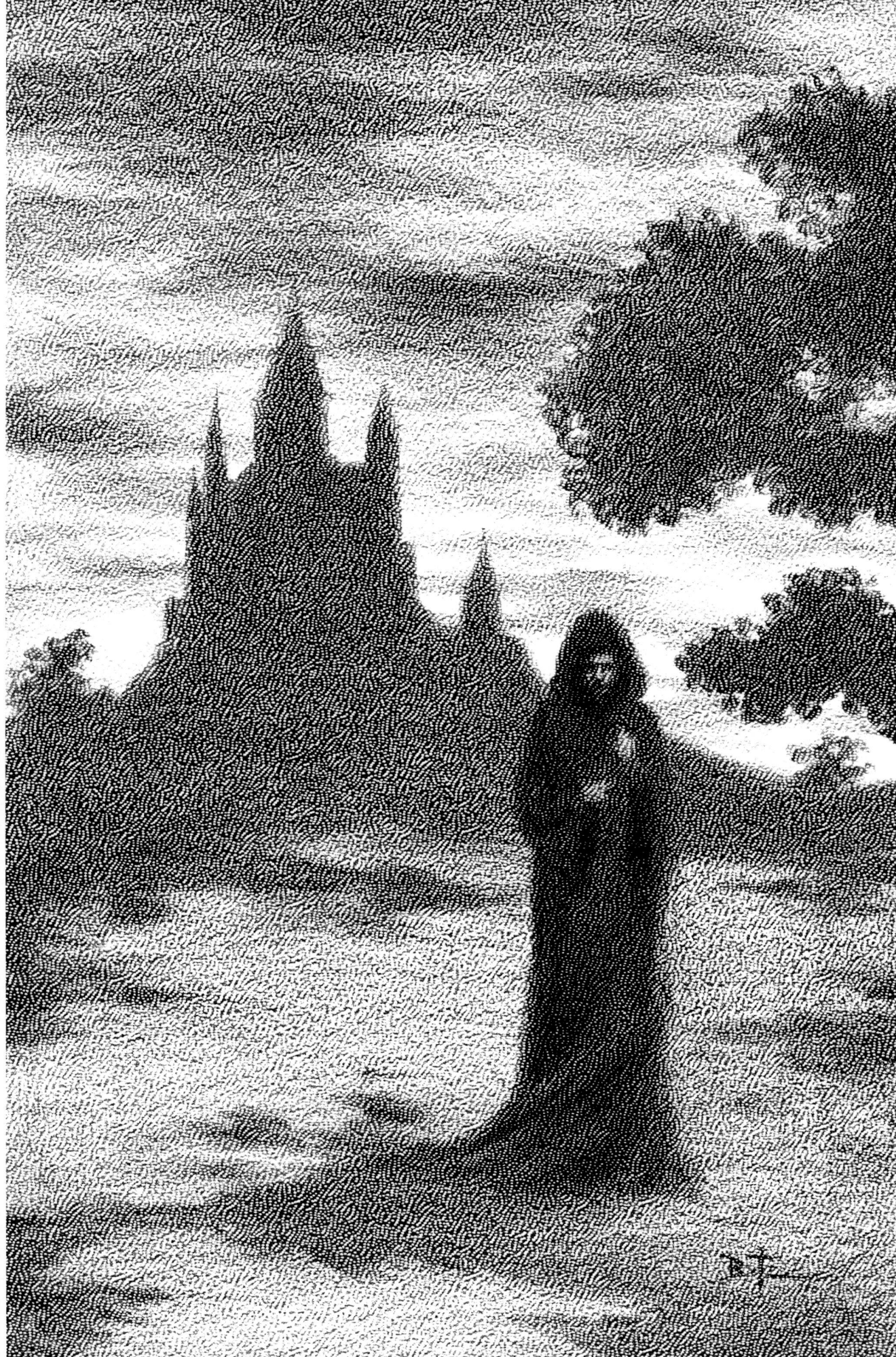

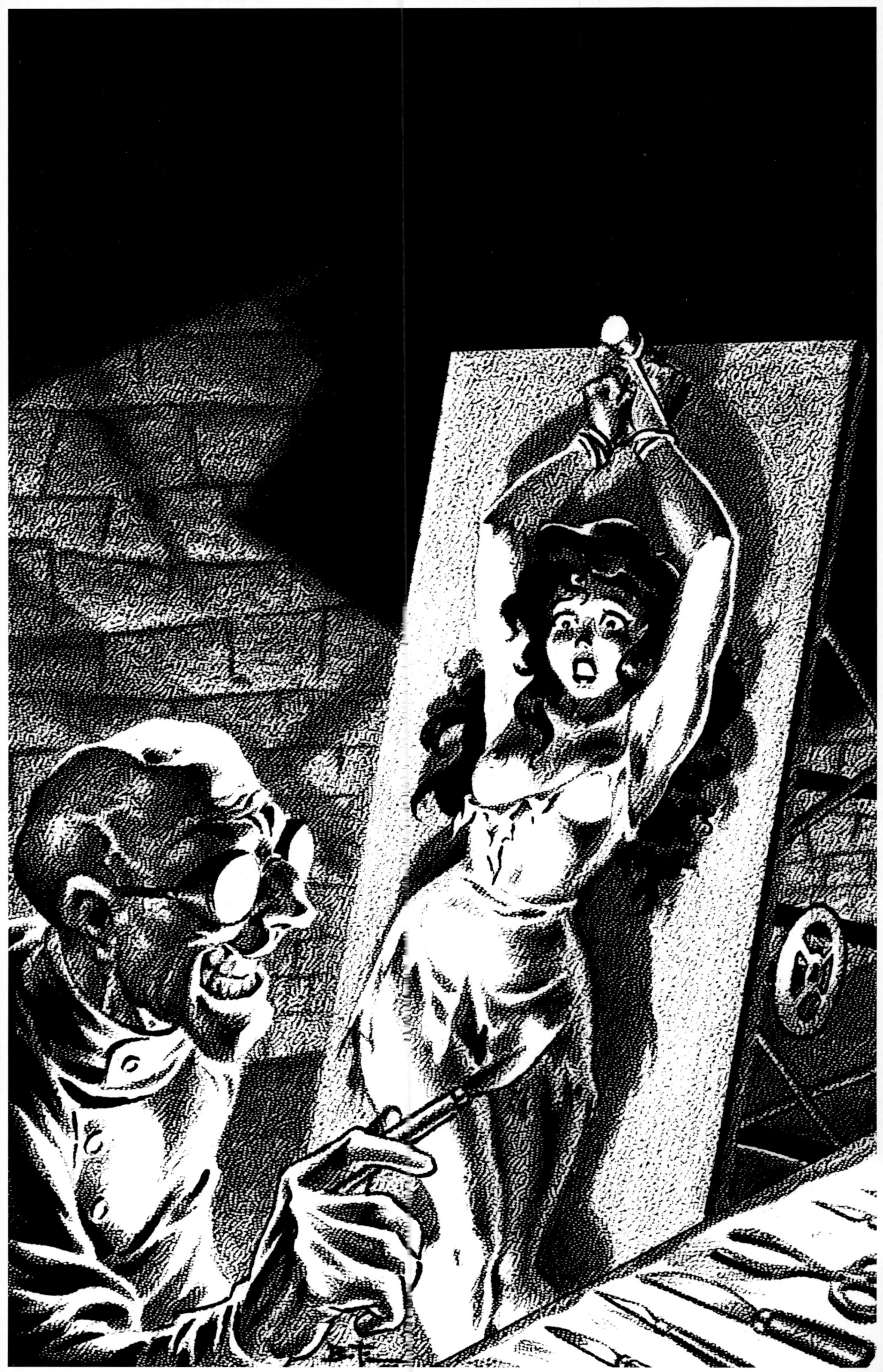

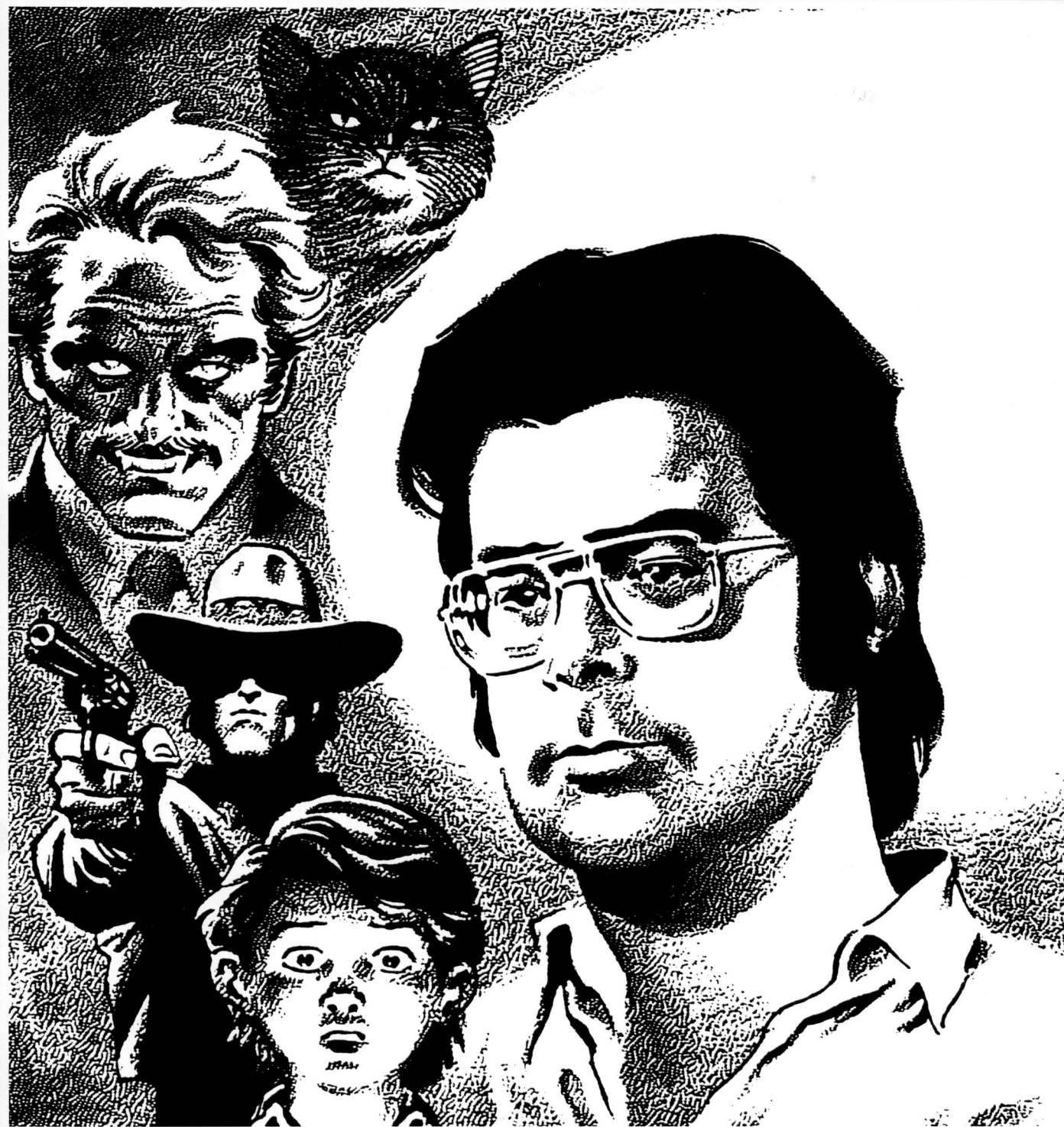

This is the inside front cover to *Pulp Magazine* #1 (opposite), another of Bob Price's Cryptic Publications. As you might guess from the title, it was something of a "pulp fiction grab-bag," not devoted to any one genre. It had a little bit of everything. Just for kicks, I decided to do a classic "Weird Menace" piece.

The piece above was done for a company called Starmont House. The publisher was a longtime science-fiction fan/editor named T.E. "Ted" Dikty. In the '80s he was doing pulp reprint collections and a variety of nonfiction reference works. He had a whole series of readers' guides to the works of science-fiction and fantasy authors like Isaac Asimov and Fritz Lieber. Many of those had really nice covers by Stephen Fabian.

Ted asked me to do this piece for a readers' guide to the works of Stephen King. I don't believe it was ever published, but I don't remember why. This is me trying to imitate Fabian's coquille-board technique.

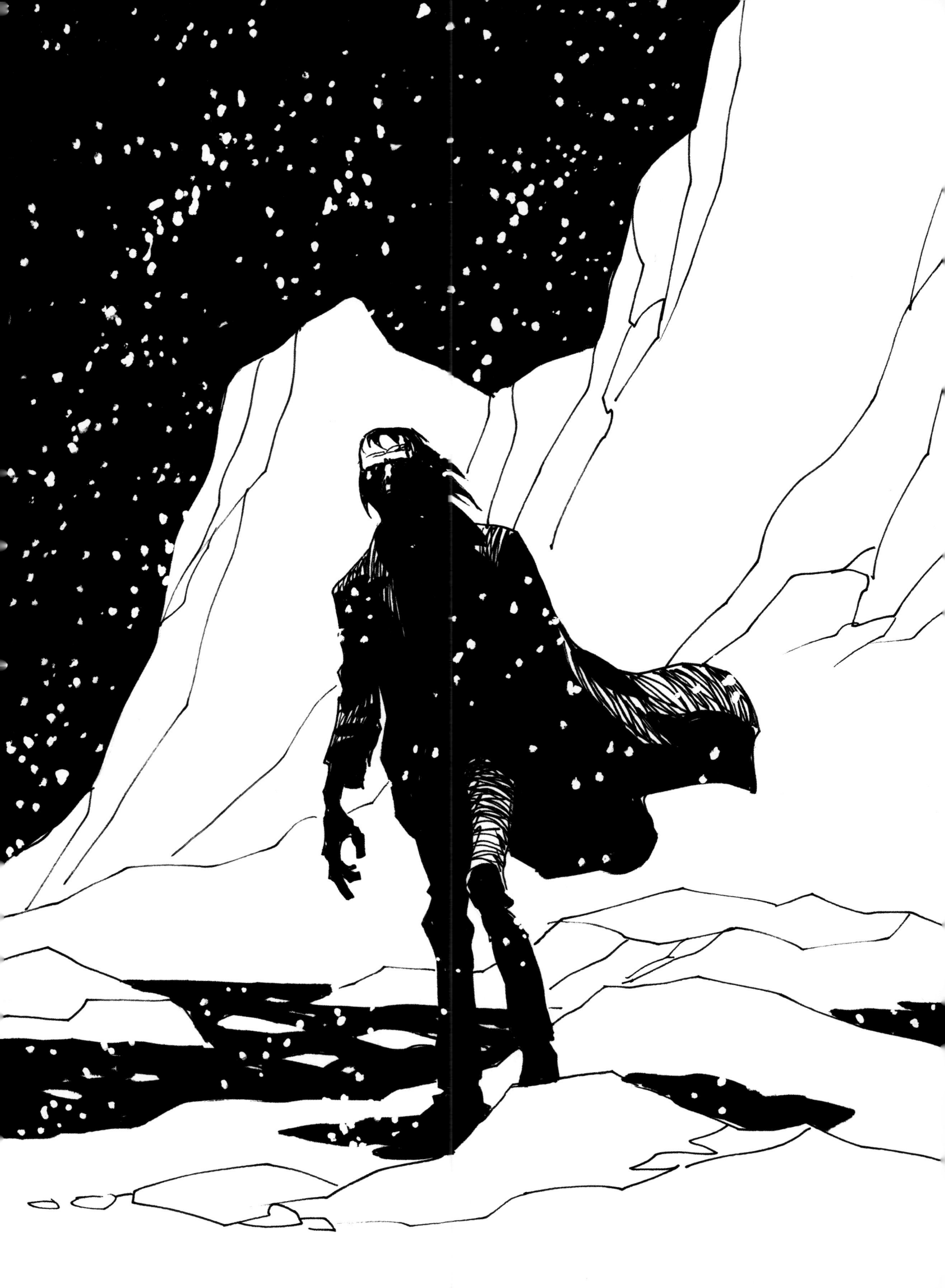

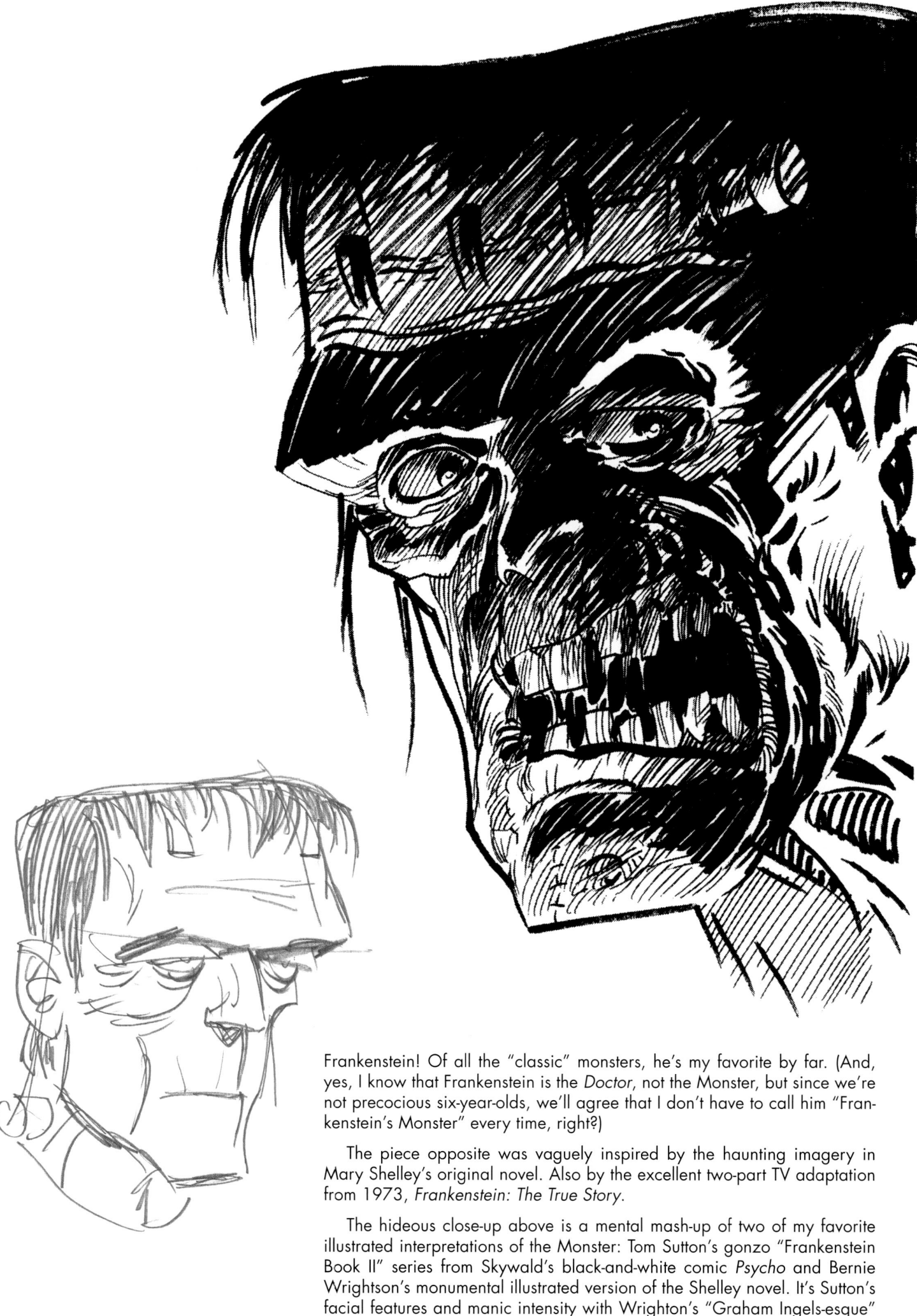

Frankenstein! Of all the "classic" monsters, he's my favorite by far. (And, yes, I know that Frankenstein is the *Doctor*, not the Monster, but since we're not precocious six-year-olds, we'll agree that I don't have to call him "Frankenstein's Monster" every time, right?)

The piece opposite was vaguely inspired by the haunting imagery in Mary Shelley's original novel. Also by the excellent two-part TV adaptation from 1973, *Frankenstein: The True Story*.

The hideous close-up above is a mental mash-up of two of my favorite illustrated interpretations of the Monster: Tom Sutton's gonzo "Frankenstein Book II" series from Skywald's black-and-white comic *Psycho* and Bernie Wrighton's monumental illustrated version of the Shelley novel. It's Sutton's facial features and manic intensity with Wrighton's "Graham Ingels-esque" rendering on top. Kinda.

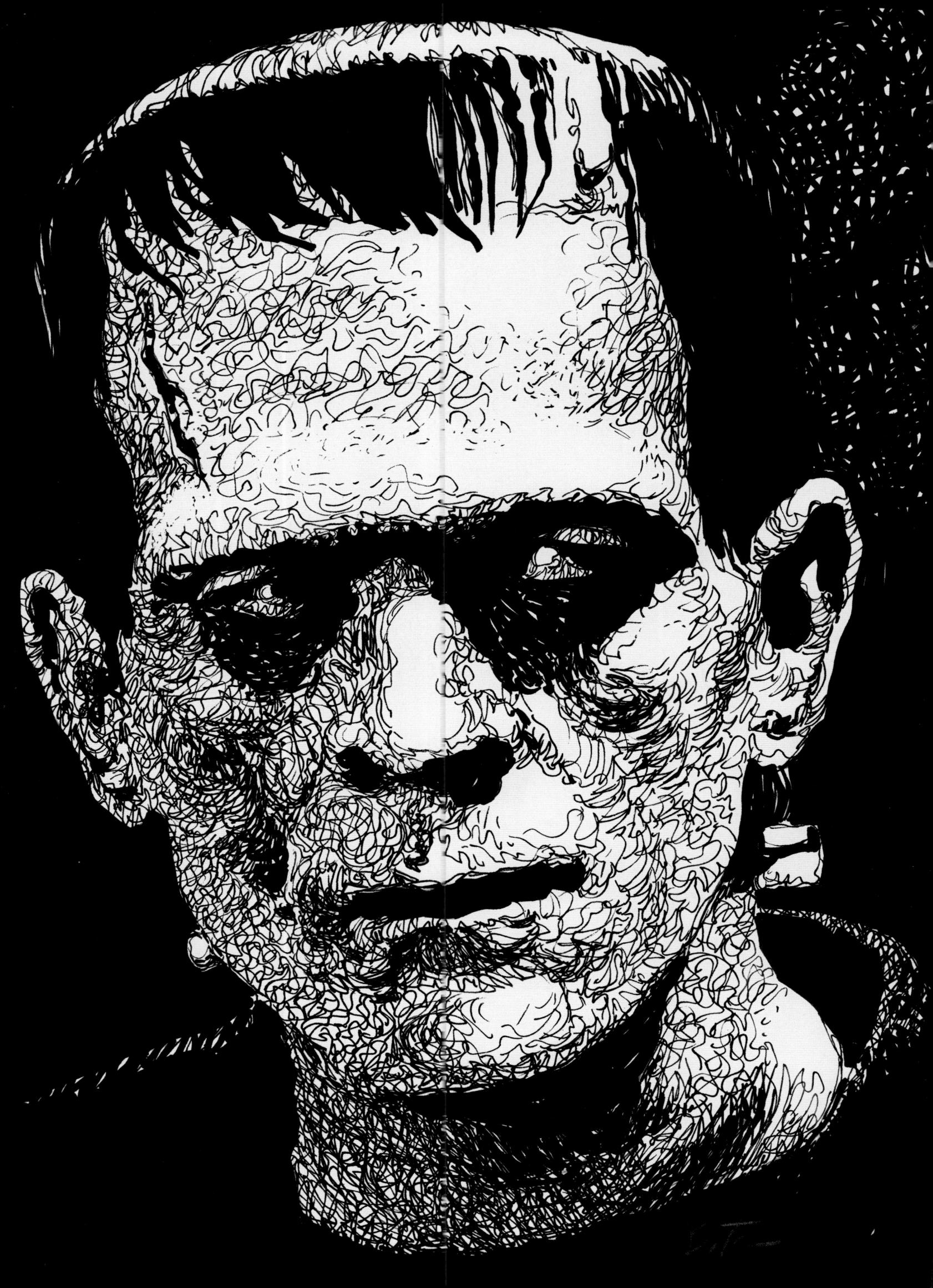

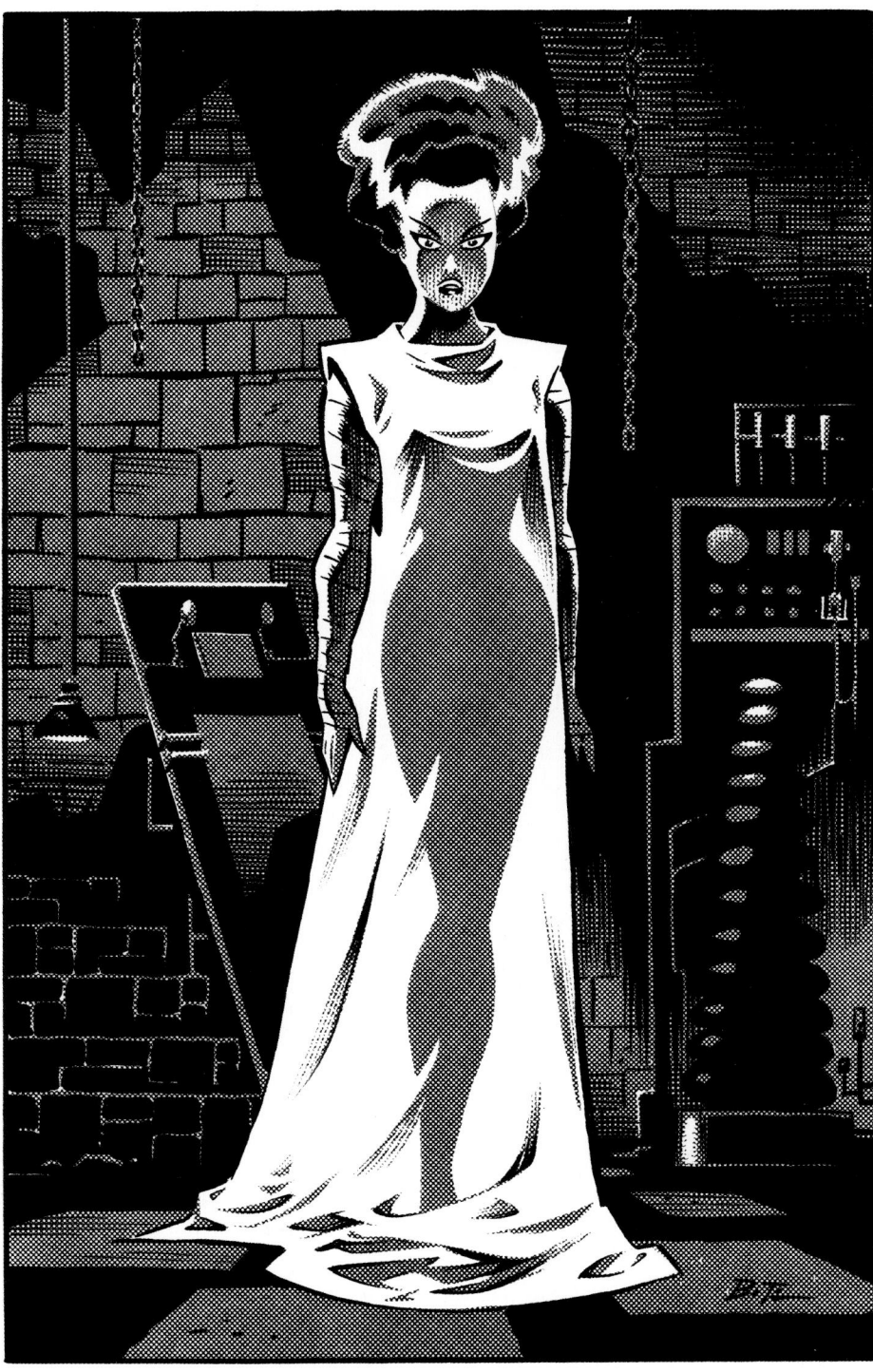

I'm a huge fan of the various Spanish artists whose lush, illustrative black-and-white artwork appeared in the Warren comics in the 1970s and '80s: Esteban Maroto, José Ortiz, Leopold Sánchez and many others. The portrait of Karloff's Monster (opposite) was subconsciously inspired by the spontaneous rendering techniques in the black-and-white work of Fernando Fernandez.

The "Bride" piece above was done around the time that Mike Mignola was writing and drawing his early *Hellboy* stories. The overall style of this piece doesn't really look anything like his, but I remember consciously thinking about the way he would break things up into these weird abstract shapes, like in the shadows on that back wall. When I look at this piece now, I'm mostly just struck by how insanely complicated that "fake Zip-A-Tone" technique was to execute. I think it looks pretty cool—but, *man*, what a pain in the ass …!

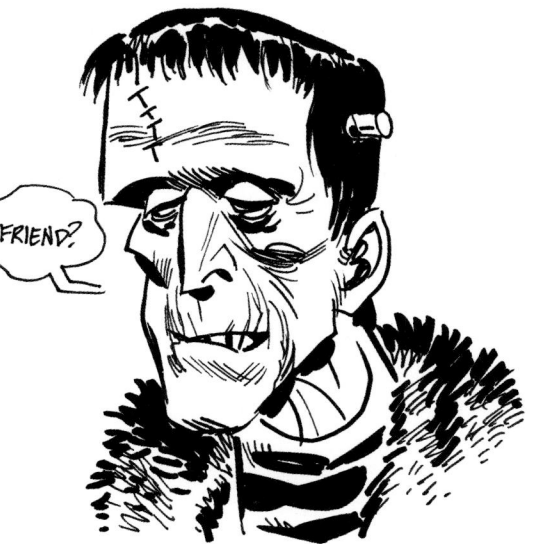

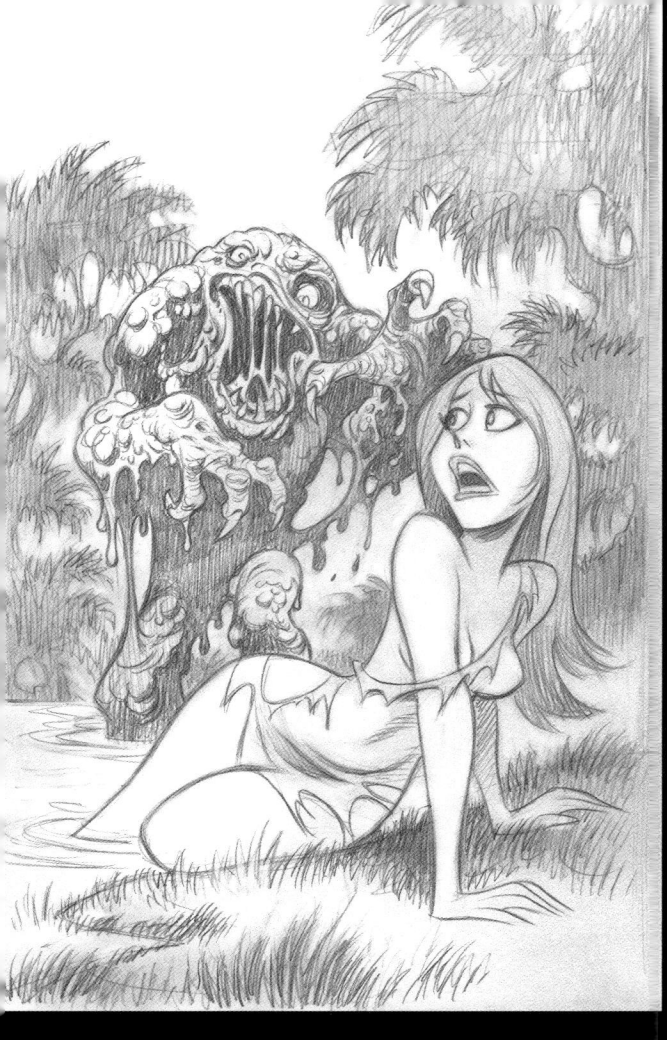

This was done for the cover of the *Monsters and Dames* charity art book (Emerald City Comic Con, 2013). It's an homage-slash-parody of the old Marvel black-and-white horror comics like *Monsters Unleashed*, *Vampire Tales*, etc. Previously seen in *The Big Tease* with my hand-drawn Gaspar Saladino-ish logo and nutty '70s-style trade dress and blurbs ("IT CAME FROM SATAN'S TOILET!"), which my font expert pal Peter Girardi executed to groovy perfection. This time around, we thought it might be nice to see it *au naturel*.

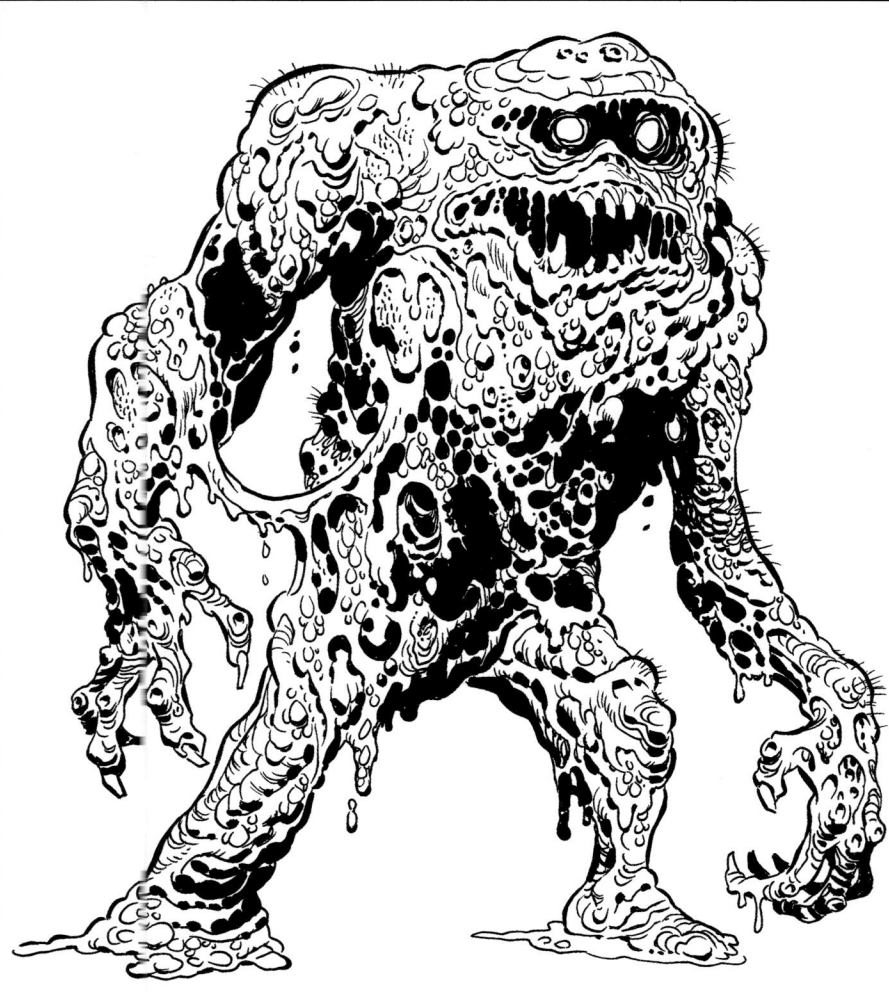

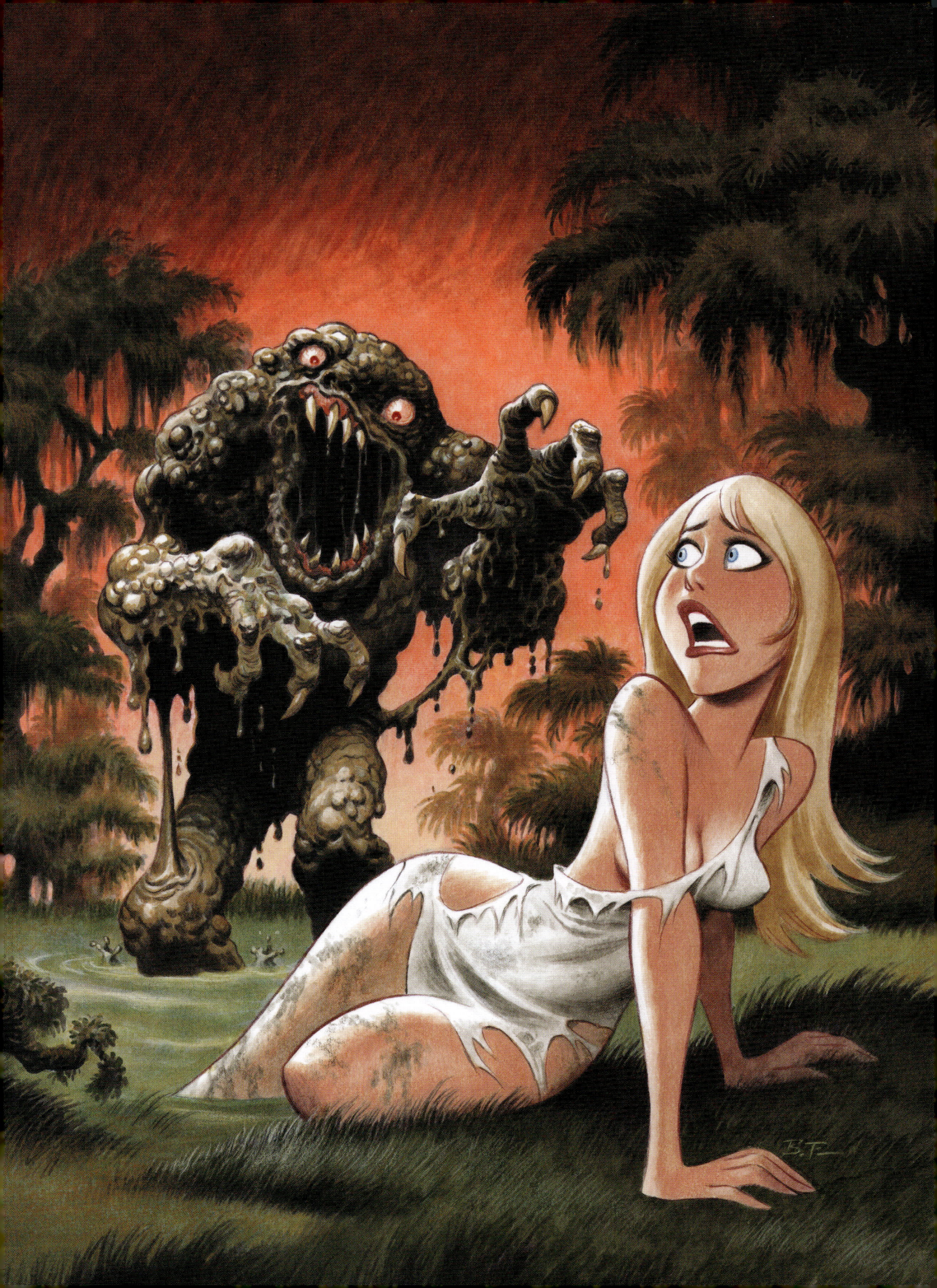

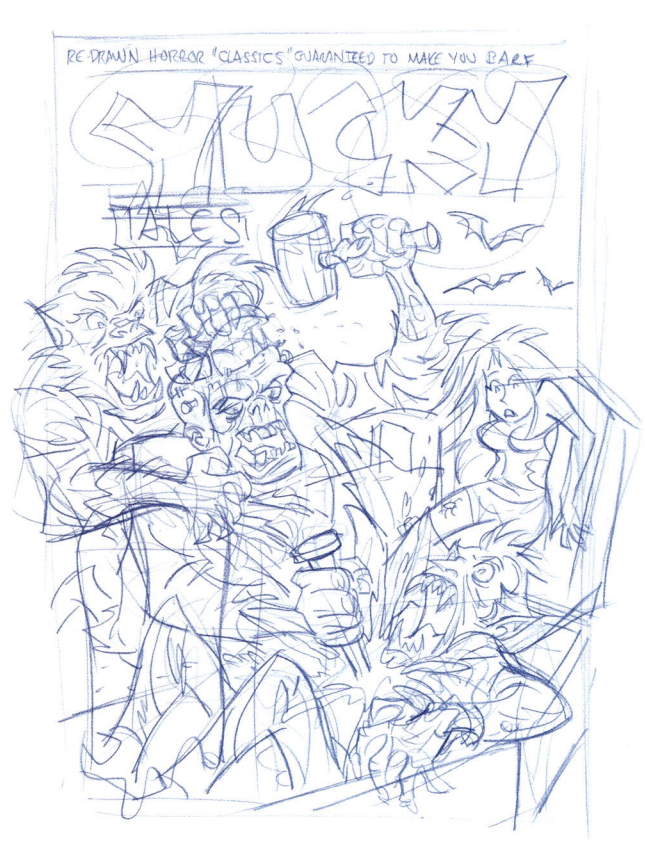

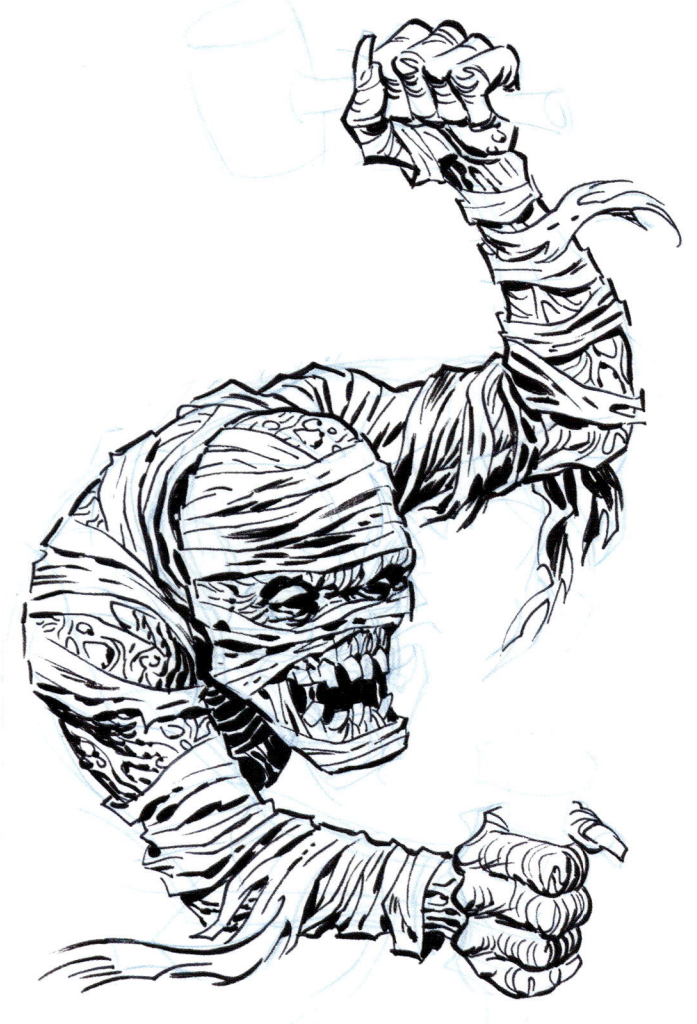

This was intended for the 2013 *Monsters and Dames* charity art book. After finishing the color version, I decided it wasn't quite right.

It's a takeoff on the notoriously gory and horrifying Eerie Publications magazines (*Terror Tales*, *Weird*, *Witches' Tales*, etc.) They were easily the most grotesque black-and-white comics on the market in the '60s and '70s. The covers were outrageous masterpieces of utterly appalling imagery—mangled body parts spilling gallons of blood, disheveled ladies in filthy, torn-up clothes being molested by monsters—all rendered without an ounce of restraint or "Good Taste." I'd see these things on newsstands while hunting for the latest issue of *Creepy* or *Vampirella* or *Savage Sword of Conan* but could never bring myself to buy a copy. They were just too gnarly!

Now, of course, as a grown-up, I kind of like them. Well, maybe "like" isn't quite the right word! But I do get a queasy kick out of how gleefully horrible they are.

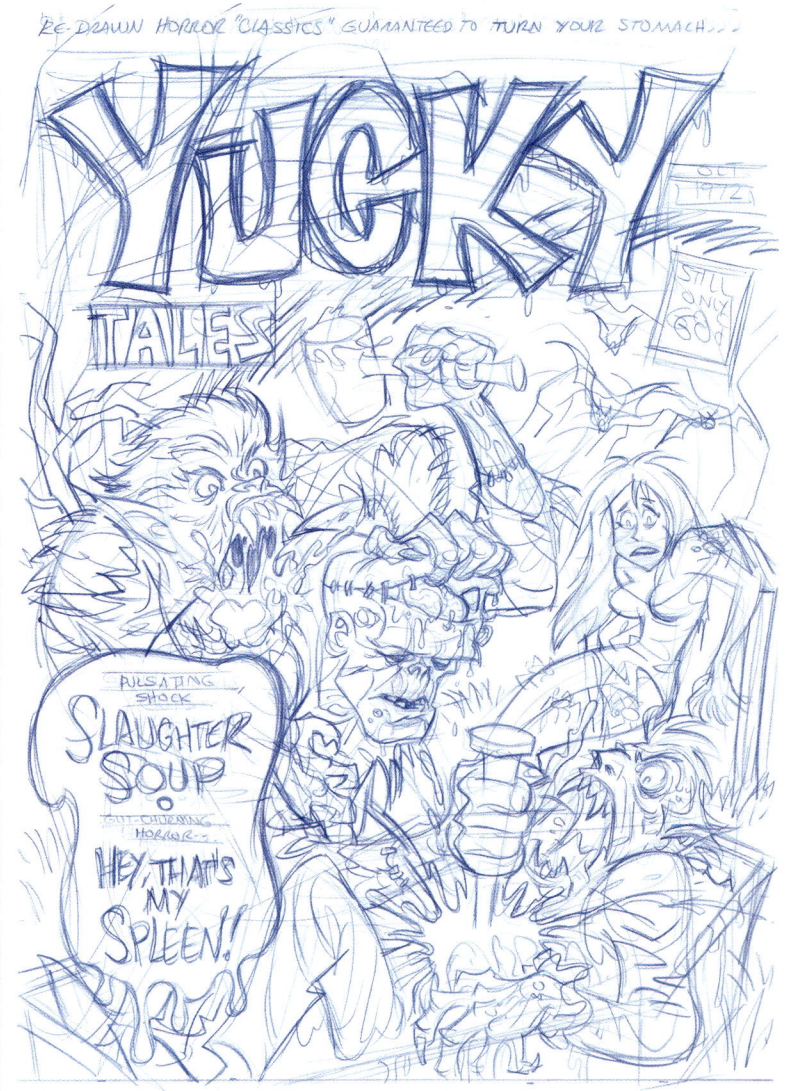

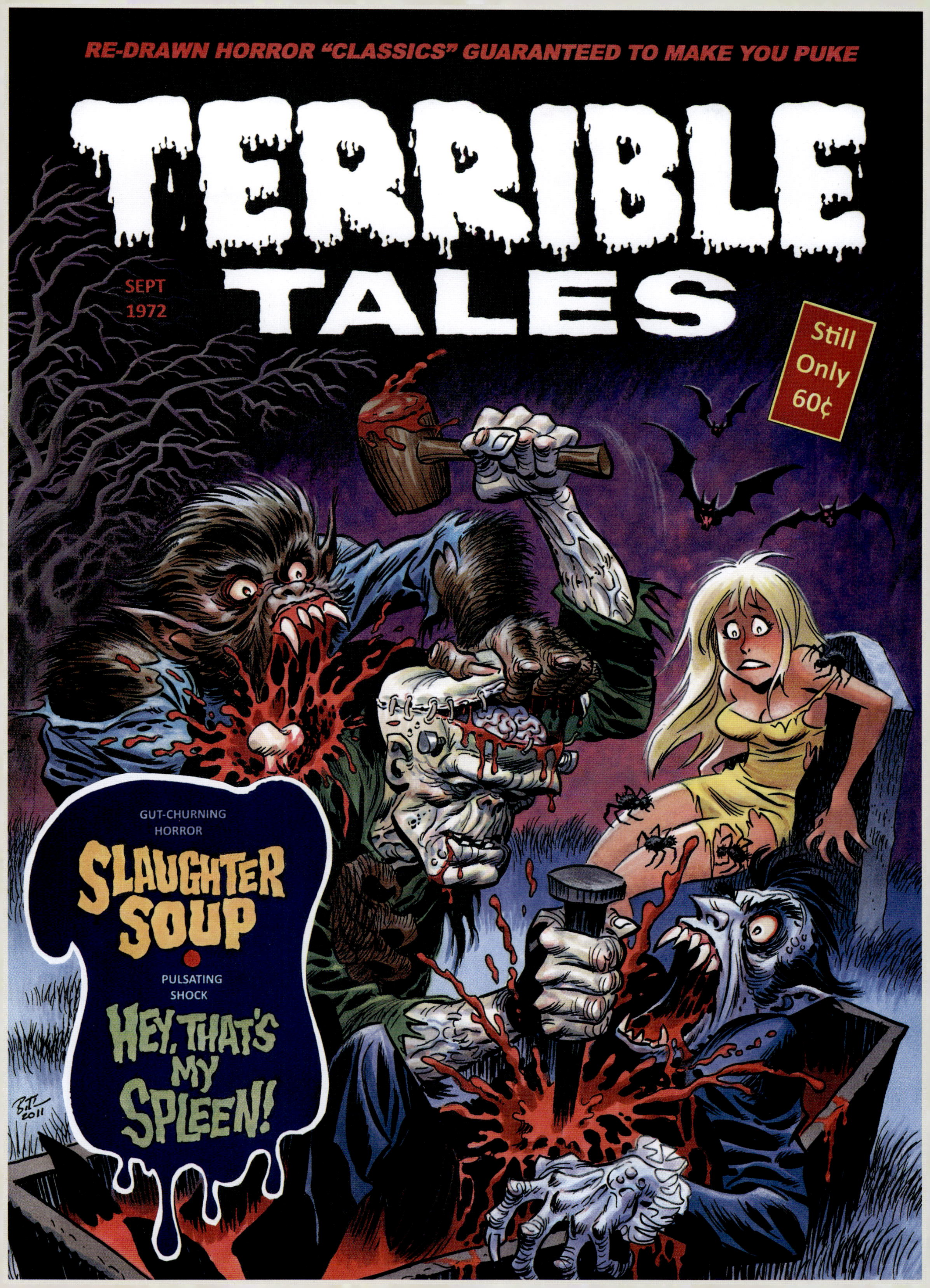
RE-DRAWN HORROR "CLASSICS" GUARANTEED TO MAKE YOU PUKE
TERRIBLE TALES
SEPT 1972
Still Only 60¢
GUT-CHURNING HORROR
SLAUGHTER SOUP
PULSATING SHOCK
HEY, THAT'S MY SPLEEN!
2011

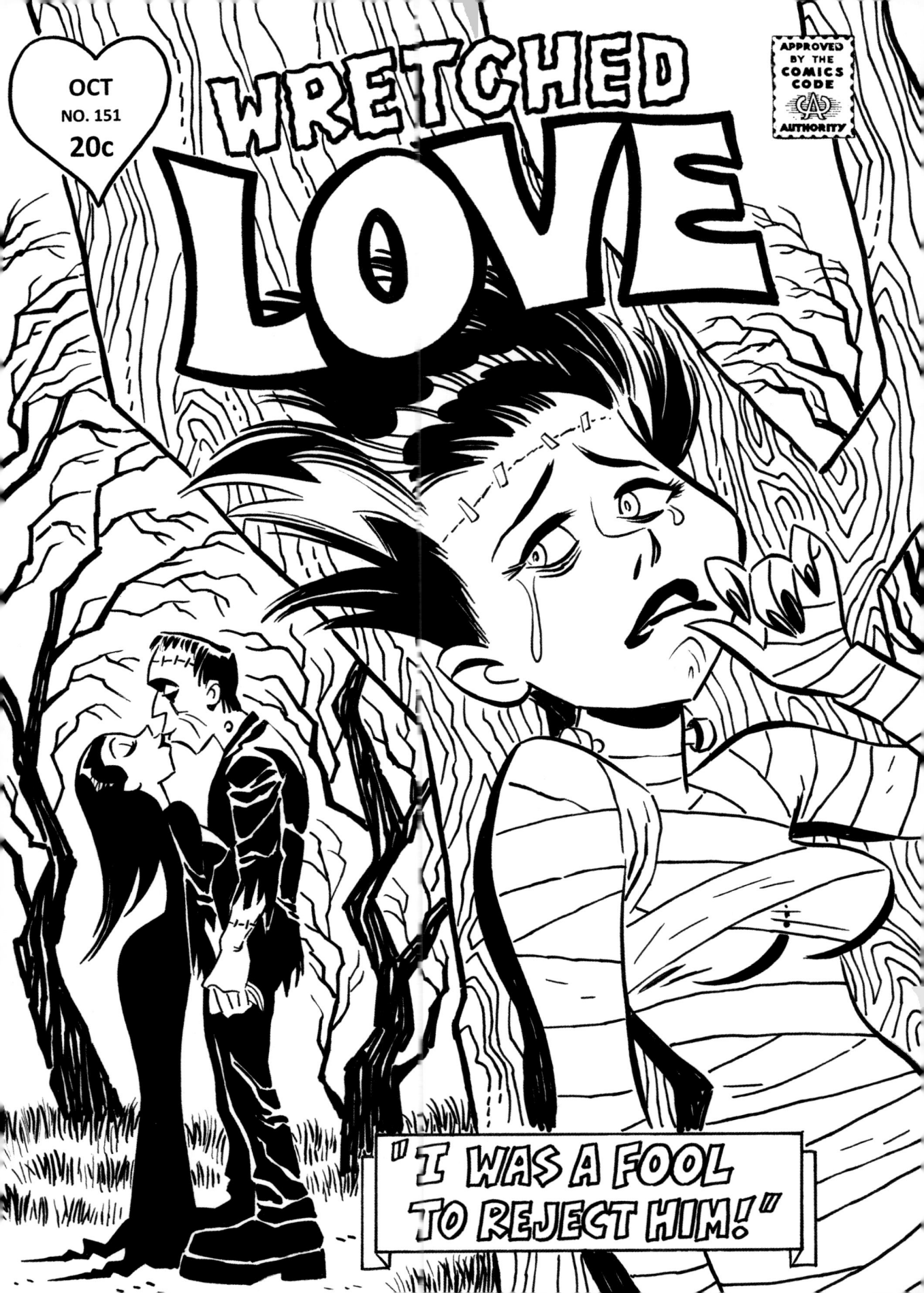

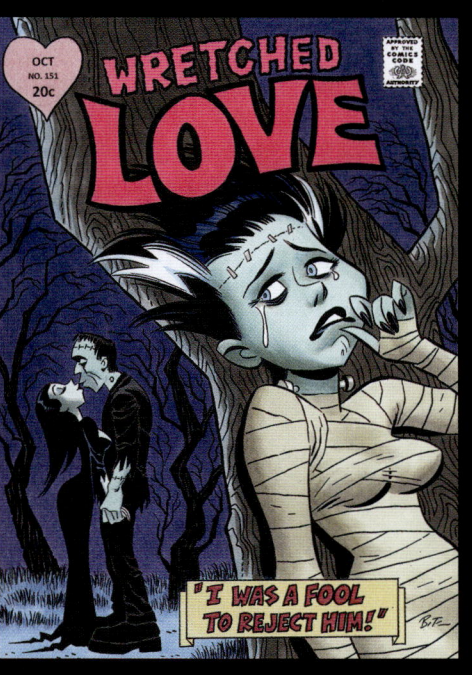

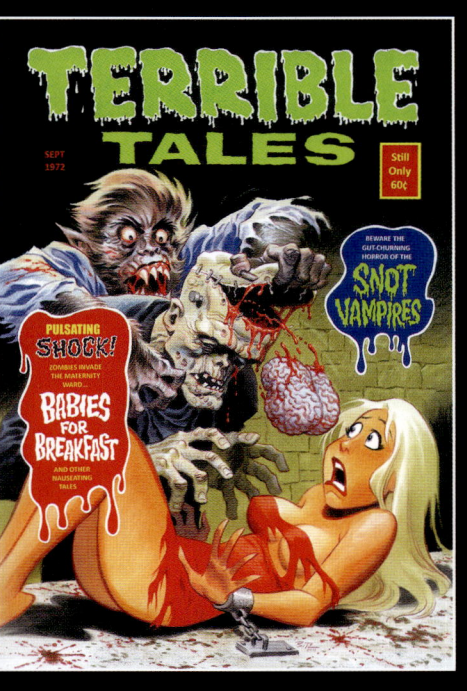

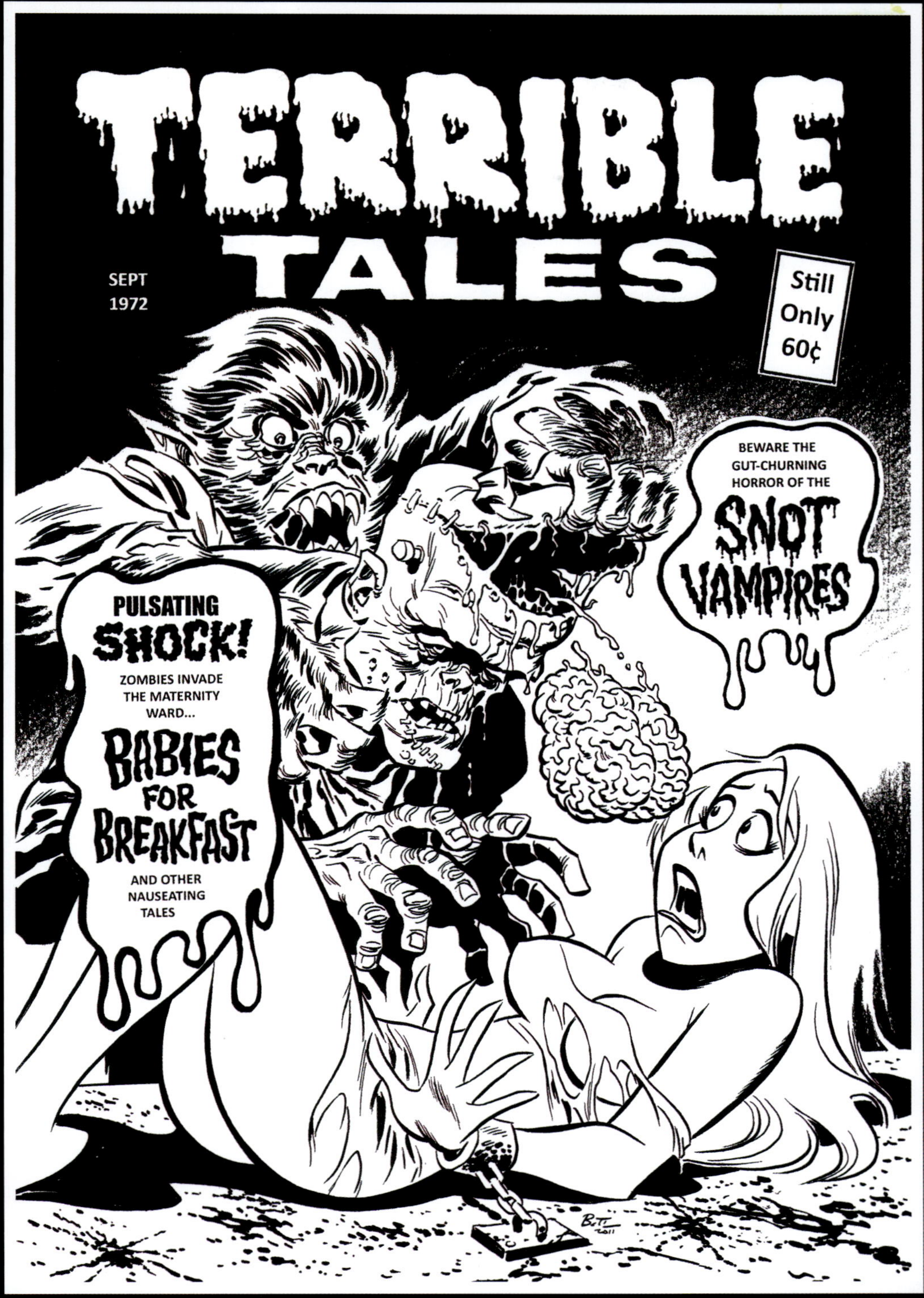

These *Wretched Love* pieces are "work in progress" variants of a monochrome piece that was published in the 2011 *Monsters and Dames* art book. That version later appeared in my previous collection, *The Big Tease*.

The two *Terrible Tales* pieces here are variants of the piece I ultimately sent for the 2012 *Monsters and Dames* art book. I like this one more than my first pass at a "Spoof Eerie Pubs" cover (on the previous spread). Having Frankenstein's brain fall out of his head—and about to plop right into the lady's face—makes it funnier. It's a *twisted* joke for sure, but at least it's a joke, not just over-the-top gore.

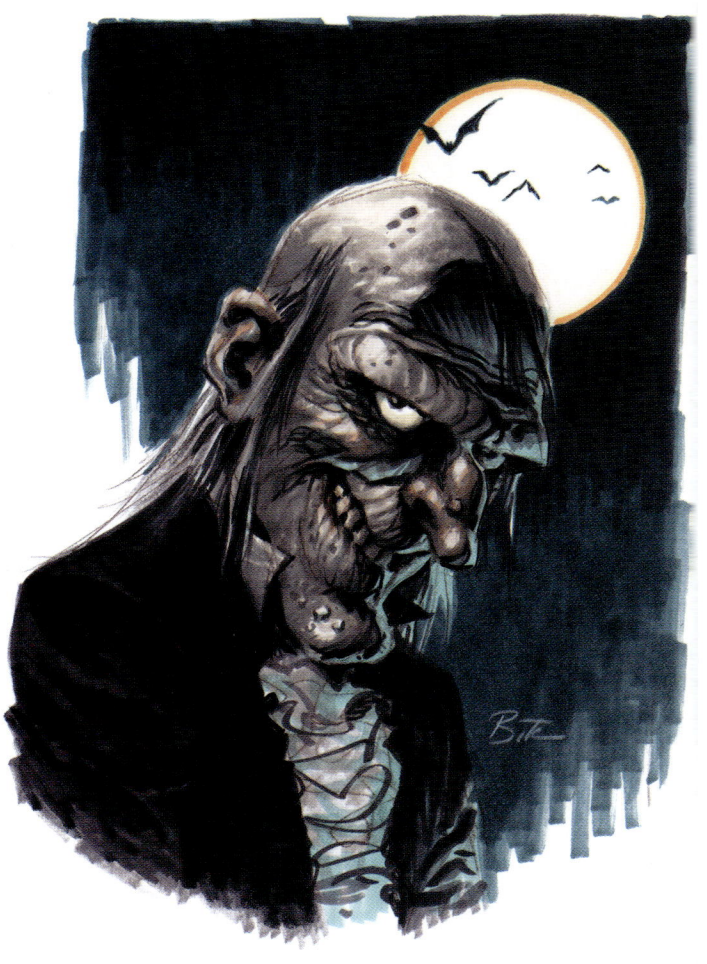

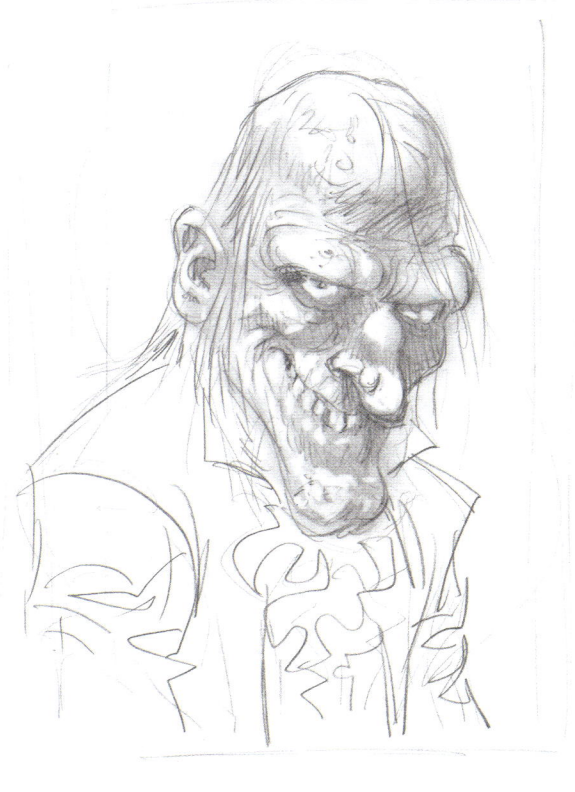

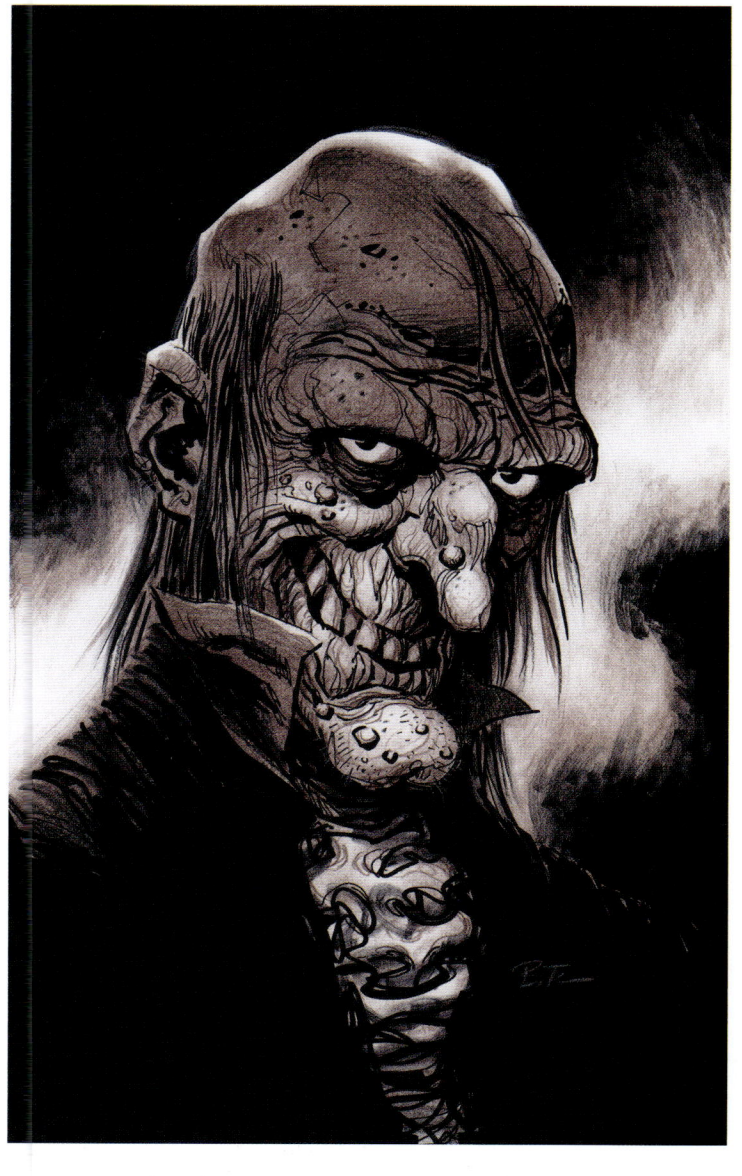

When the current rights holders of *Creepy* and *Eerie* asked me if I'd be interested in doing a frontispiece for their newly revived *Creepy* comic book, I couldn't say no. I've been a huge fan of the Warren horror comics since I was a kid, so getting paid to draw my all-time favorite Horror Host was pretty dang cool.

I like the portrait at the lower right—he just looks so depraved and disgusting! A pretty good Jack Davis-style Uncle Creepy. But as often happens, I wasn't 100 percent satisfied. Then I hit on the idea of doing a "group portrait" with Uncle Creepy surrounded by Frankenstein, a werewolf, an "old school" Haitian-style zombie, a mummy, a cute vampire girl … and, for good measure, I threw Cthulhu in there in the background. Rendered it all in grayscale halftones as "painterly" as I could manage. I'm pretty happy with how it came out.

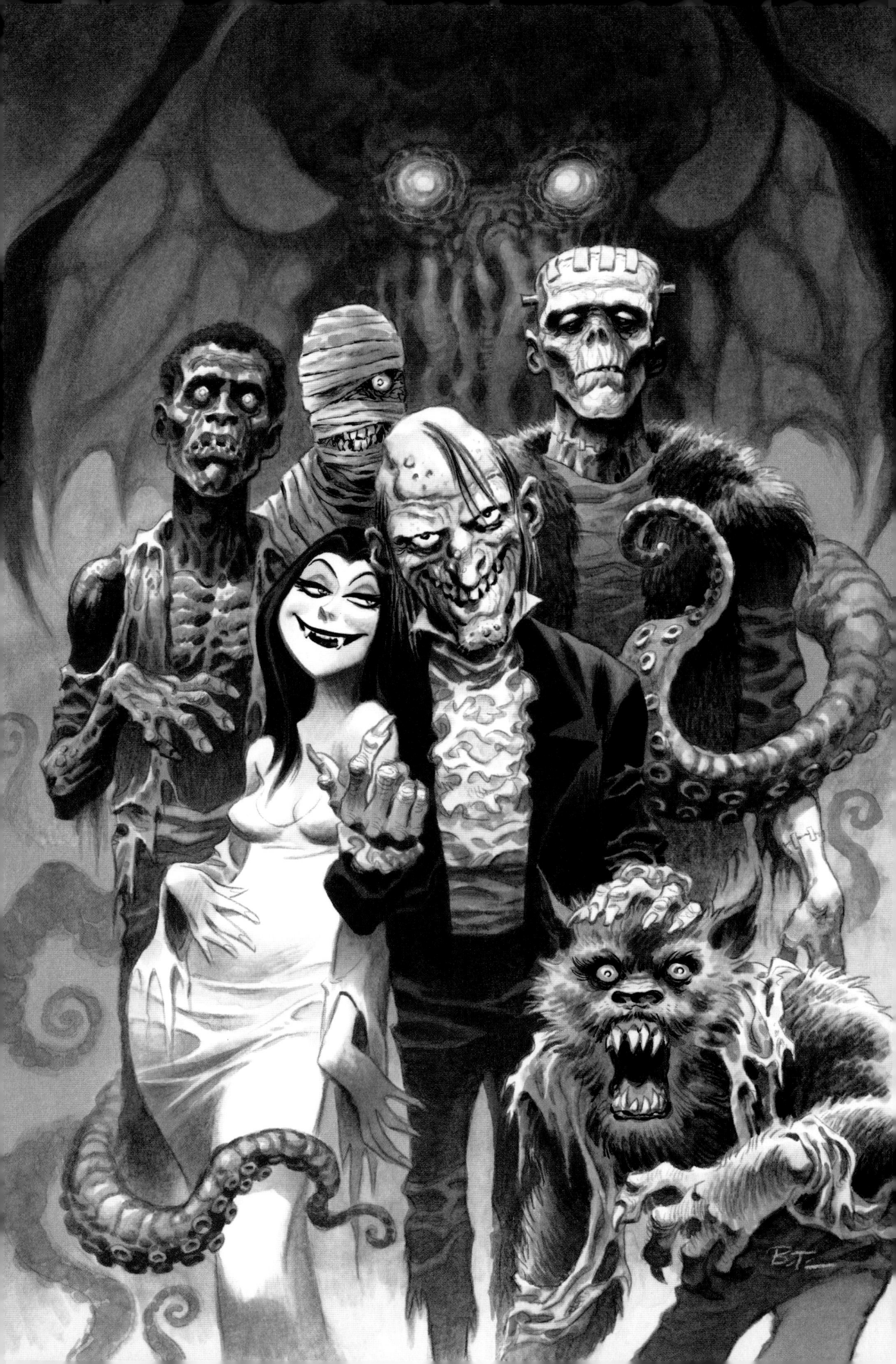

FLESH AND BLOOD

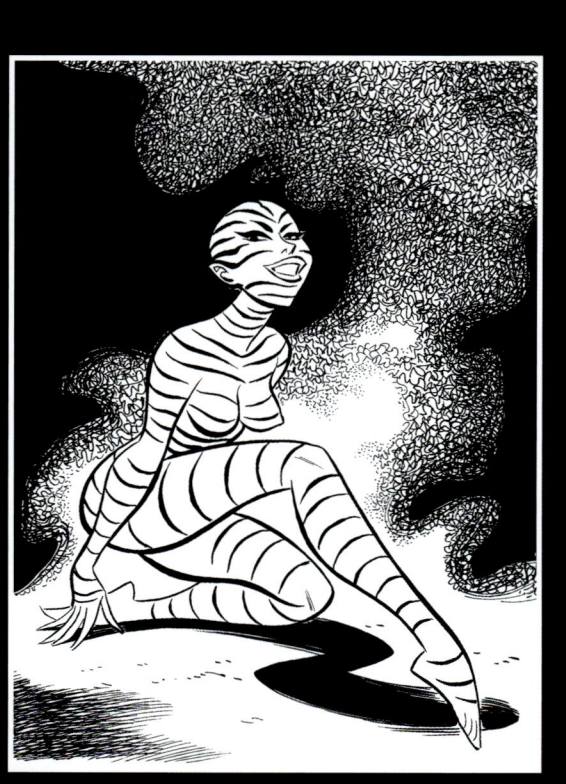

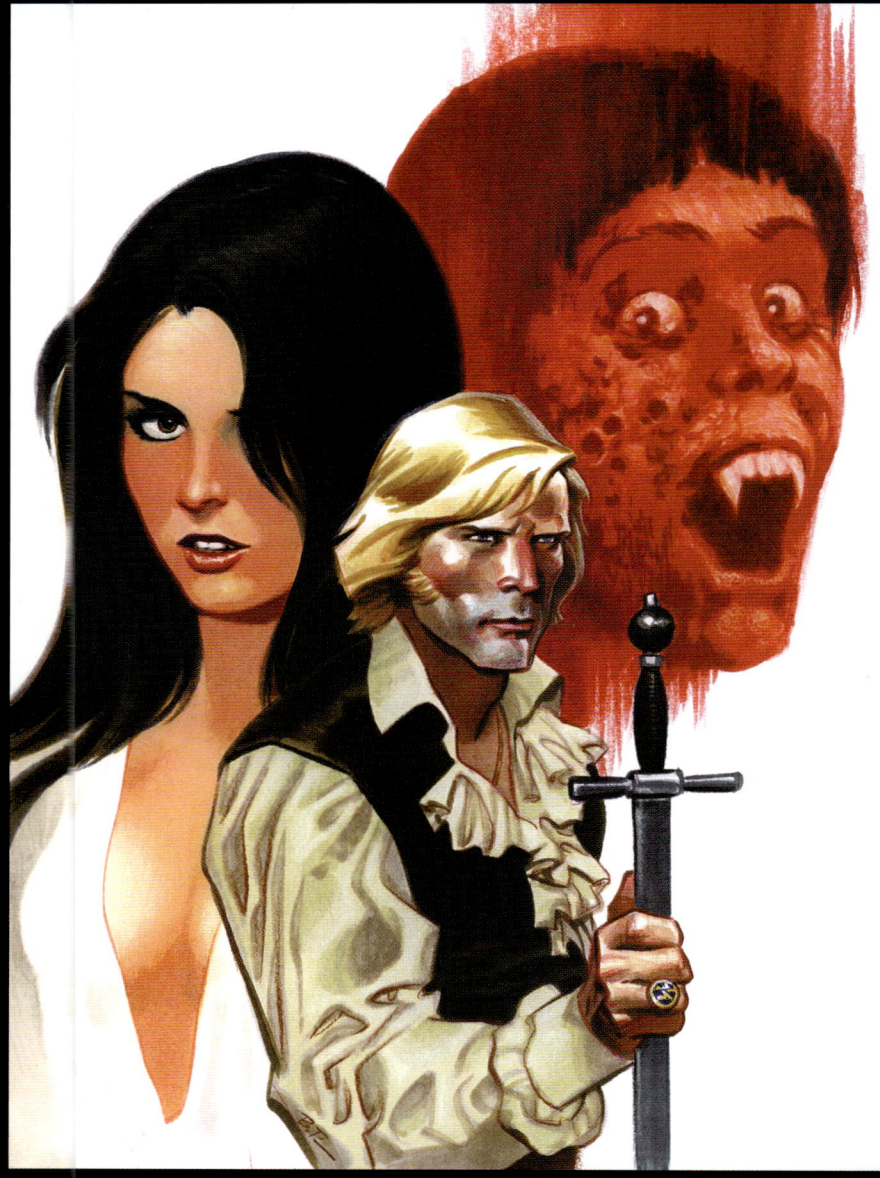

In the early 1990s, the combination of two things happening simultaneously reignited my interest in the Hammer movies. I saw a copy of Richard "Dick" Klemensen's *Little Shoppe of Horrors* magazine at a great little monster specialty shop in Burbank called Creature Features. Flipping through it, I discovered the entire mag was devoted to in-depth articles about Hammer, generously illustrated with photos and art. Got it home, read it front-to-back and *loved* it.

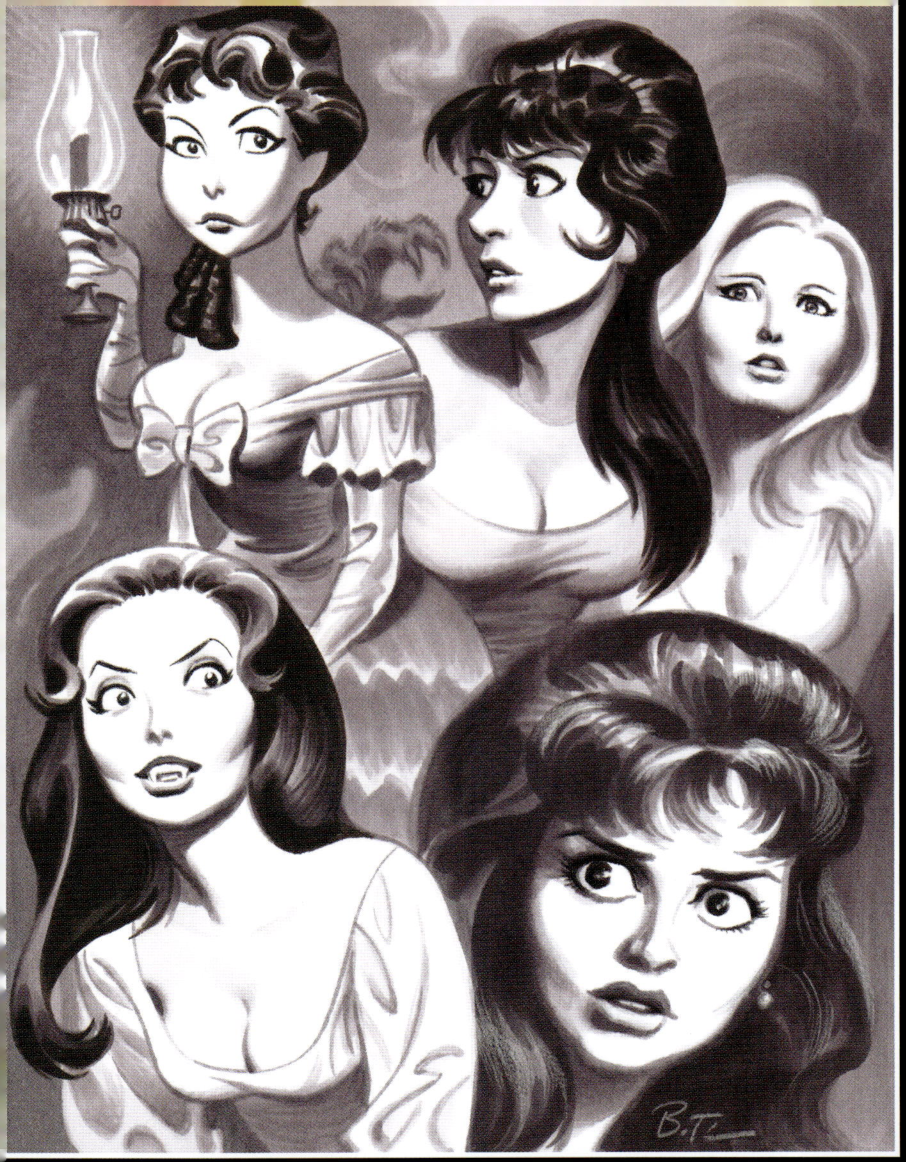

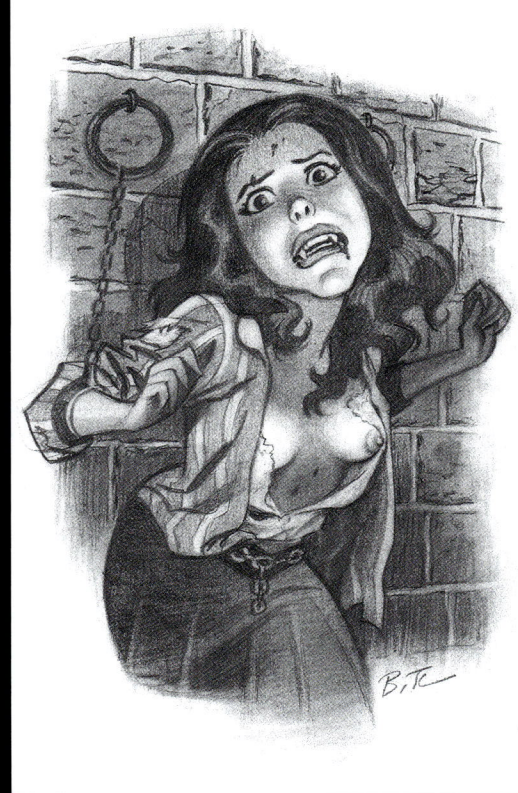

Right around the same time, TNT began running restored prints of a bunch of Hammer movies, many of which I'd heard of but had never actually seen before, like *The Devil Rides Out* and *The Reptile*. As a kid, I'd grown up on a steady diet of Universal monster movies and wasn't really sure how I felt about the Hammers. It probably didn't help that the prints I'd see on TV were usually in pretty poor shape—chopped-up, washed-out and dupe-y. Watching those gorgeous restored prints and reading about the movies in Dick's wonderful mag opened my eyes to how cool the Hammers could be.

I wrote Dick a fan letter, introduced myself and sent him some art pieces. He responded by inviting me to do something for his magazine. For the next twenty-plus years, practically every issue of *Little Shoppe* contained some art of mine—sometimes as many as three or four black-and-white pieces per issue and even an occasional cover.

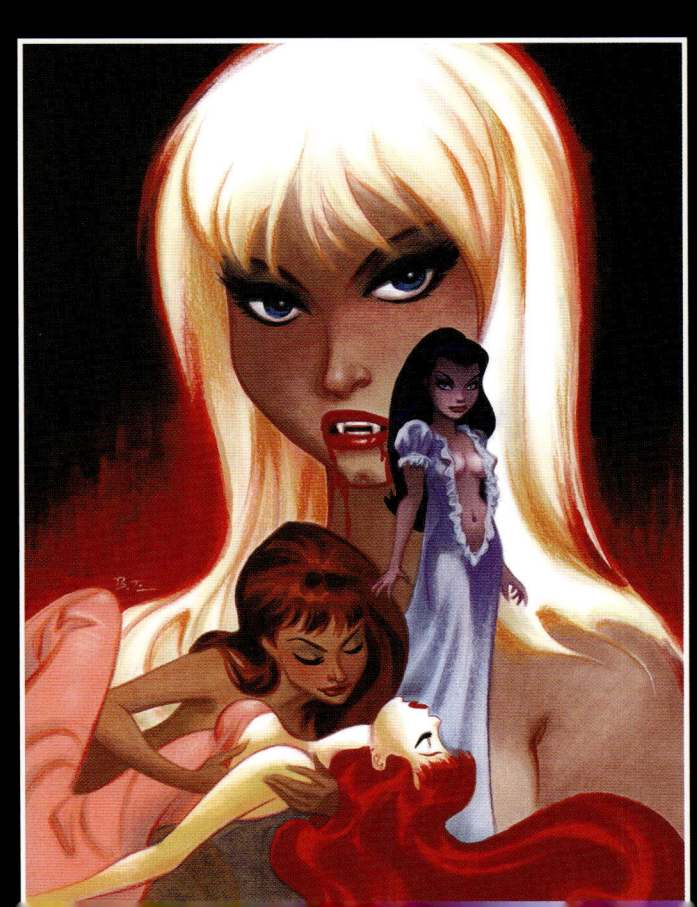

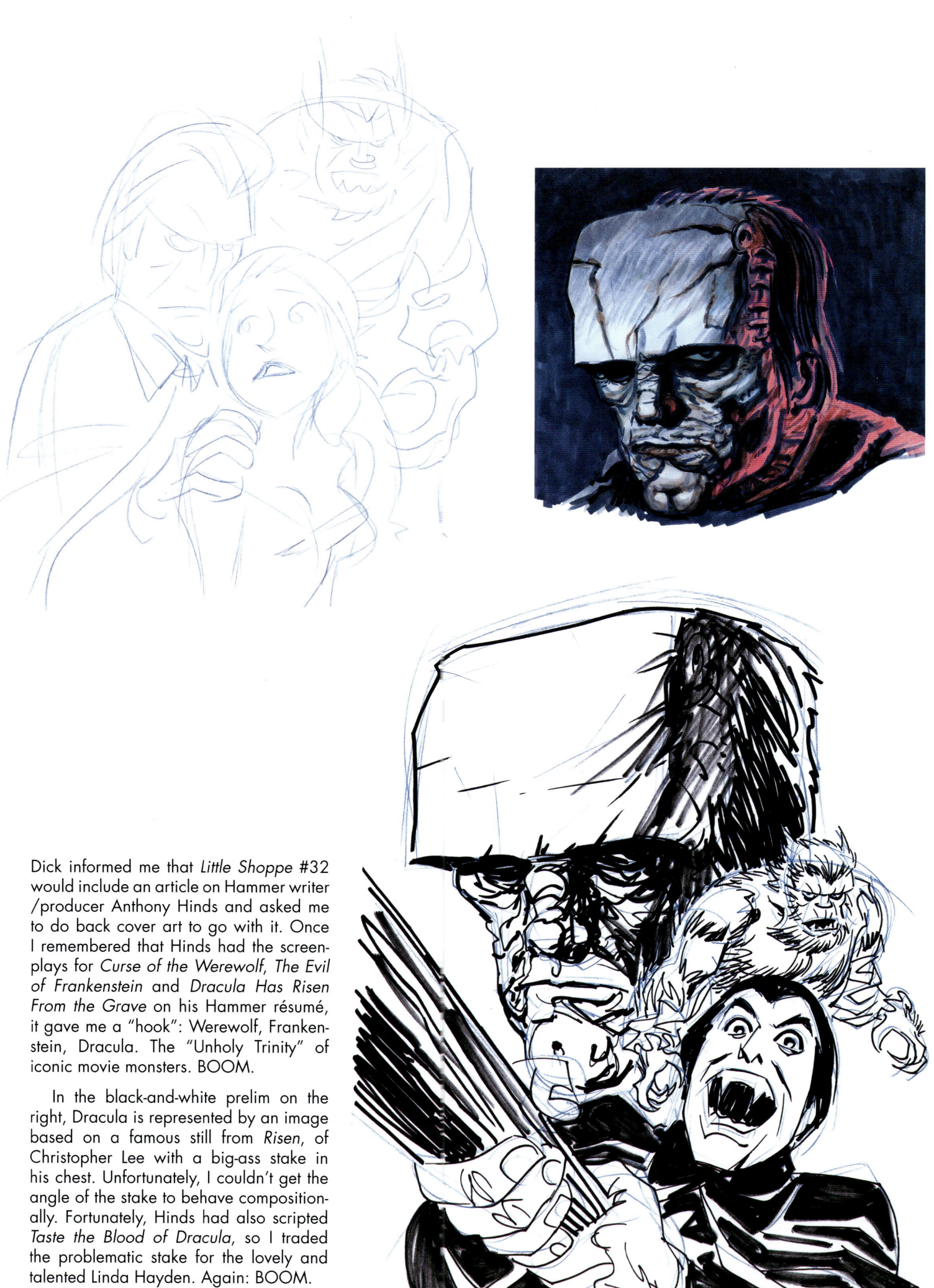

Dick informed me that *Little Shoppe* #32 would include an article on Hammer writer/producer Anthony Hinds and asked me to do back cover art to go with it. Once I remembered that Hinds had the screenplays for *Curse of the Werewolf*, *The Evil of Frankenstein* and *Dracula Has Risen From the Grave* on his Hammer résumé, it gave me a "hook": Werewolf, Frankenstein, Dracula. The "Unholy Trinity" of iconic movie monsters. BOOM.

In the black-and-white prelim on the right, Dracula is represented by an image based on a famous still from *Risen*, of Christopher Lee with a big-ass stake in his chest. Unfortunately, I couldn't get the angle of the stake to behave compositionally. Fortunately, Hinds had also scripted *Taste the Blood of Dracula*, so I traded the problematic stake for the lovely and talented Linda Hayden. Again: BOOM.

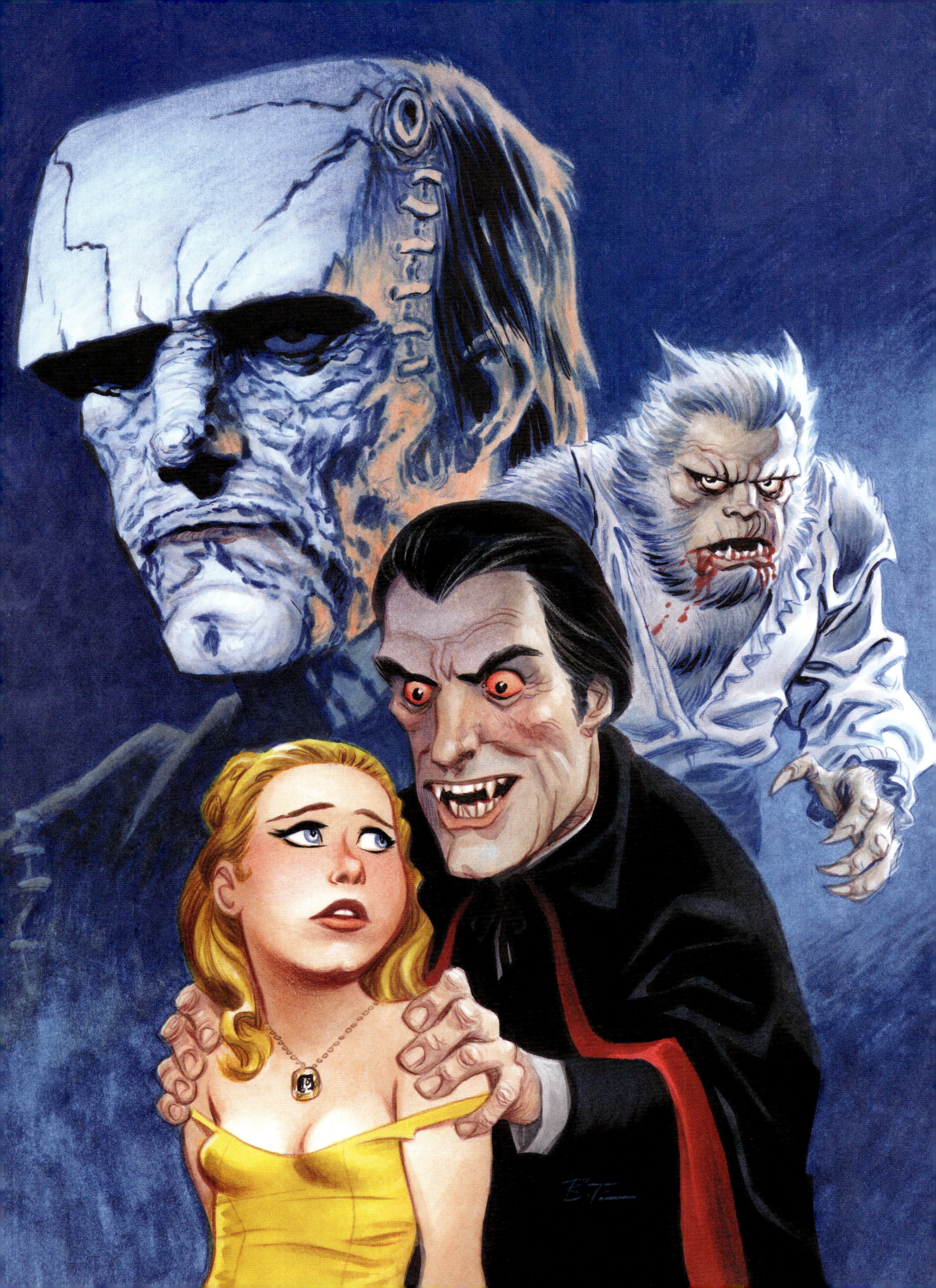

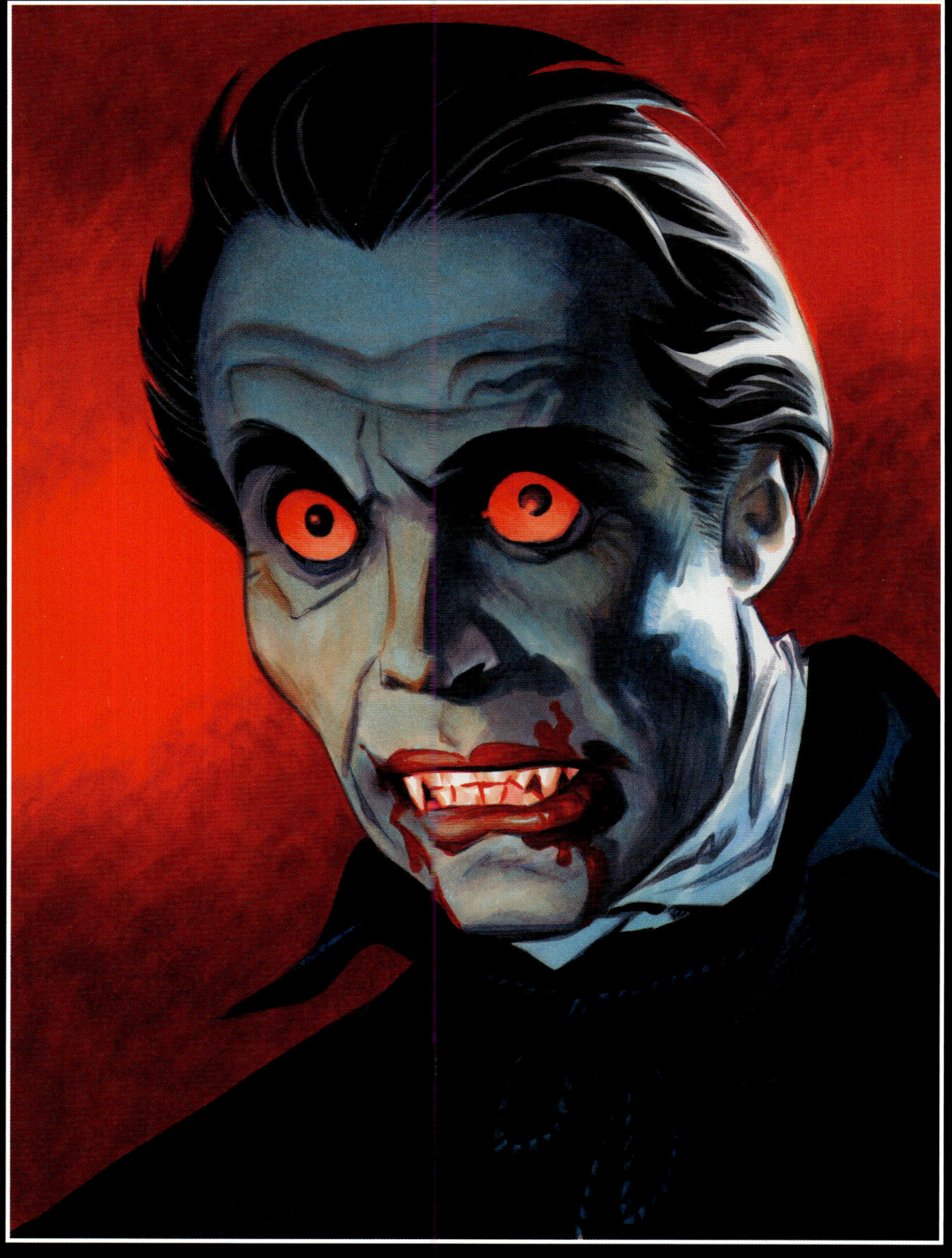

Doing an illustration based on photo reference is always a challenge. It can be tricky to find that sweet spot between realism and stylization. The Dracula face above is fairly exaggerated and "cartoony," but it's rendered in a semi-painterly way. The one on page 27 is more "flat" and graphic all around. I thought that approach looked more unusual—and also more "Me"—so that's the one I sent to Dick. But I do like 'em both.

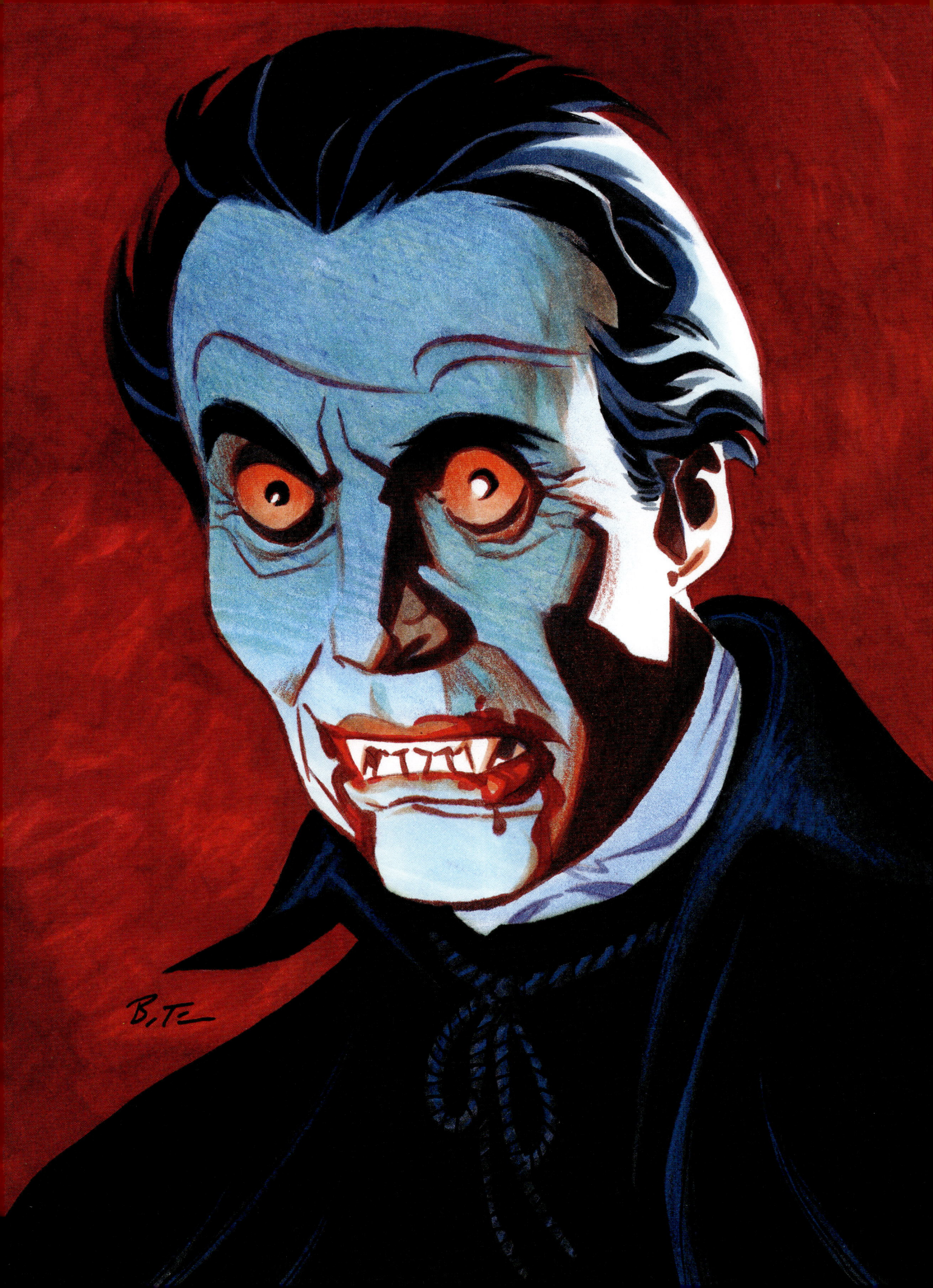

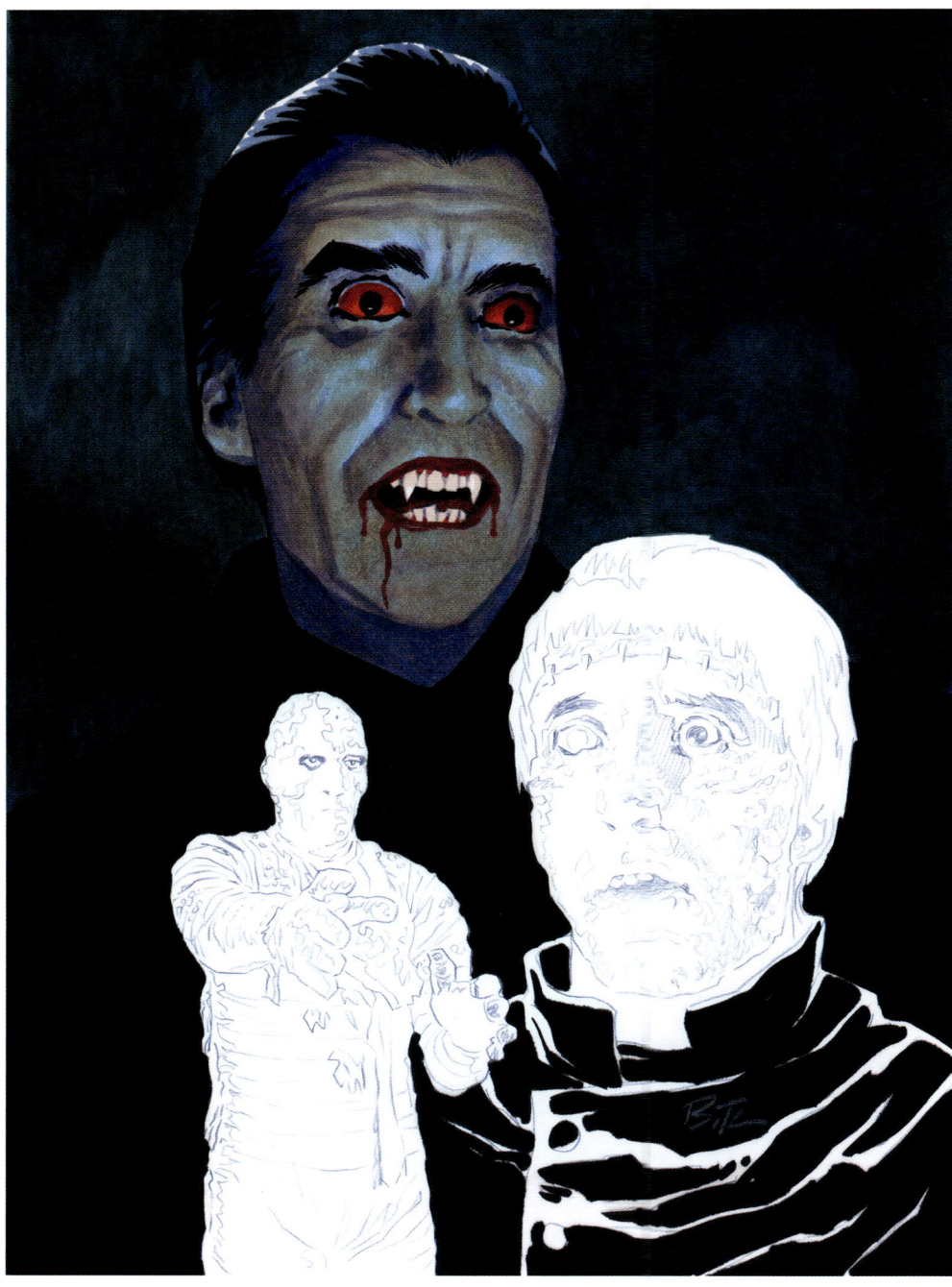

This was done for the issue of *Little Shoppe* immediately following the death of Christopher Lee in 2015. The half-finished piece above was my first attempt at a "Lee at Hammer" tribute montage. I wasn't loving it at the time— but now I think the full-color Dracula face actually looks kinda cool. D'oh!

Overall, I do like the one on the facing page better, so I don't totally regret abandoning the first one. I think I may have been subconsciously trying to channel the brilliant Spanish illustrator Manuel Sanjulian, specifically his splendid cover for Warren's *Eerie* #46. This one's definitely more "realistic" than my usual work and quite obviously based on photo-reference, but I think it came out pretty nice.

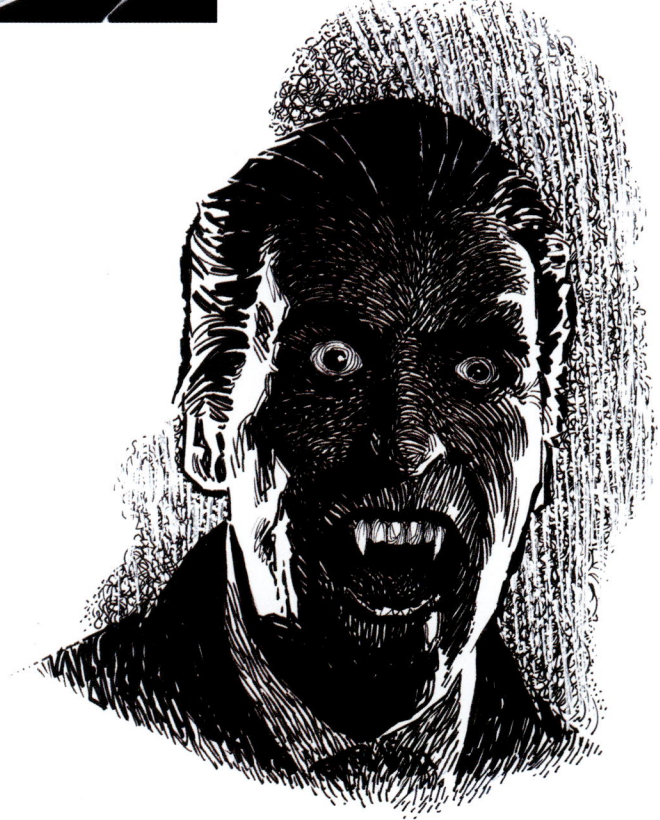

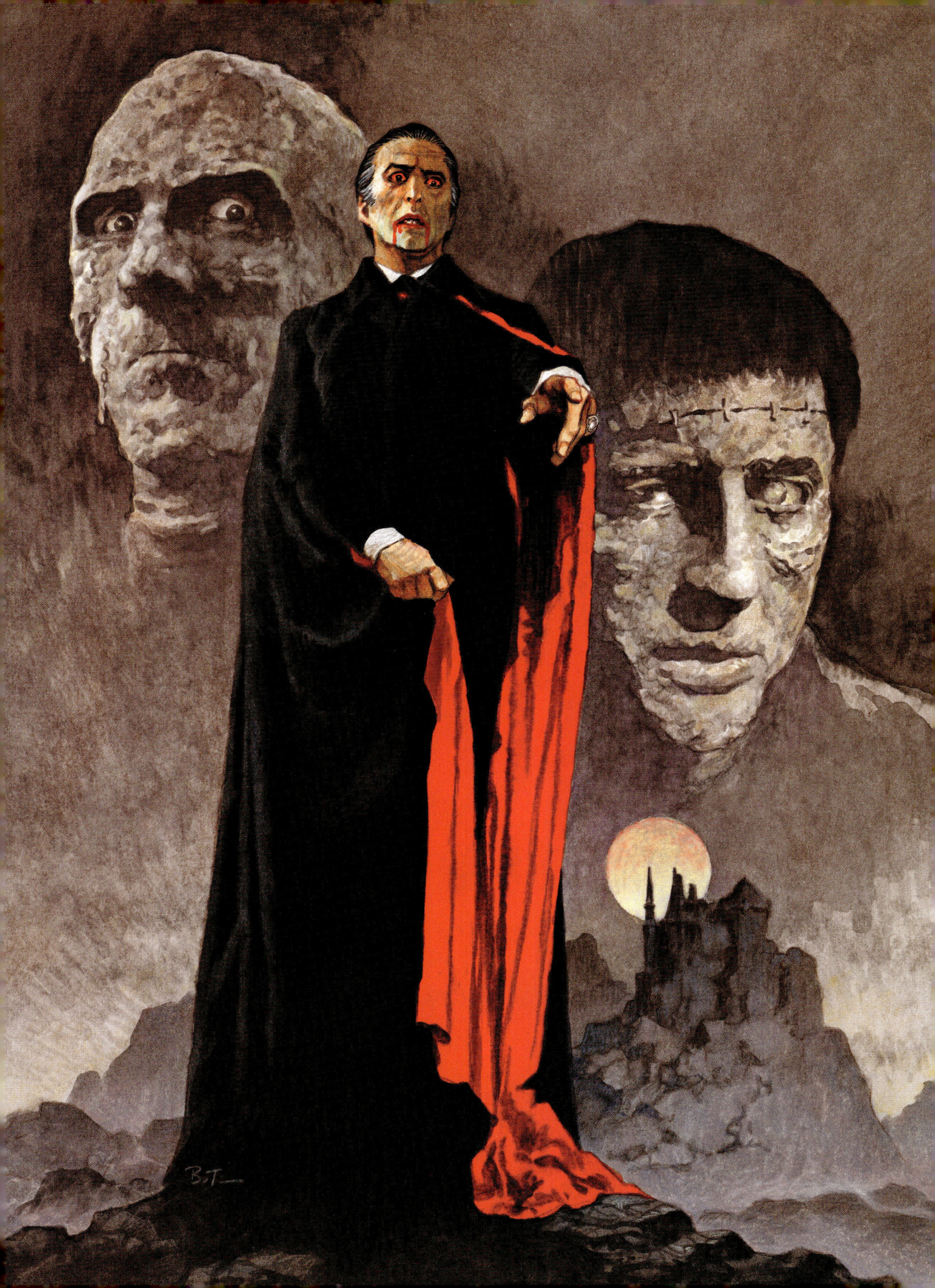

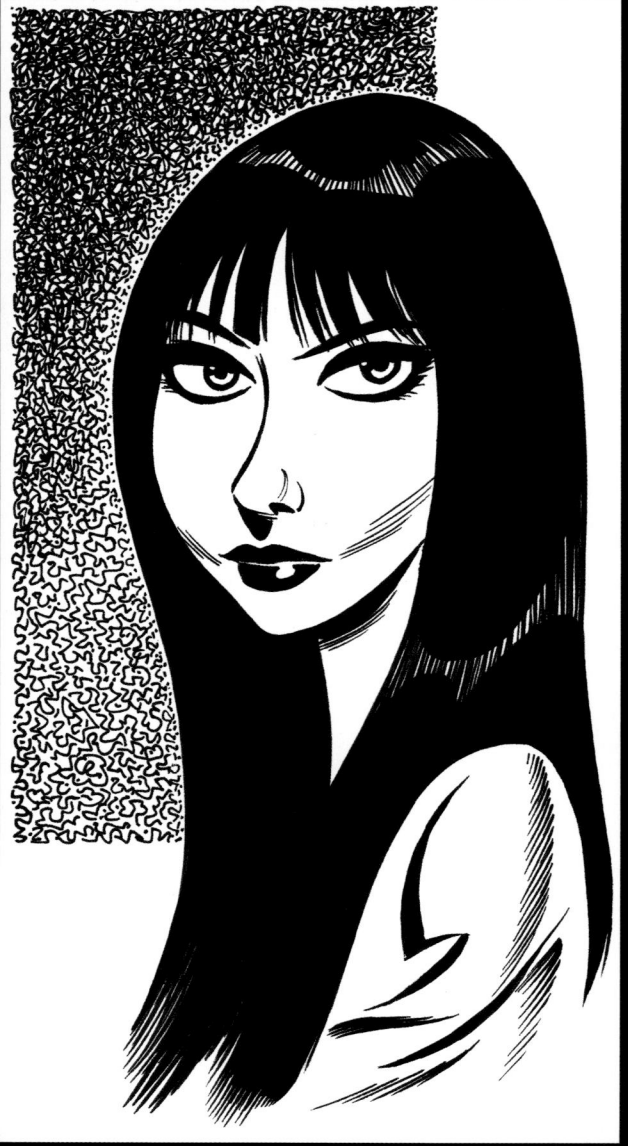

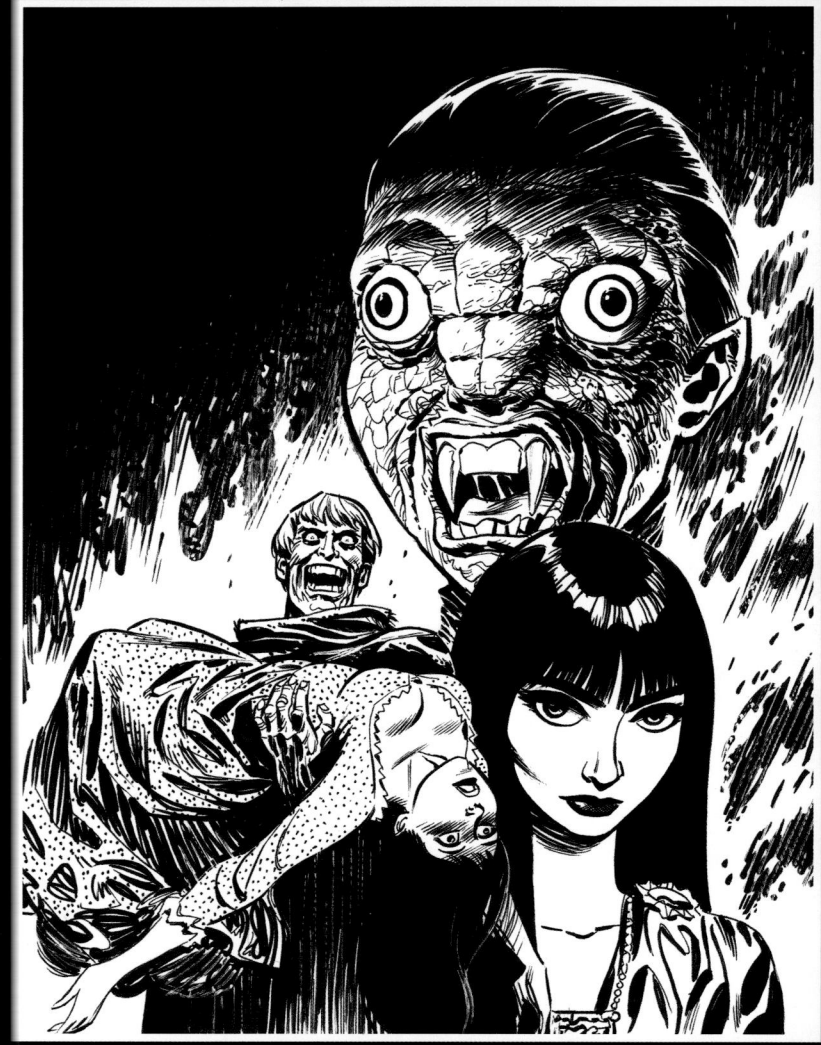

The Reptile and *The Plague of the Zombies* were two fairly unusual "off-trail" Hammer Horrors set in Cornwall but actually filmed on the backlot at Bray Studios. Both were directed by John Gilling, and both featured Jacqueline Pearce and Hammer stalwart Michael Ripper.

The striking Pearce gets a lot more screen time in *The Reptile,* and she's mesmerizing as the title character (Oops—spoiler alert!) I like it a bit more than *Plague,* but I think they're both quite good.

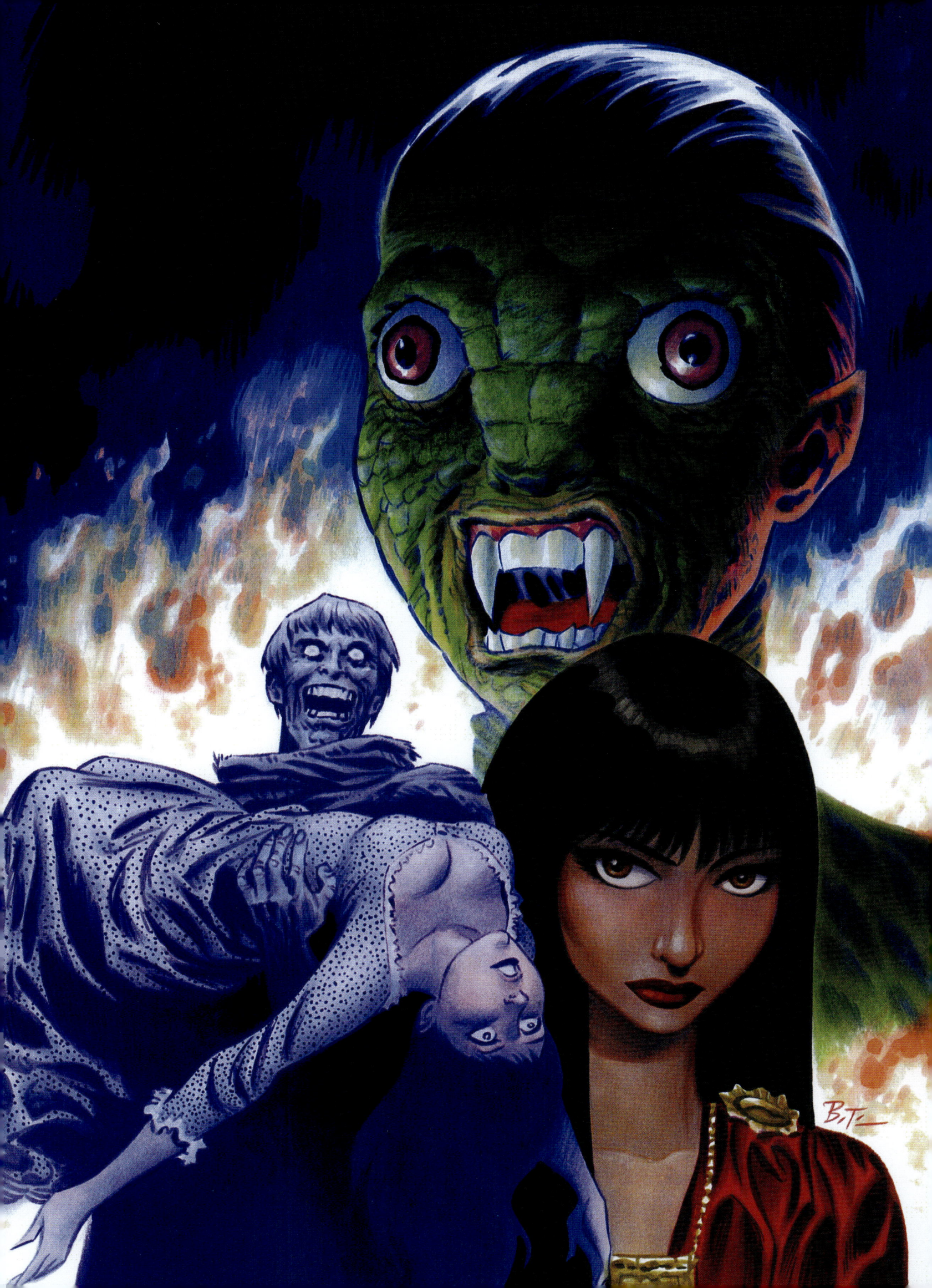

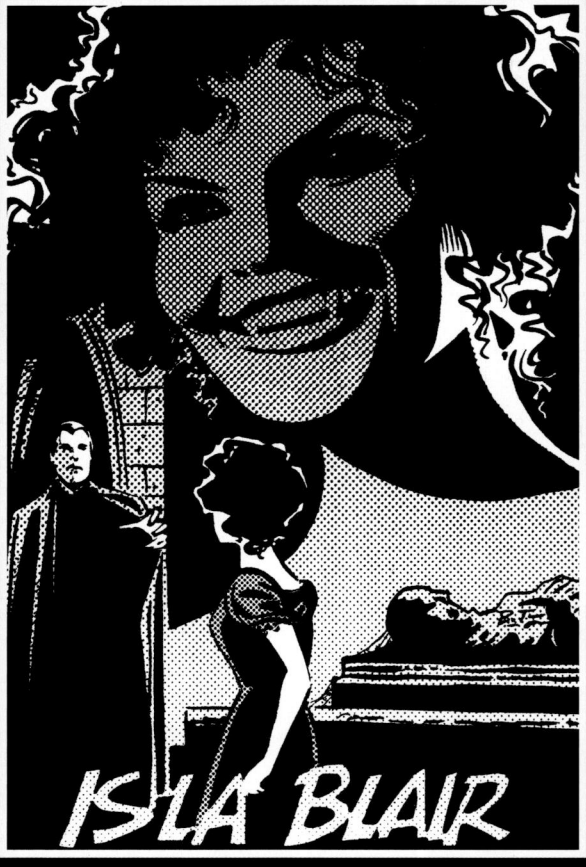

ISLA BLAIR

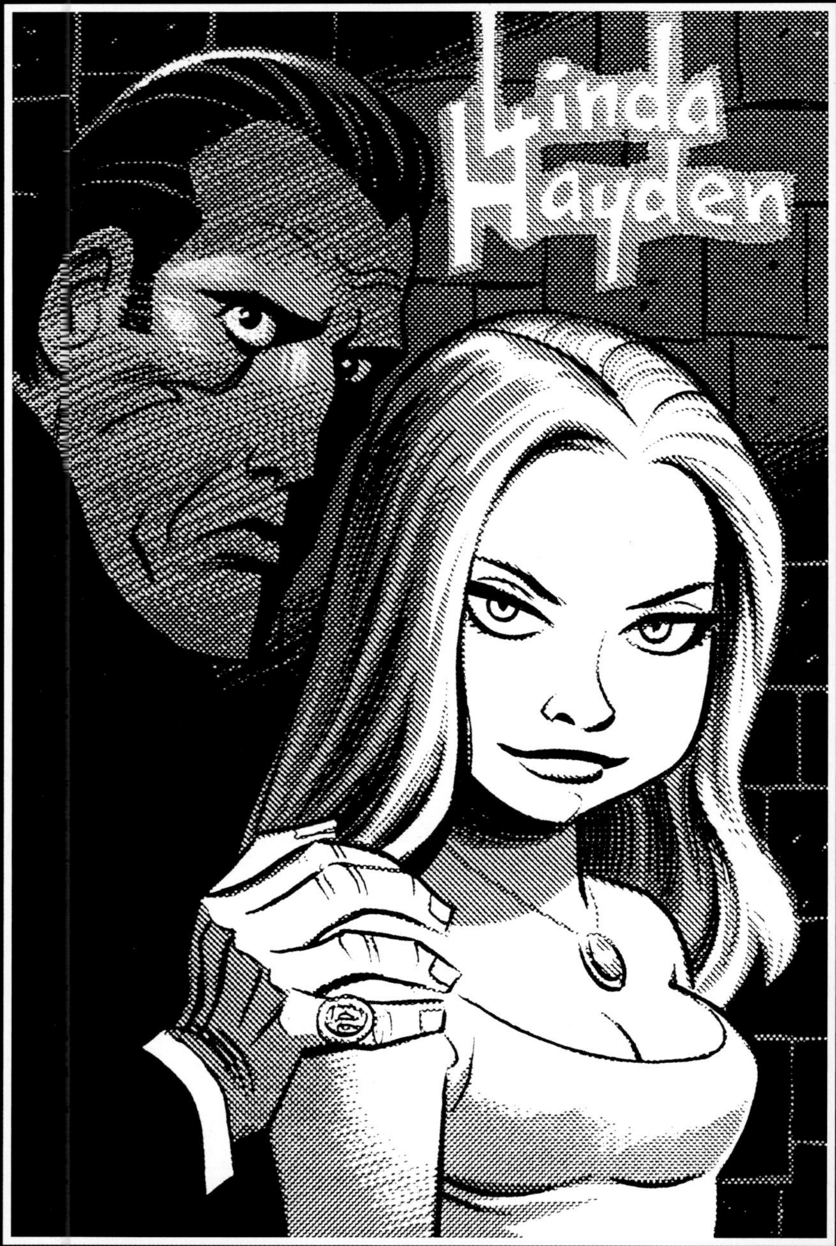

Lynda Hayden

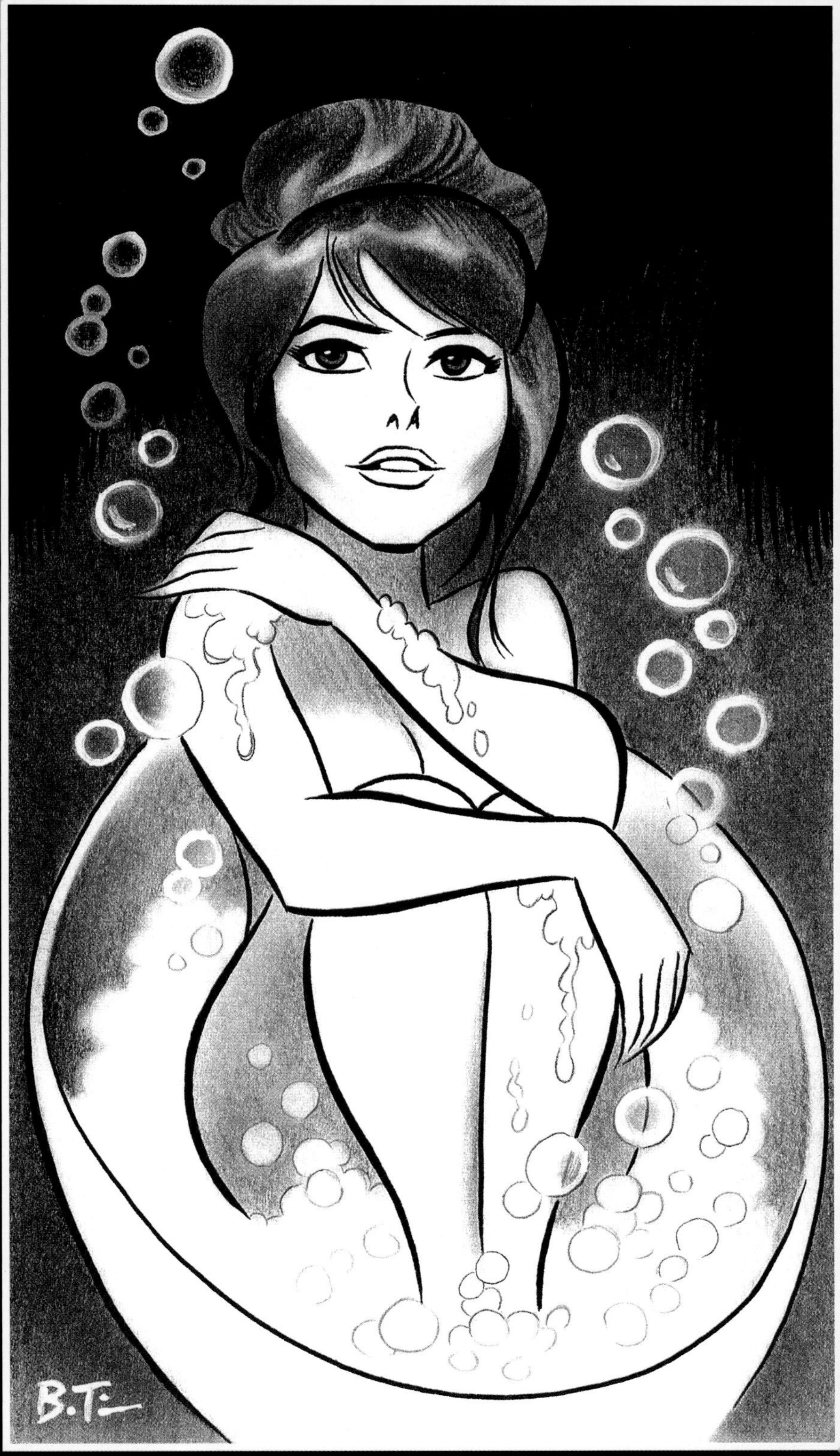

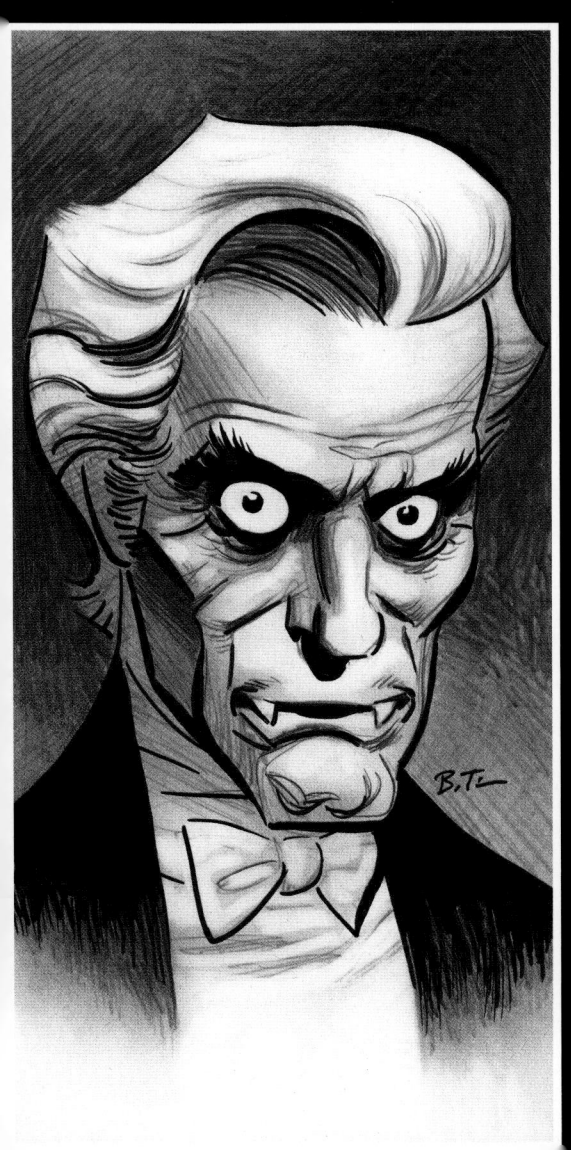

At some point, I realized that—since Dick ran halftone photos and continuous-tone grayscale art in *Little Shoppe* all the time—I could just do pieces rendered with gray markers or even a soft number 2 pencil and let Dick and his team convert the images to halftone. SO much easier! Duh.

In addition to all the coverage of Hammer films, Dick also occasionally spotlighted non-Hammer movies. *Little Shoppe #27* was one such "special issue," focusing on Roman Polanski's *Dance of the Vampires* a.k.a. *The Fearless Vampire Killers*, starring Ferdy Mayne and the spectacularly beautiful Sharon Tate.

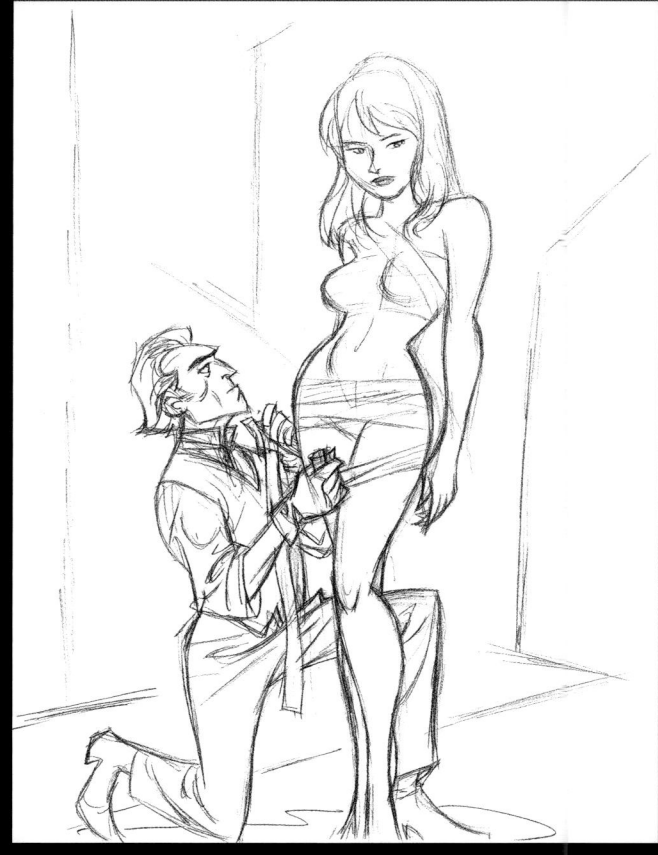

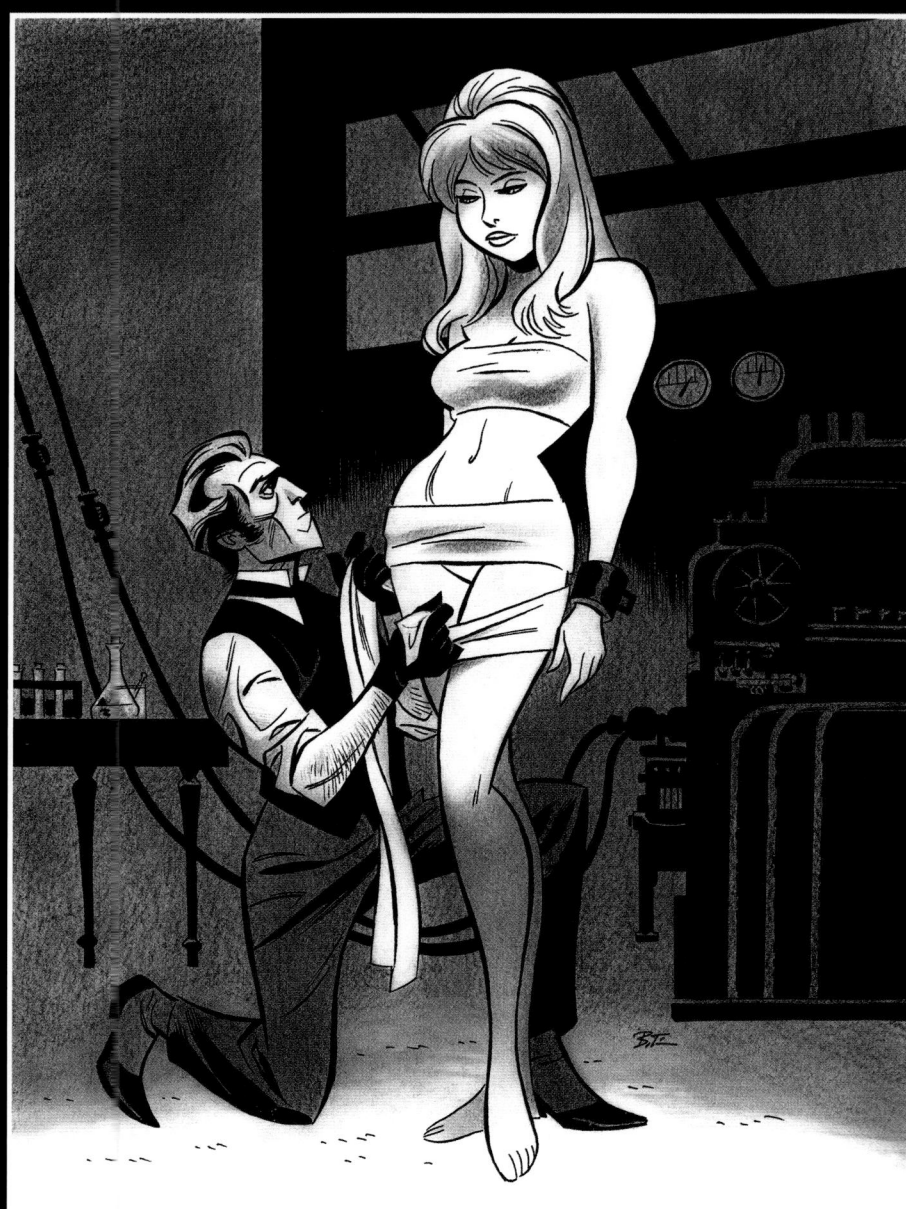

Hammer's *Frankenstein Created Woman* has always bugged me. The P.R. people shot a bunch of publicity stills of Peter Cushing as Baron Frankenstein posing with the movie's lead actress, former *Playboy* Playmate Susan Denberg as the "Woman" of the title. In the photos, she's wrapped in a kind of gauze bikini, suggesting a sort of sexed-up *Bride of Frankenstein*. Thing is, she never appears in the movie dressed like this. Not once. And there's not even a creation scene! They definitely "sold the sizzle" with this one. It's a perfectly fine movie, but when you see the stills, it's hard not to think, "Aww, I want to see *that* movie!"

Anyhow. A friend of mine saw my black-and-white illustration in *Little Shoppe* and commissioned me to do the color version you see here.

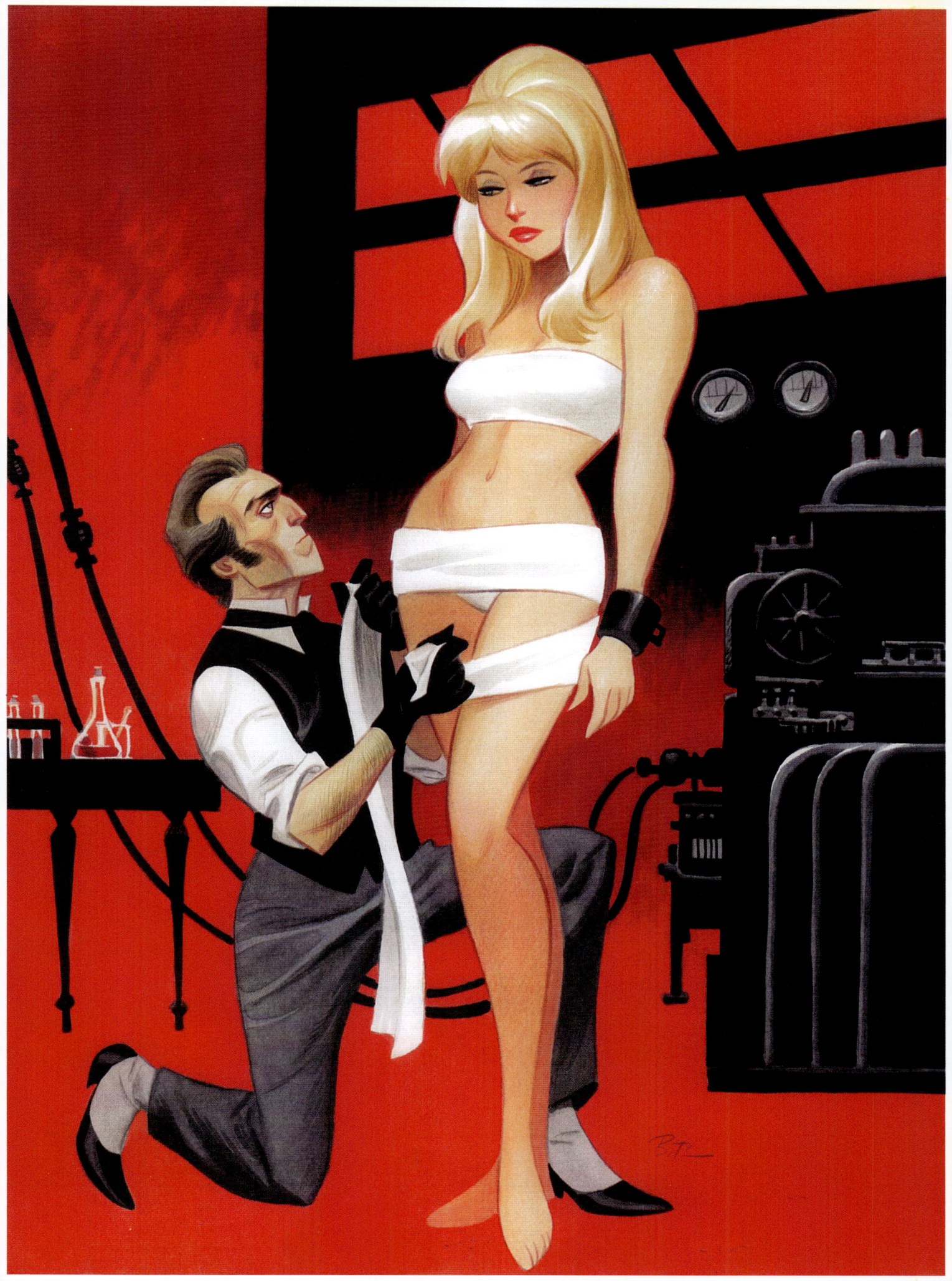

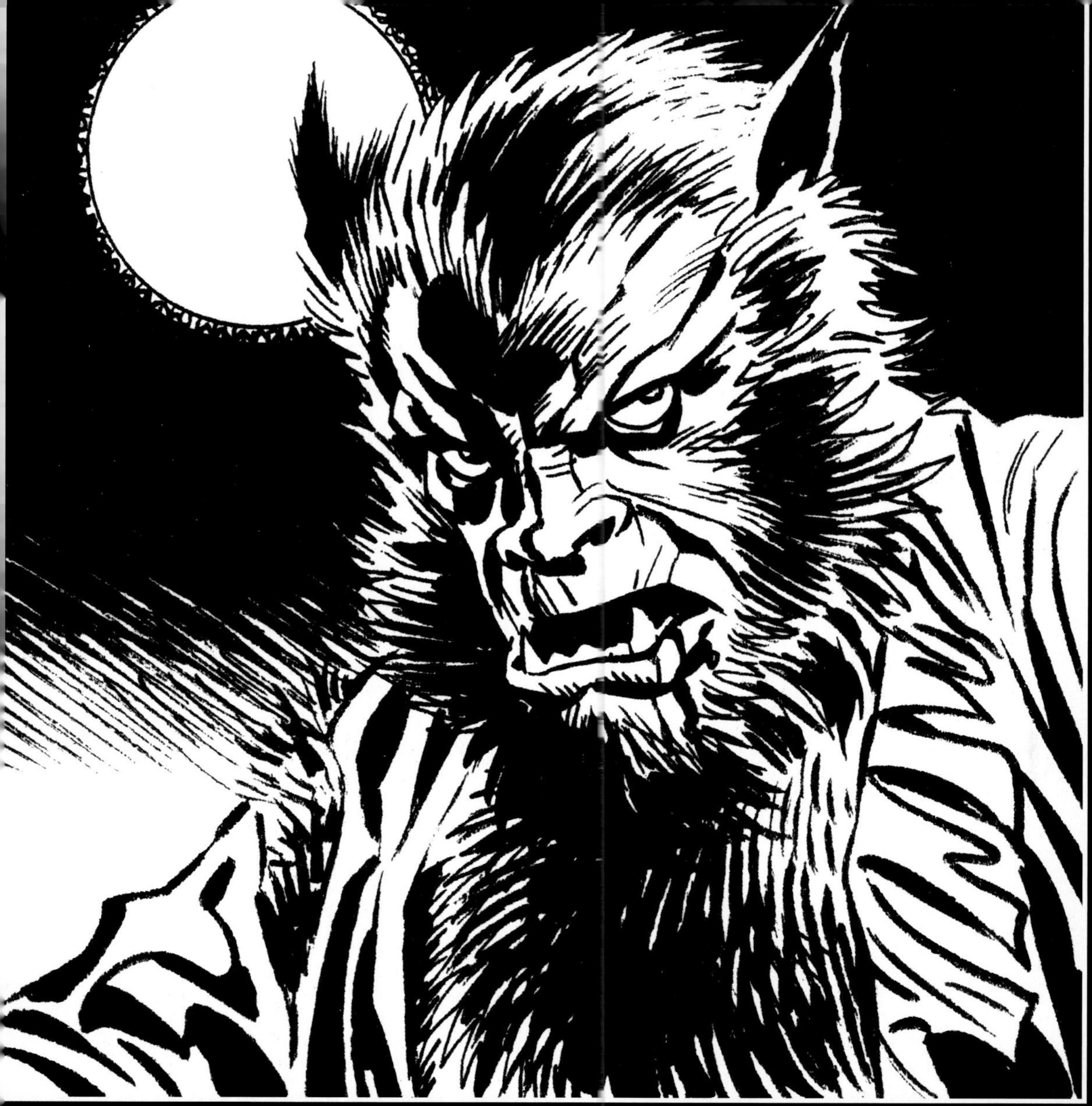

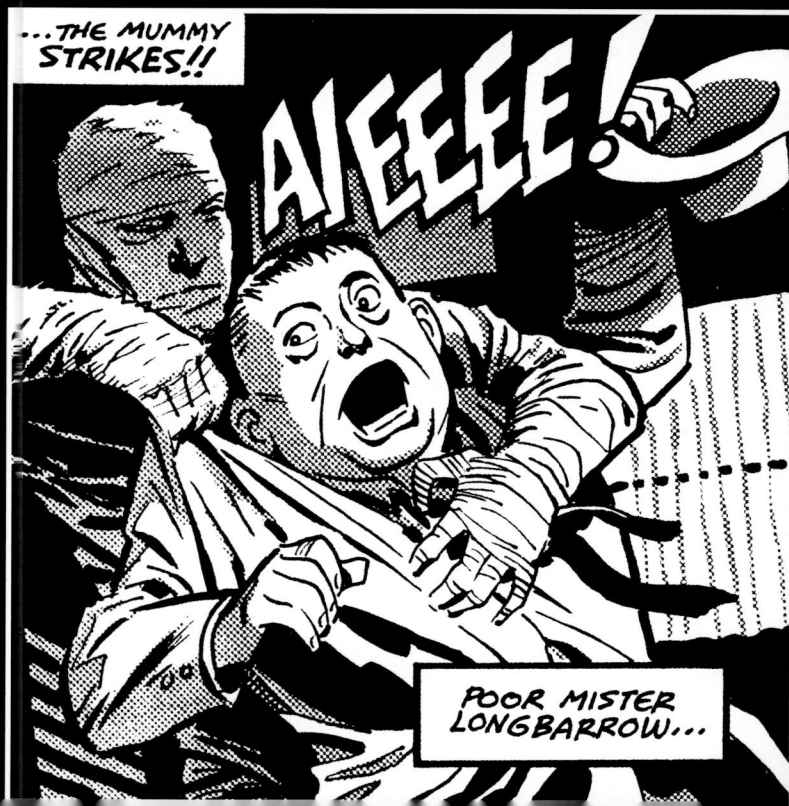

Sometimes I run out of ideas. The shot of Oliver Reed as the title character from *Curse of the Werewolf* is a pretty basic head-and-shoulders medium close-up. Nothing fancy, but I think it works. Same thing with the portrait of lovely Caroline Munro as Carla from *Captain Kronos: Vampire Hunter*. No fake Zip-A-Tone, just crisp black-and-white line art with some scribbly texture in the background. But it's a pretty decent likeness of her, and since she's one of the most popular and iconic actresses of fantasy cinema, what more do you need?

For the Michael Ripper piece, I drew his character's death scene from *The Mummy's Shroud* as if it was a panel from a comics adaptation of the film. Because why not. A bit of fake Zip shading gives it a little Wally Wood flavor.

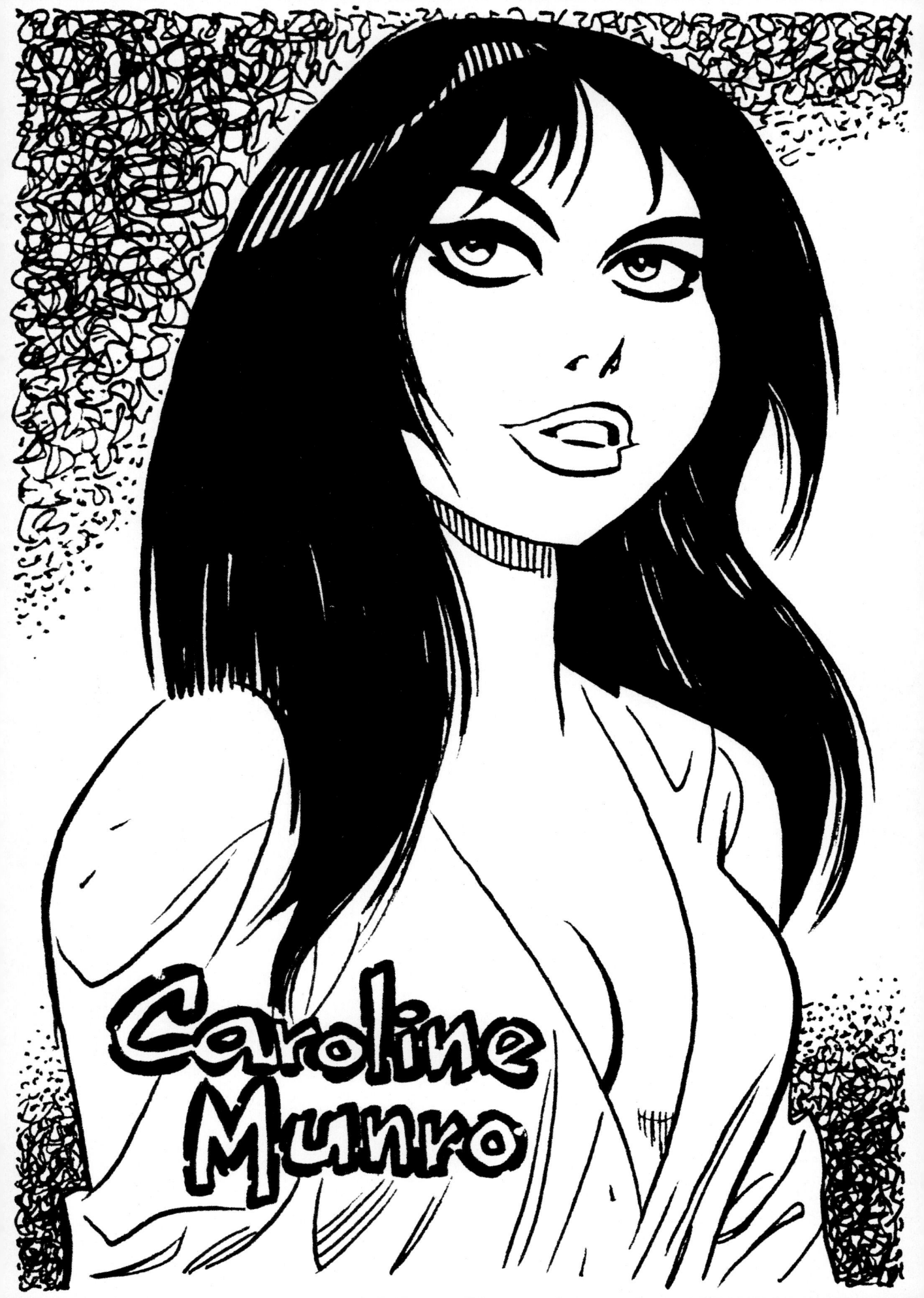

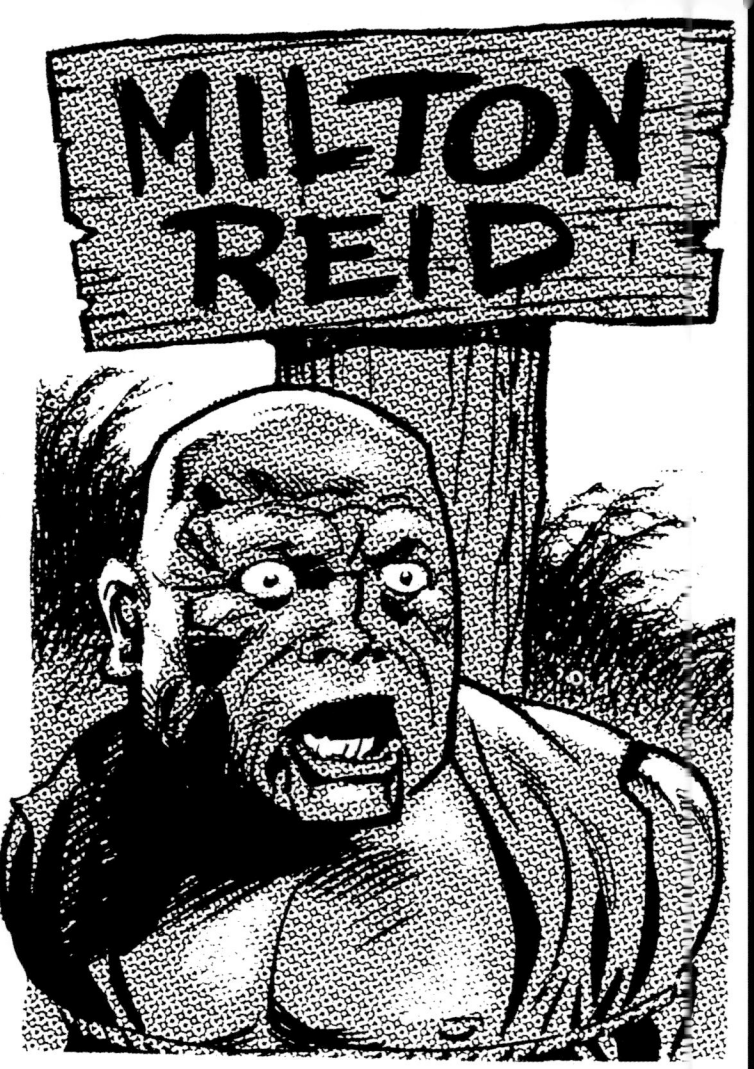

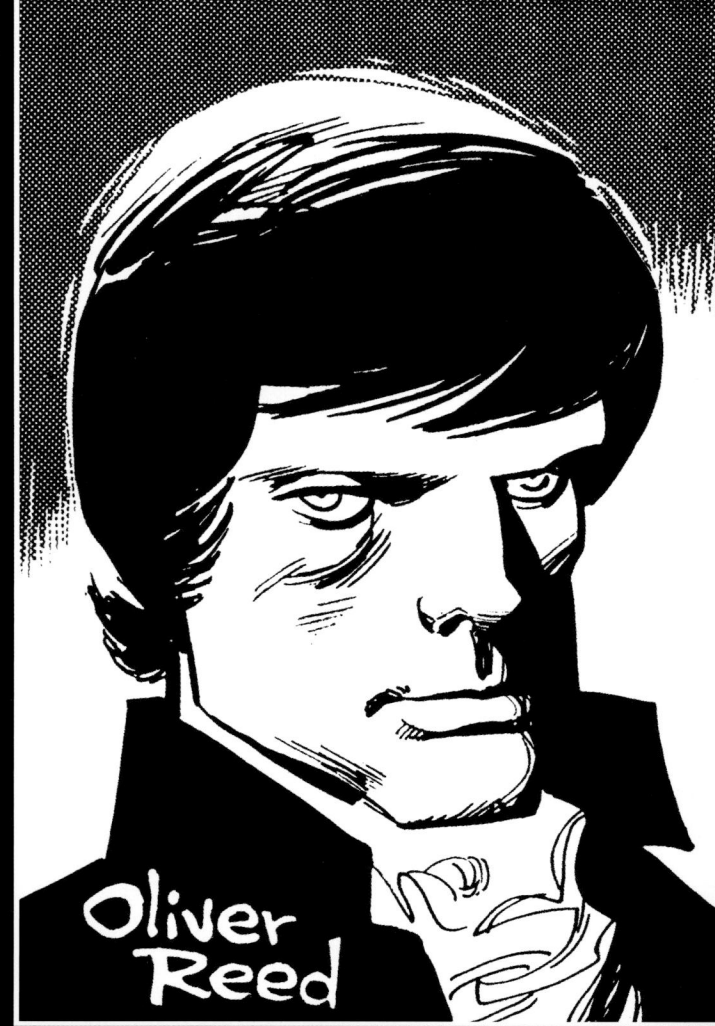

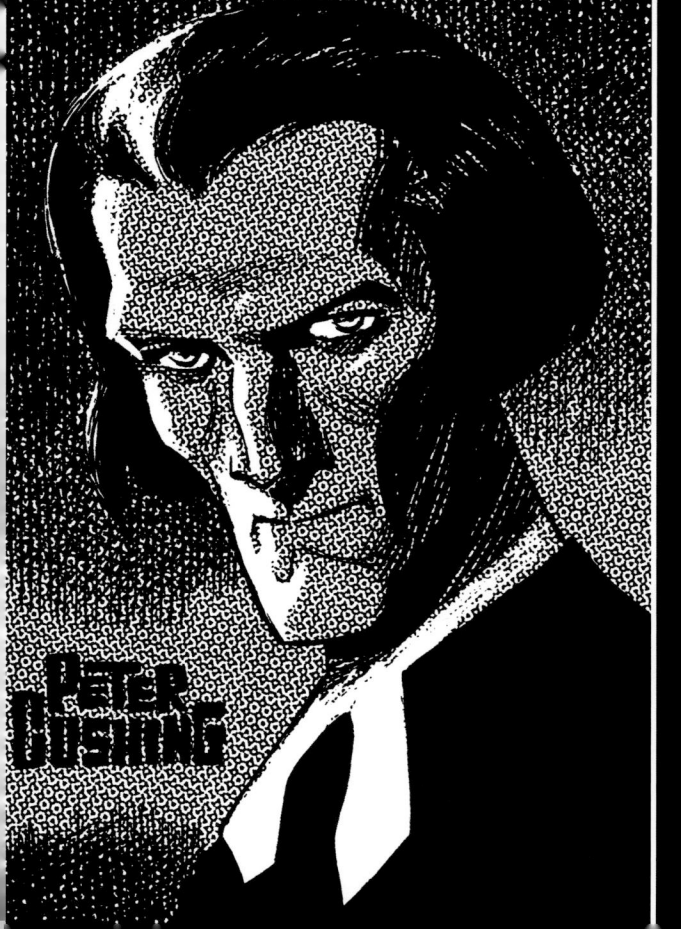

Milton Reid and Peter Cushing in *Captain Clegg* aka *Night Creatures*: Ai-yi-yi—it's fake Zip-A-Tone on top of fake Zip-A-Tone on top of fake Zip-A-Tone! Taking that technique about as far as it could go. I used a much simpler fake Zip treatment for the Oliver Reed piece from the same film.

Little Shoppe #20 is another of Dick's "non-Hammer specials," this time devoted to Hammer's rival, Amicus Films. Inspired by arguably the best of Amicus's many "portmanteau movies," *Tales From the Crypt*, I had a blast doing my best Jack Davis impression. "EC Comics homage covers" are a dime a dozen in comic book-land—practically a cliché—but I couldn't resist. It's one of my absolute favorite pieces that I did for *Little Shoppe*.

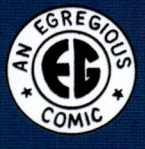

AMICUS ISSUE

LITTLE SHOPPE OF HORRORS

NO. 20

$8.95

FEATURING...

THE MAD SCIENTIST

THE SEXY VAMPIRE

THE CRAWLING HAND

BE MY VALENTINE

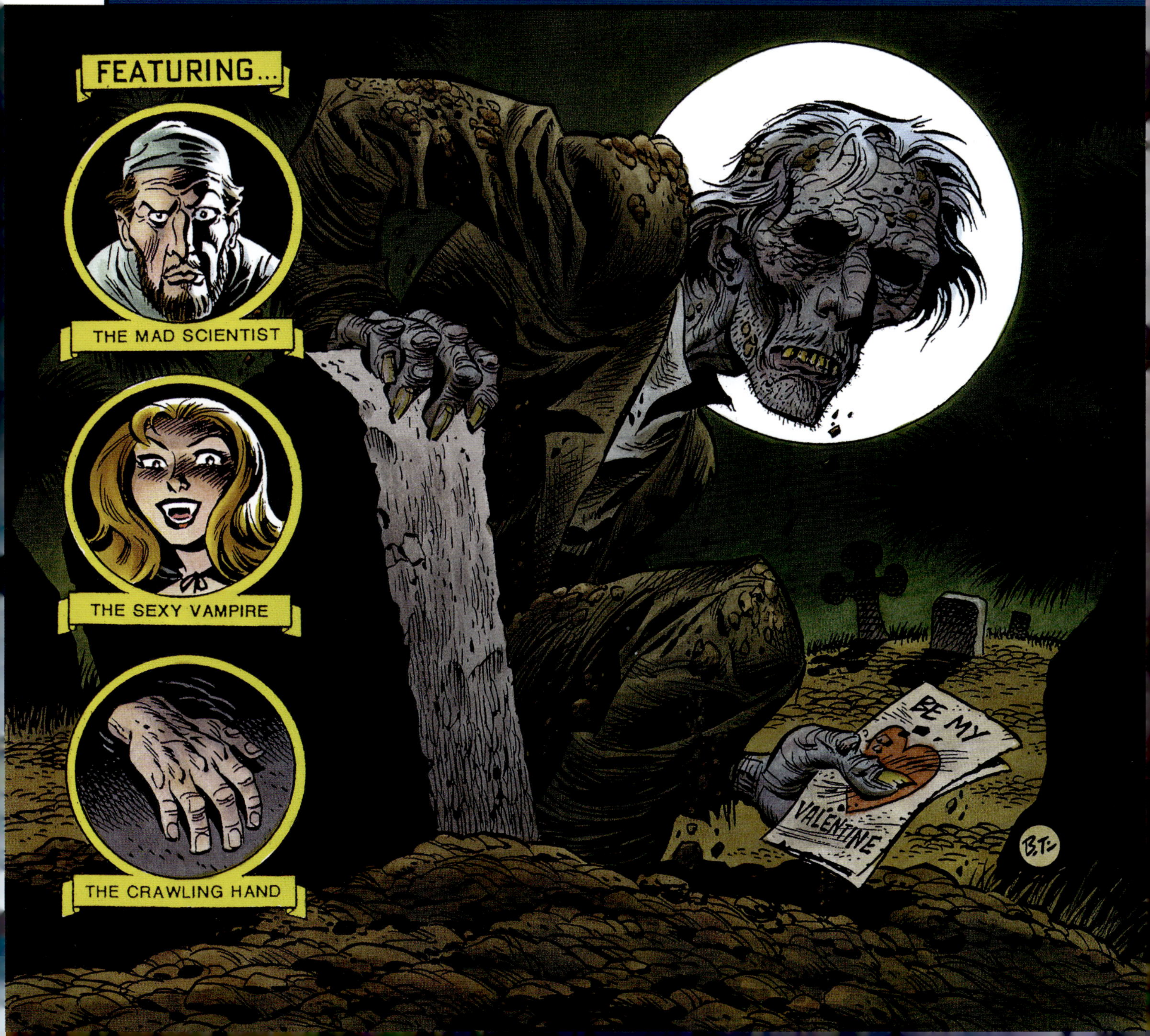

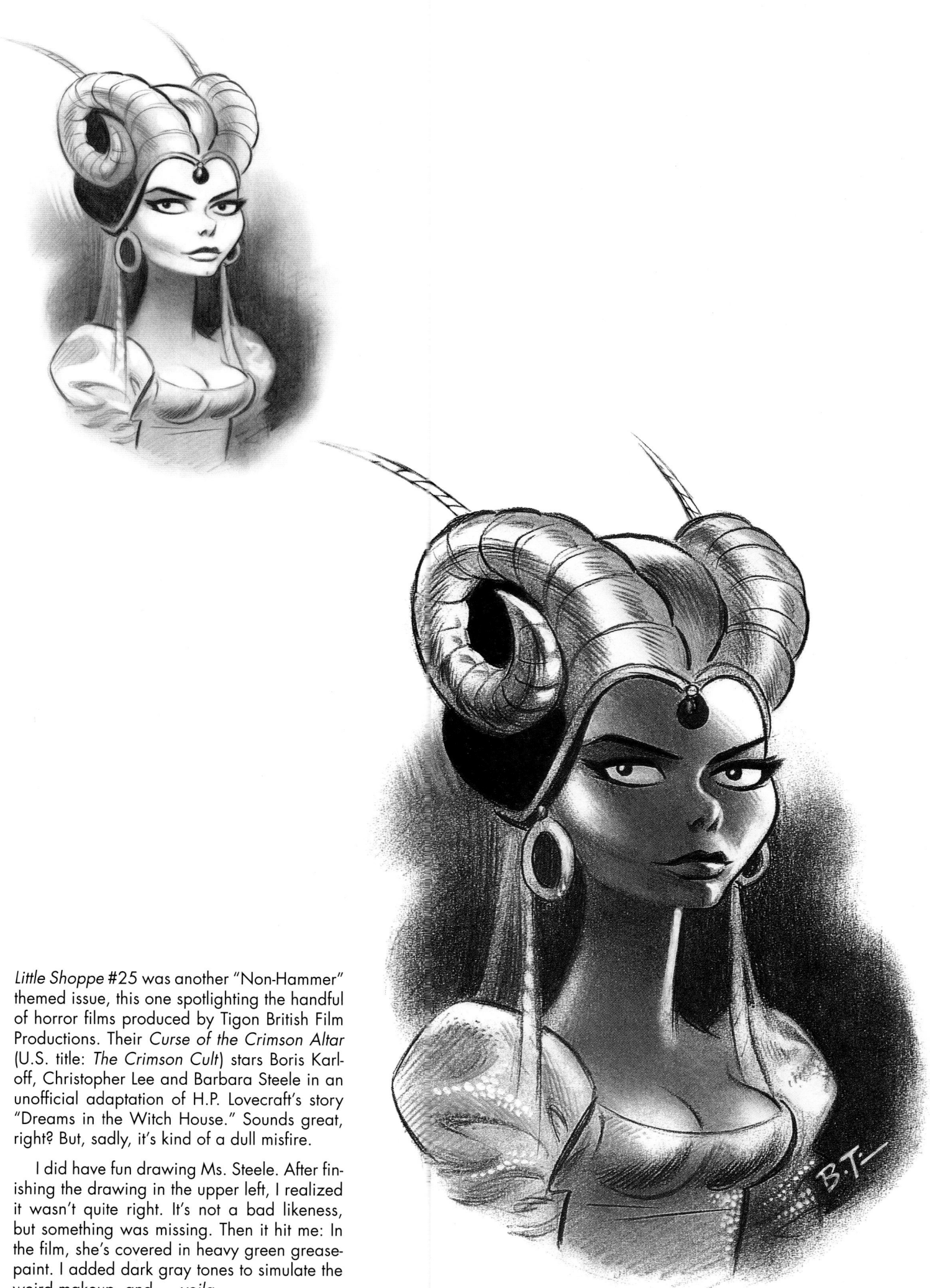

Little Shoppe #25 was another "Non-Hammer" themed issue, this one spotlighting the handful of horror films produced by Tigon British Film Productions. Their *Curse of the Crimson Altar* (U.S. title: *The Crimson Cult*) stars Boris Karloff, Christopher Lee and Barbara Steele in an unofficial adaptation of H.P. Lovecraft's story "Dreams in the Witch House." Sounds great, right? But, sadly, it's kind of a dull misfire.

I did have fun drawing Ms. Steele. After finishing the drawing in the upper left, I realized it wasn't quite right. It's not a bad likeness, but something was missing. Then it hit me: In the film, she's covered in heavy green grease-paint. I added dark gray tones to simulate the weird makeup, and … *voila*.

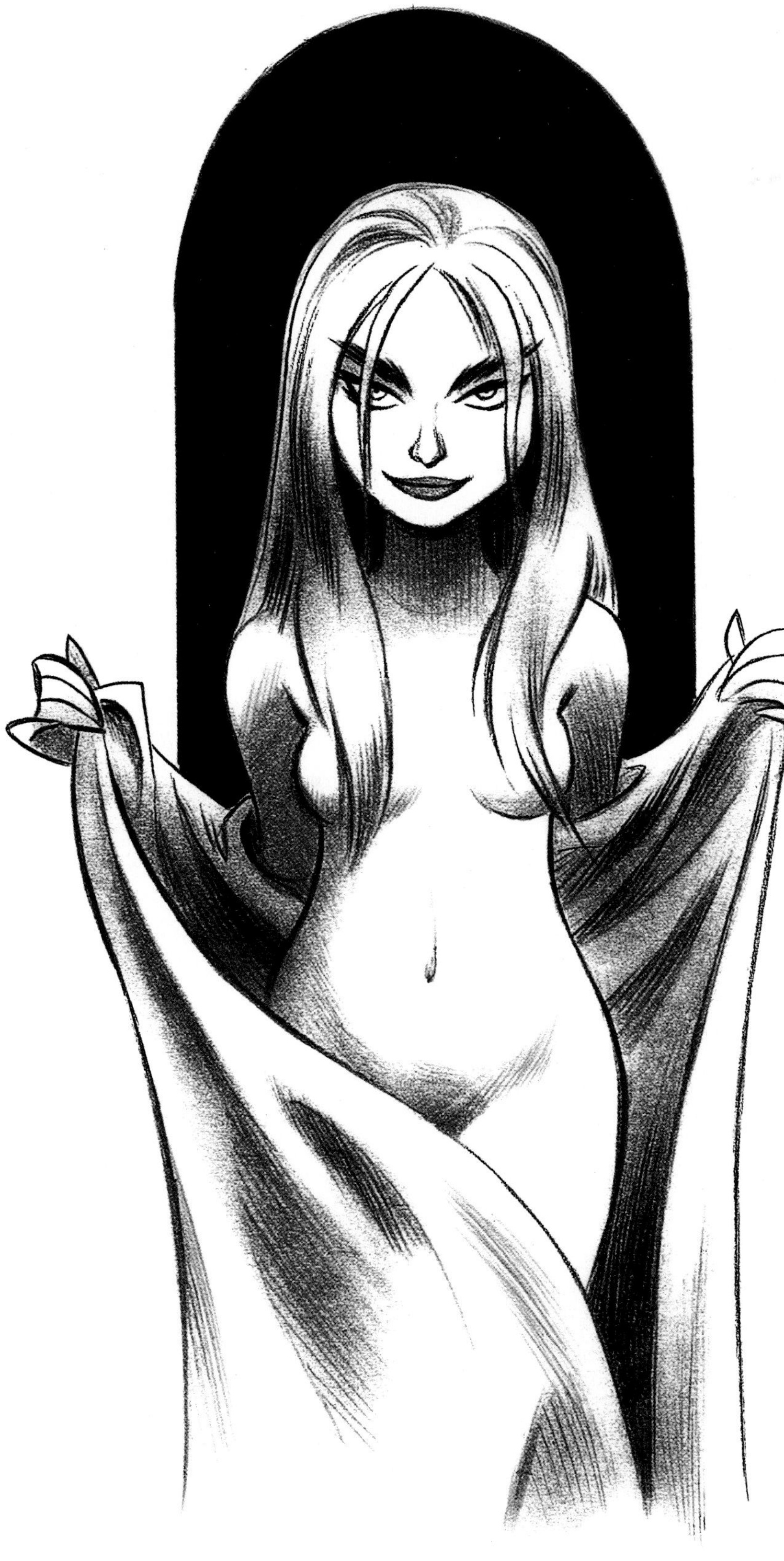

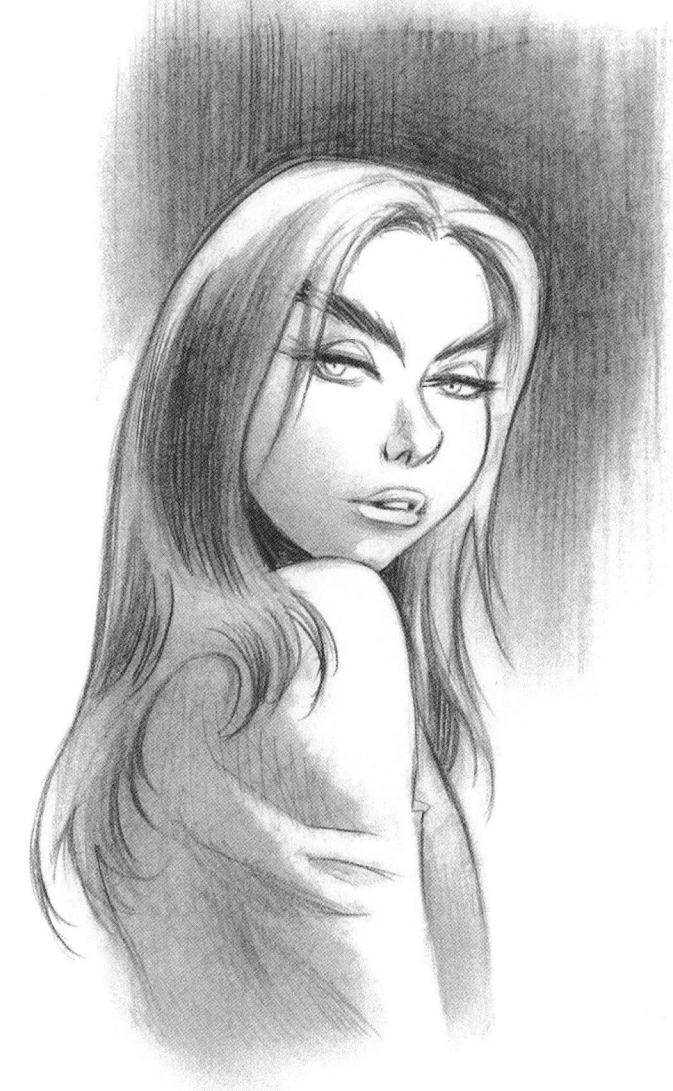

The *Blood on Satan's Claw* is probably my favorite Tigon movie, about an early 18th-century English village that comes under the influence of demonic forces. On its original release, it got middling reviews and performed poorly at the box office, but its reputation has grown over the years.

Linda Hayden is the village "Bad Girl" who gets possessed by the devil and gets "badder." At one point she tries to seduce the village's priest, right there in the church. Oh my.

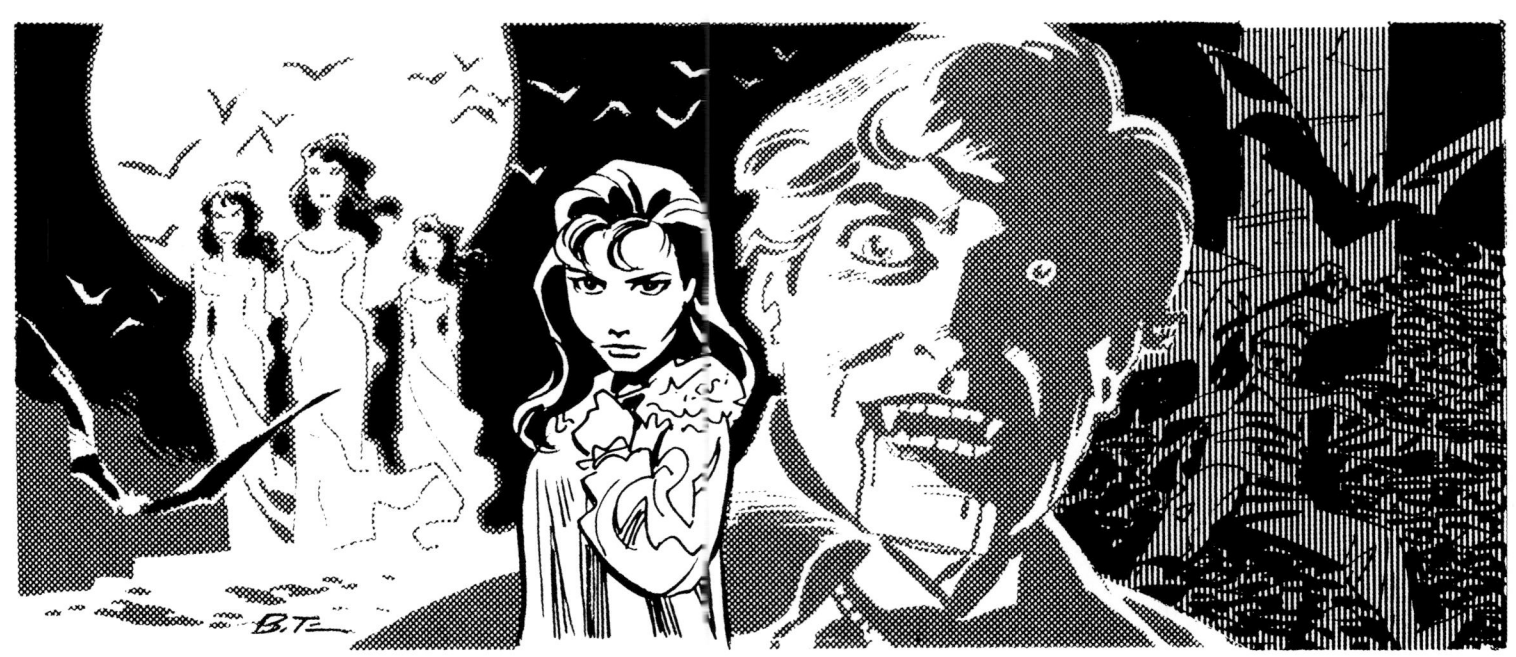

THE · BRIDES · OF
DRACULA

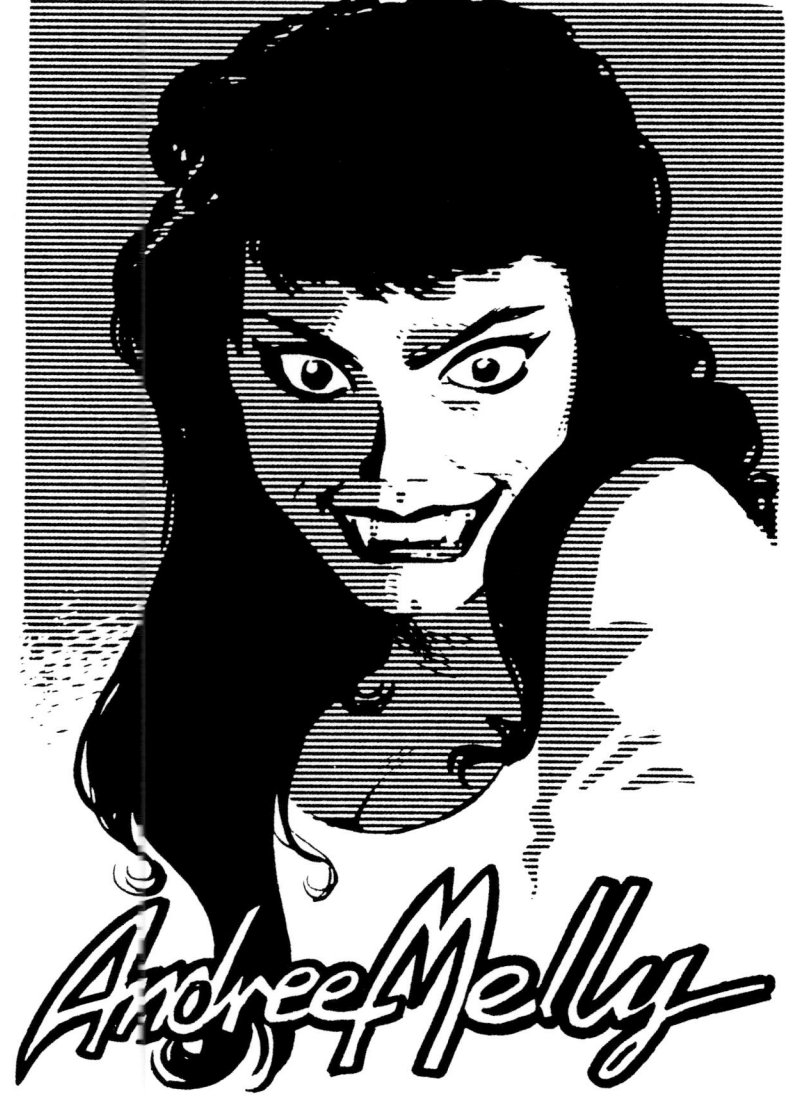

Andrée Melly

I avoided seeing *The Brides of Dracula* for years. A Hammer Dracula movie without Christopher Lee? Without *Dracula*?? How good could it be? Well … blatant bait-and-switch title aside, it's actually pretty great! In fact, it's on my short list of "All-Time Best Hammer Horrors." For one thing, it's one of the most beautiful horror films Hammer ever made. The cinematography is *gorgeous*. David Peel as substitute vampire Baron Meinster is surprisingly very good: He's handsome and charming but also genuinely menacing. There are memorable supporting performances by Martita Hunt and Freda Jackson; Marie Deveraux and Andrée Melly are the fetching undead "brides" of the title; Yvonne Monlaur is the lovely French ingenue; and Peter Cushing is back as Dr. Van Helsing.

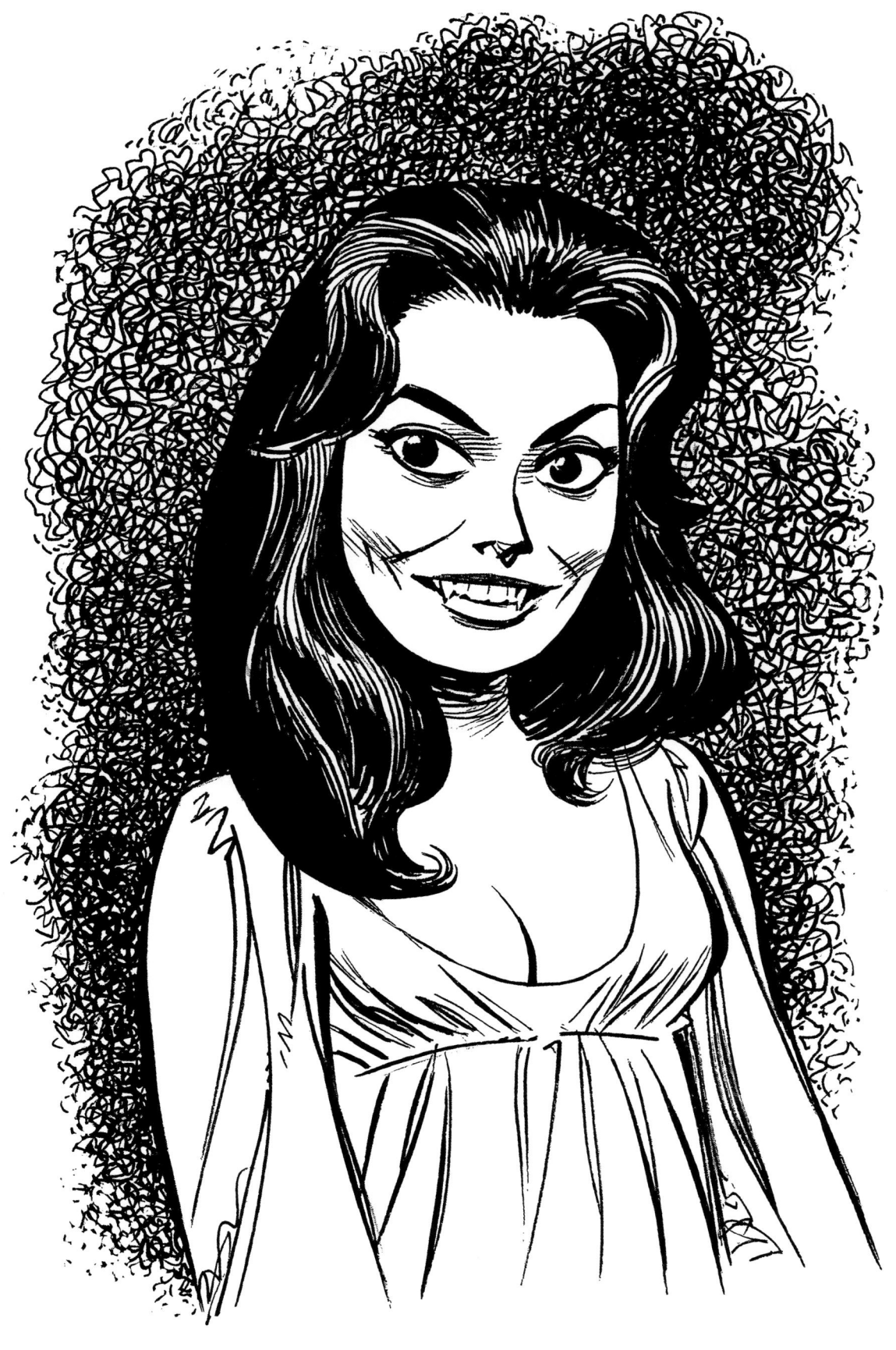

Christopher Lee returned as Dracula six years later, in *Dracula: Prince of Darkness*. Barbara Shelley's convincing transformation from sourpuss spinster to super-sexy seductress (after being exsanguinated by Dracula) is one of the film's highlights.

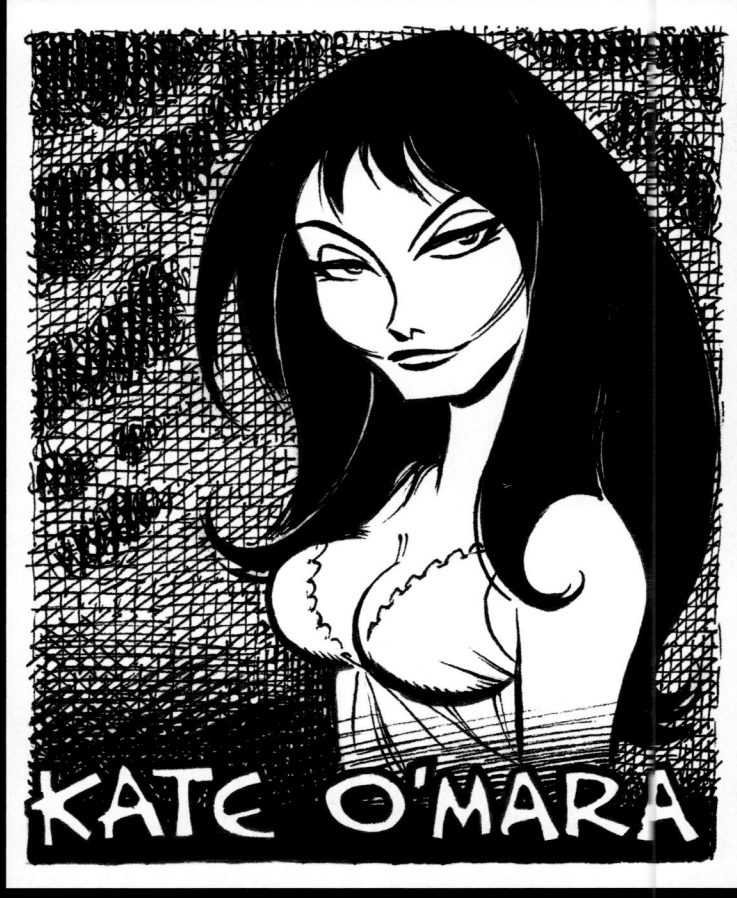

KATE O'MARA

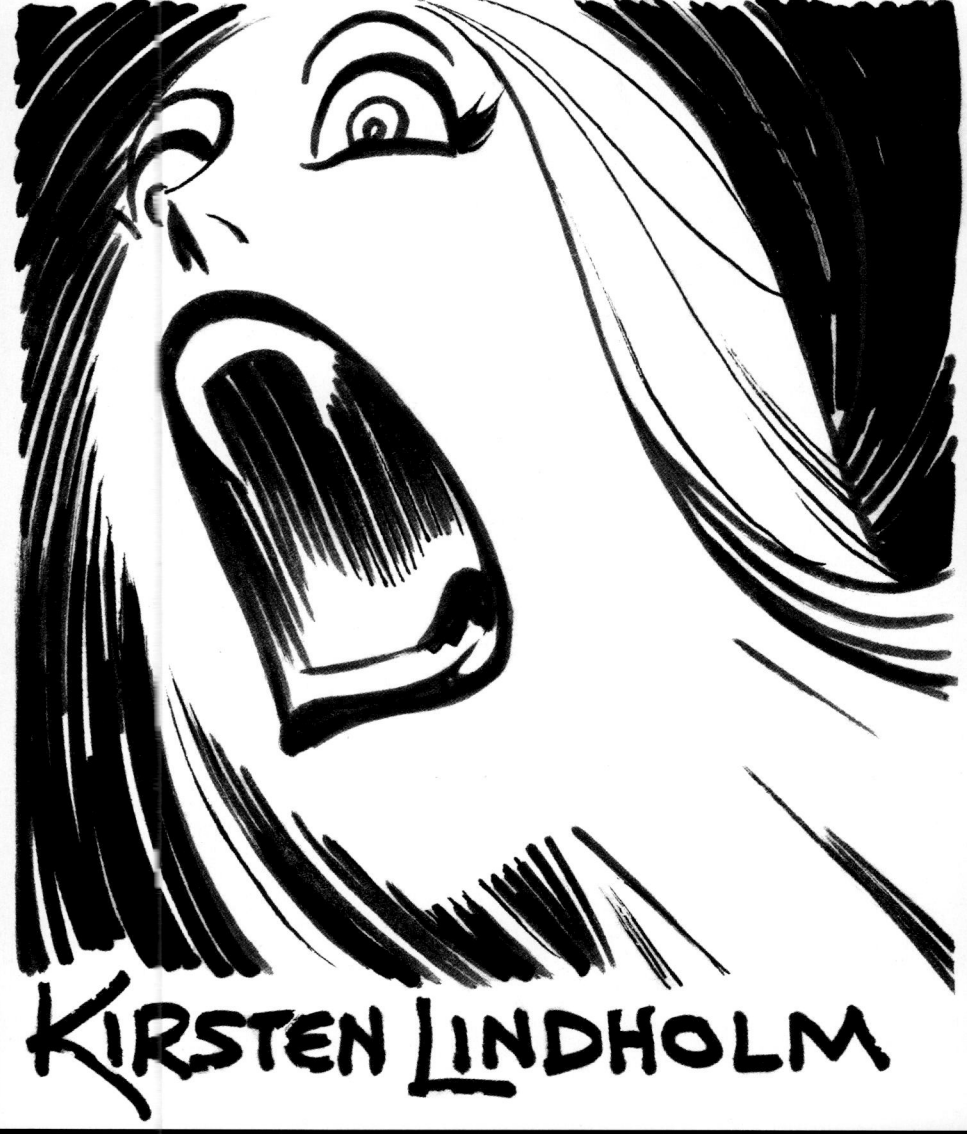

KIRSTEN LINDHOLM

It's much easier to do a decent likeness if the actor I'm drawing has distinctive facial features. Kate O'Mara in *The Vampire Lovers* was almost a parody of a beautiful woman, with her witchy "cat eyes," prominent cheekbones and full bosom. She was a lot of fun to draw.

Kirsten Lindholm was more of a challenge. She was a very, very pretty young woman, but her facial features were much less exaggerated than Ms. O'Mara's. Her character in *The Vampire Lovers* attacks Peter Cushing's character almost like a striking snake, so I tried to capture that specific motion more than her exact likeness.

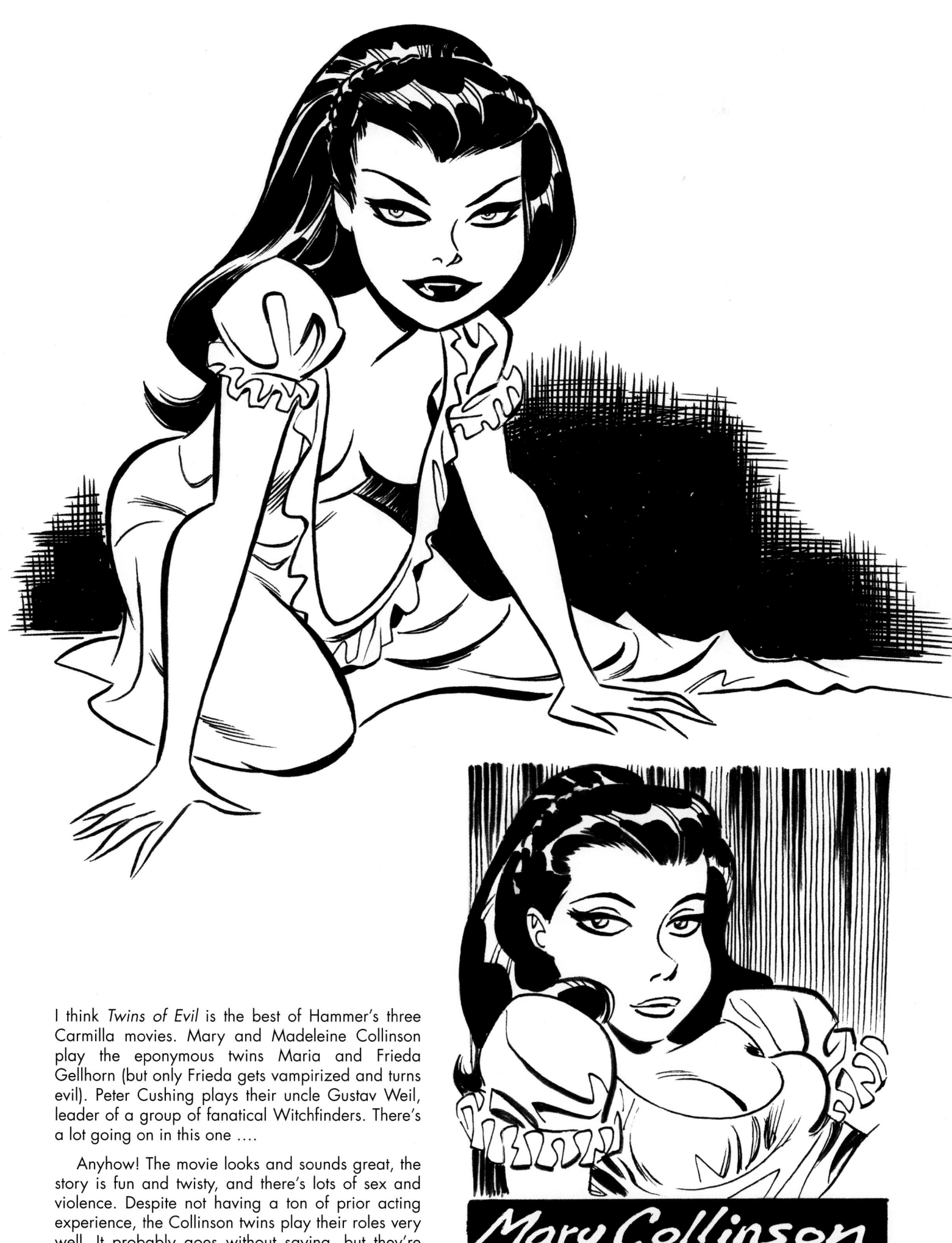

I think *Twins of Evil* is the best of Hammer's three Carmilla movies. Mary and Madeleine Collinson play the eponymous twins Maria and Frieda Gellhorn (but only Frieda gets vampirized and turns evil). Peter Cushing plays their uncle Gustav Weil, leader of a group of fanatical Witchfinders. There's a lot going on in this one ....

Anyhow! The movie looks and sounds great, the story is fun and twisty, and there's lots of sex and violence. Despite not having a ton of prior acting experience, the Collinson twins play their roles very well. It probably goes without saying, but they're both also quite beautiful.

Mary Collinson

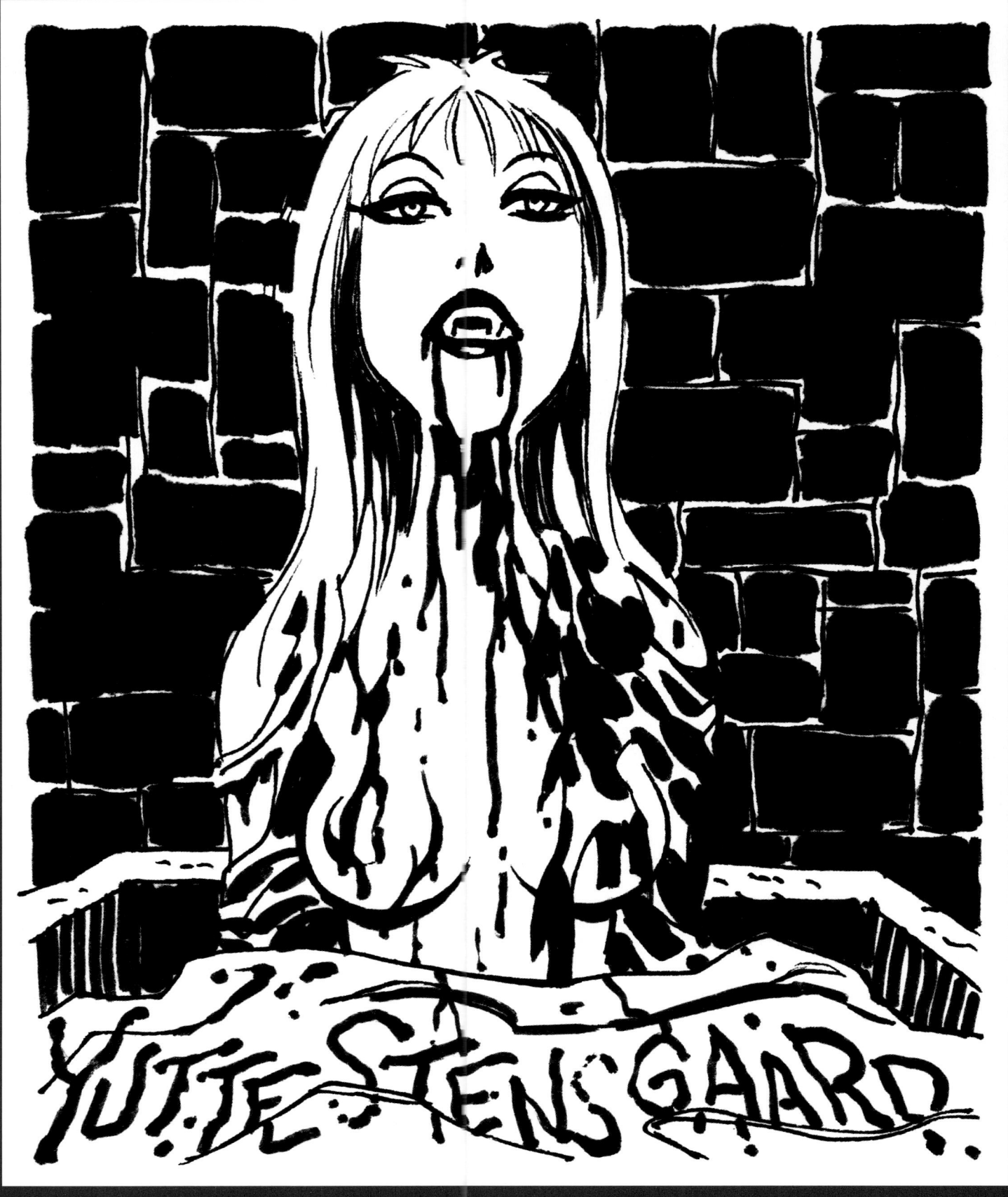

YUTTE STENSGAARD

As a kid, I'd often heard that the Hammer movies were sexier and bloodier than, say, the Universal classics, but the Hammers that ran on TV all seemed really tame. Then I saw a publicity still of Yutte Stensgaard from *Lust for a Vampire* in a coffee table book on Horror movies, with blood dripping off her fangs and all over her naked chest. Ah. So *that's* what they were talking about ….

The piece on page 47 was inspired by *The Vampire Lovers* but not an exact recreation of any specific scene from that film.

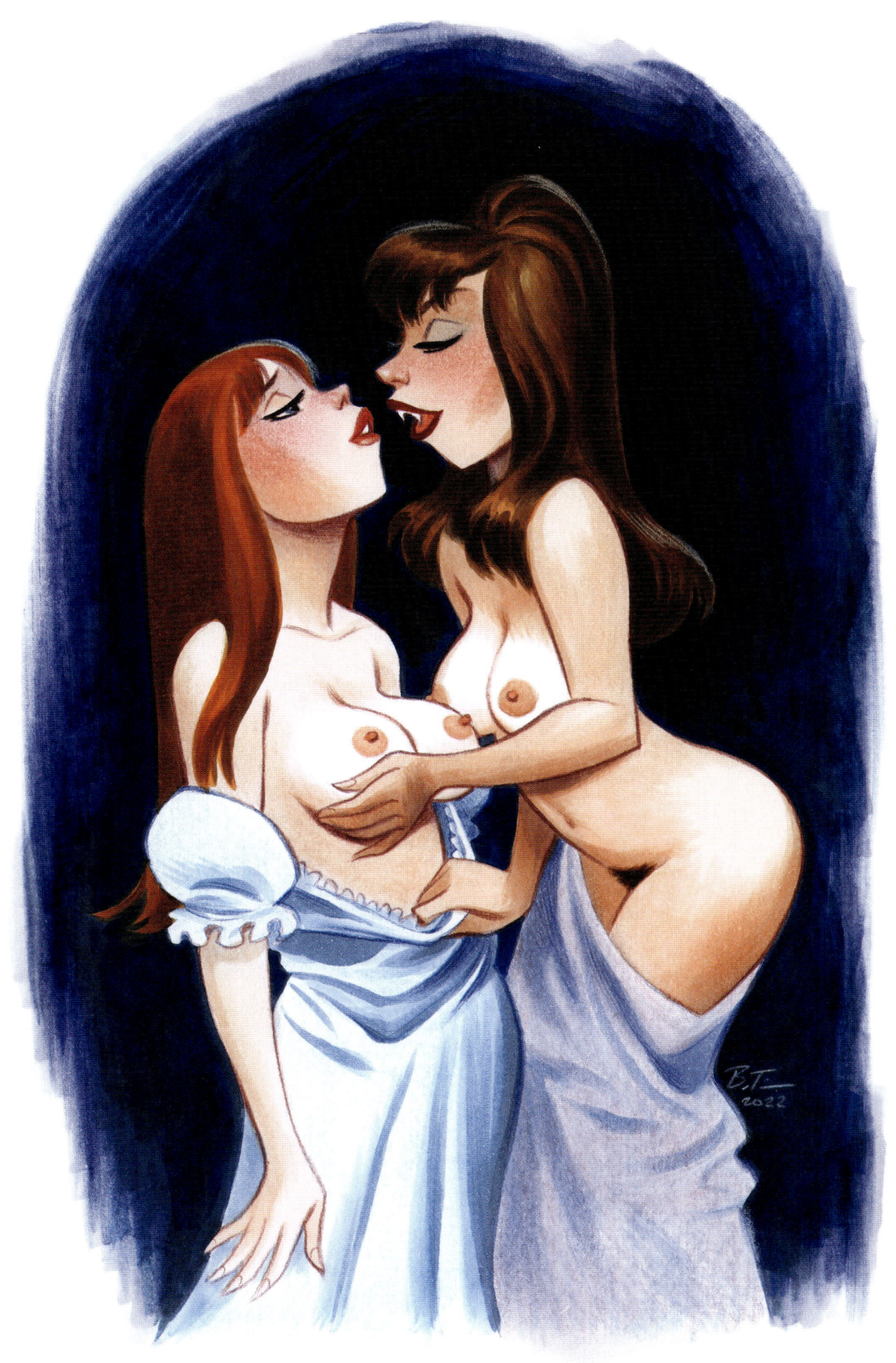

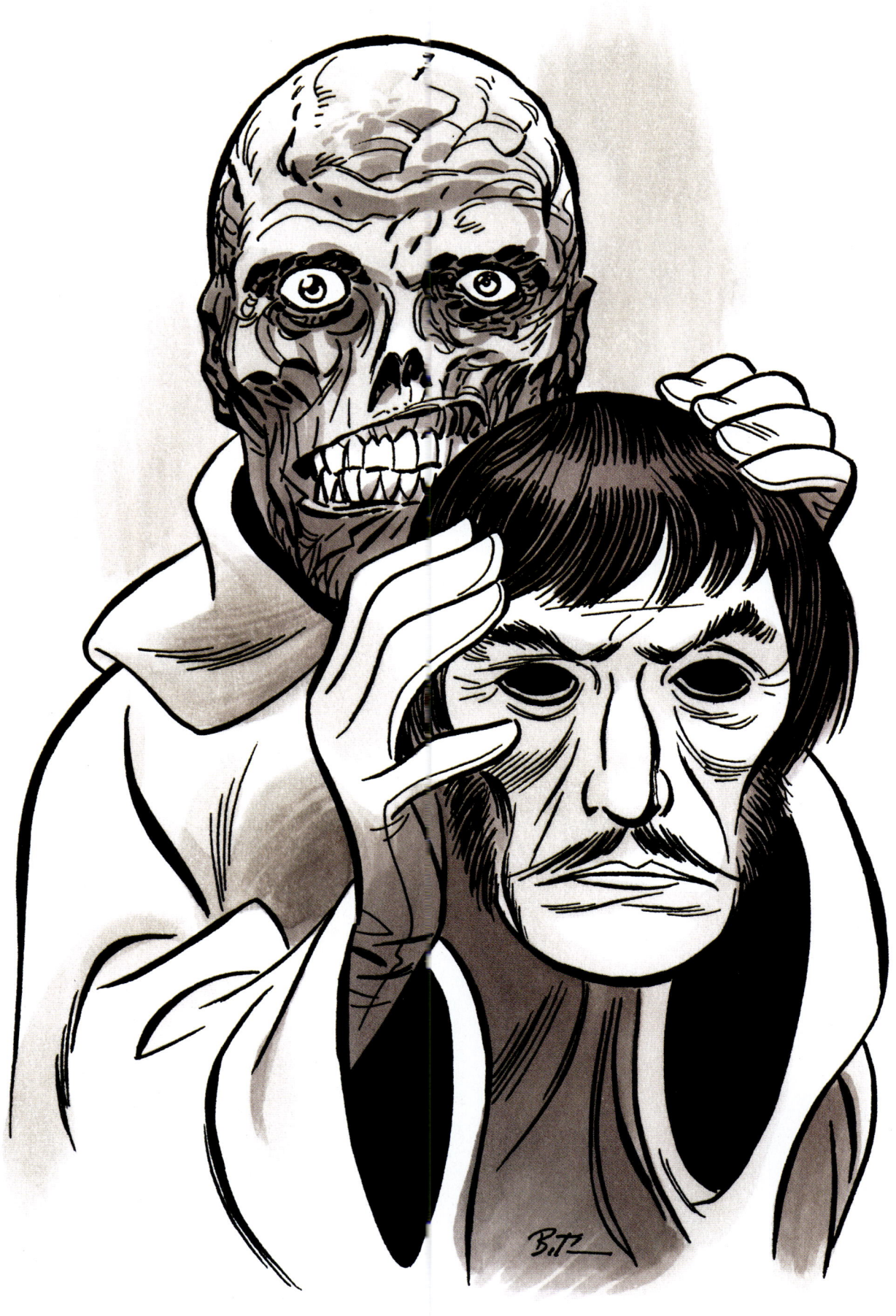

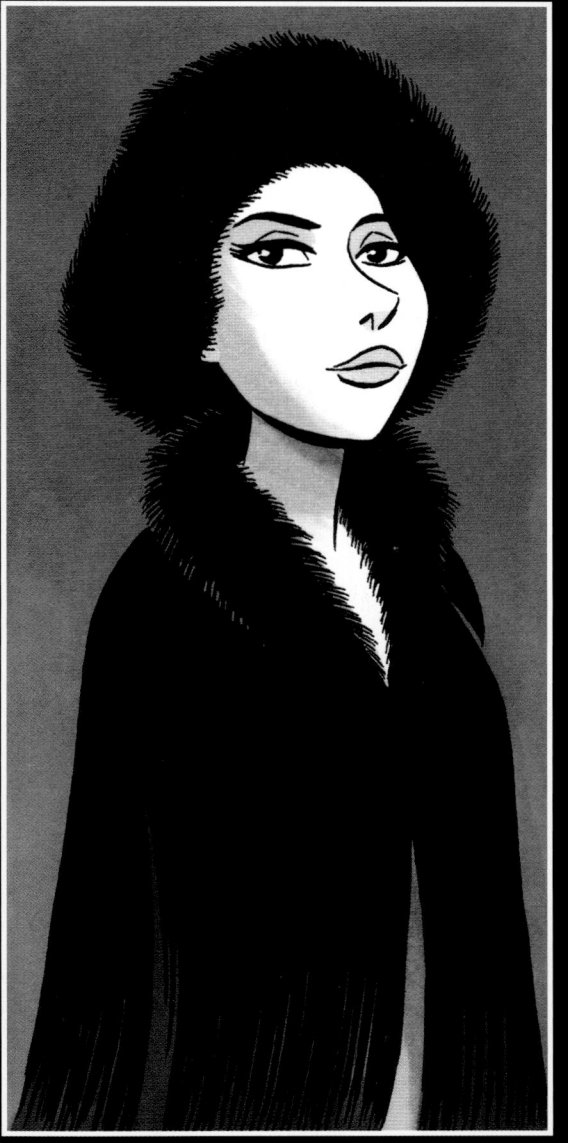

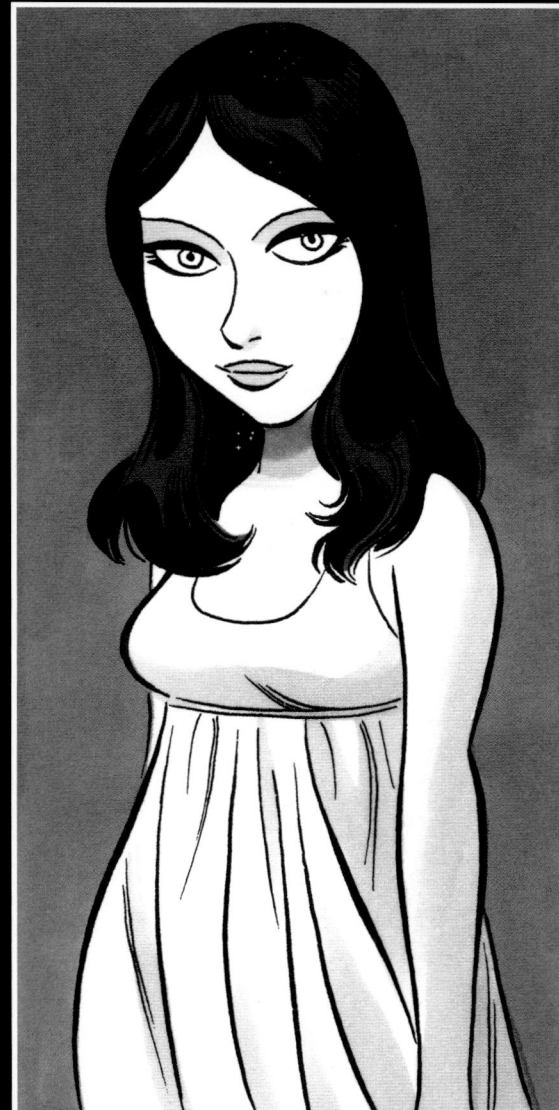

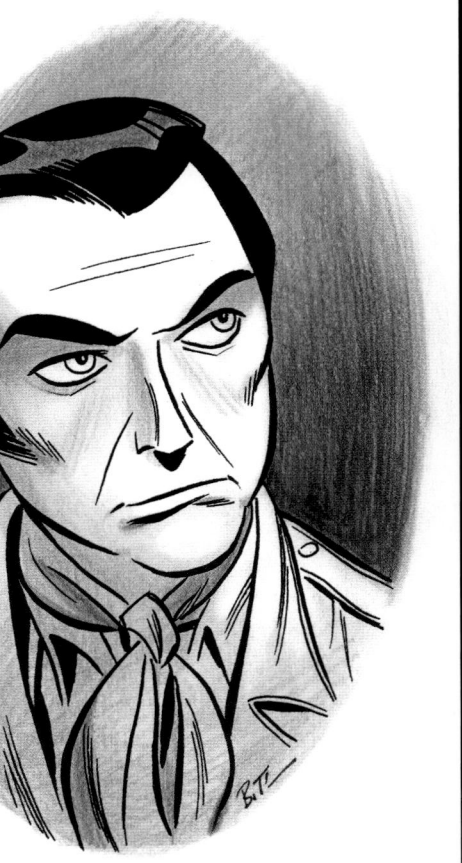

Little Shoppe #29 was the "Dr. Phibes Special." I didn't se[e]
the two Phibes movies when I was a kid, but I remember
paperback novelization of *The Abominable Dr. Phibes* on
rack at the grocery store and hearing the radio ads. Vin[cent]
swearing vengeance on his enemies in his sinister, metalli[c]
Holy crap! The whole Phibes thing seriously gave me the cree[ps]
I finally saw them years later, I was surprised to find that th[ey]
really all that scary and that they both had strong elements [of]
They're still great fun, though. Most "Phibes Phans" seem to
first film, but I like 'em both about equally.

The part of Phibes' assistant, Vulnavia, was recast for t[he]
Dr. Phibes Rises Again. I decided to draw the two ladies
"contrasting bookends"—Virginia North in her heavy furs,
in her silky nightgown.

Robert Quarry as Darrus Biederbeck (left), Phibes' nem[esis]
Phibes Rises Again.

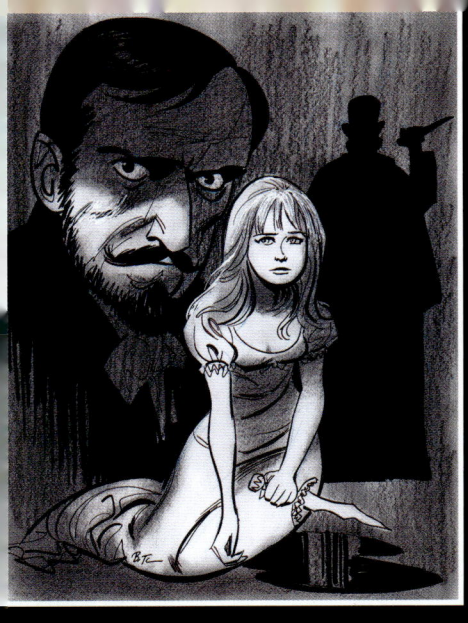

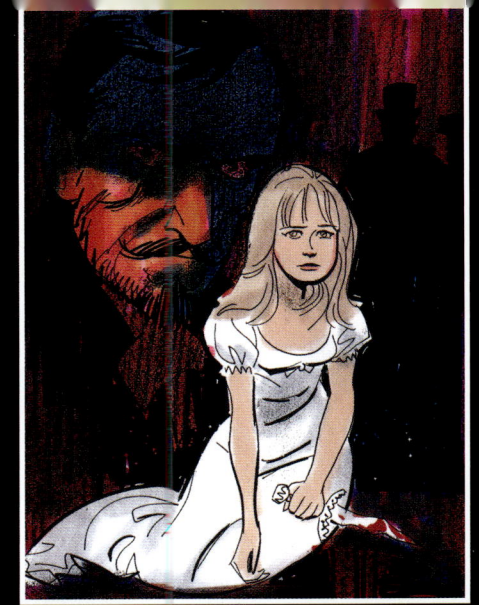

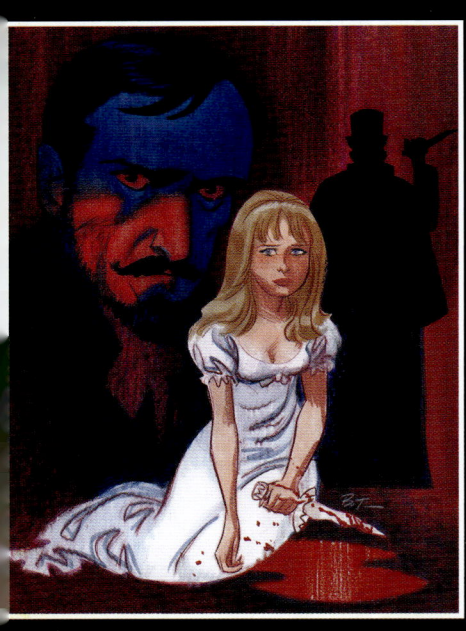

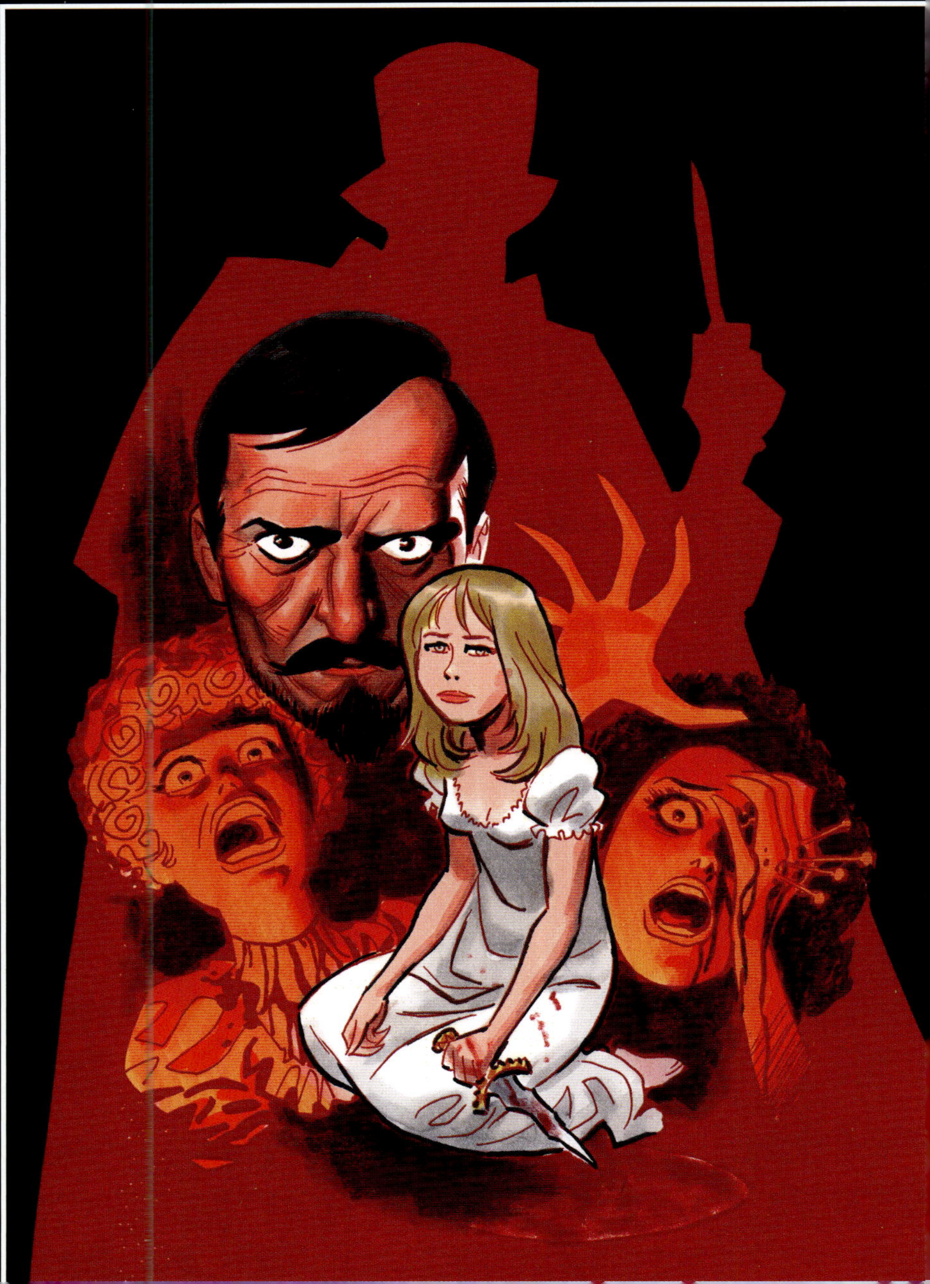

Hands of the Ripper is another of my "Top Ten Hammers." It's smart, stylish and suspenseful. Angharad Rees and Eric Porter are superb in it. The finale actually chokes me up a bit, and I can't think of any other Hammer film that affects me that way. When Dick asked me to do the back cover, it was an automatic "yes."

Once I settled on a layout that I liked, I ended up doing a "Red" version and a "(Mostly) Blue (But With Some Red)" version. I like aspects of each one, but overall I do like the "Blue" version better. I love the "reverse silhouette" of The Ripper in the "Red" version but couldn't figure out how to make that work in the "Blue" one. Oh well.

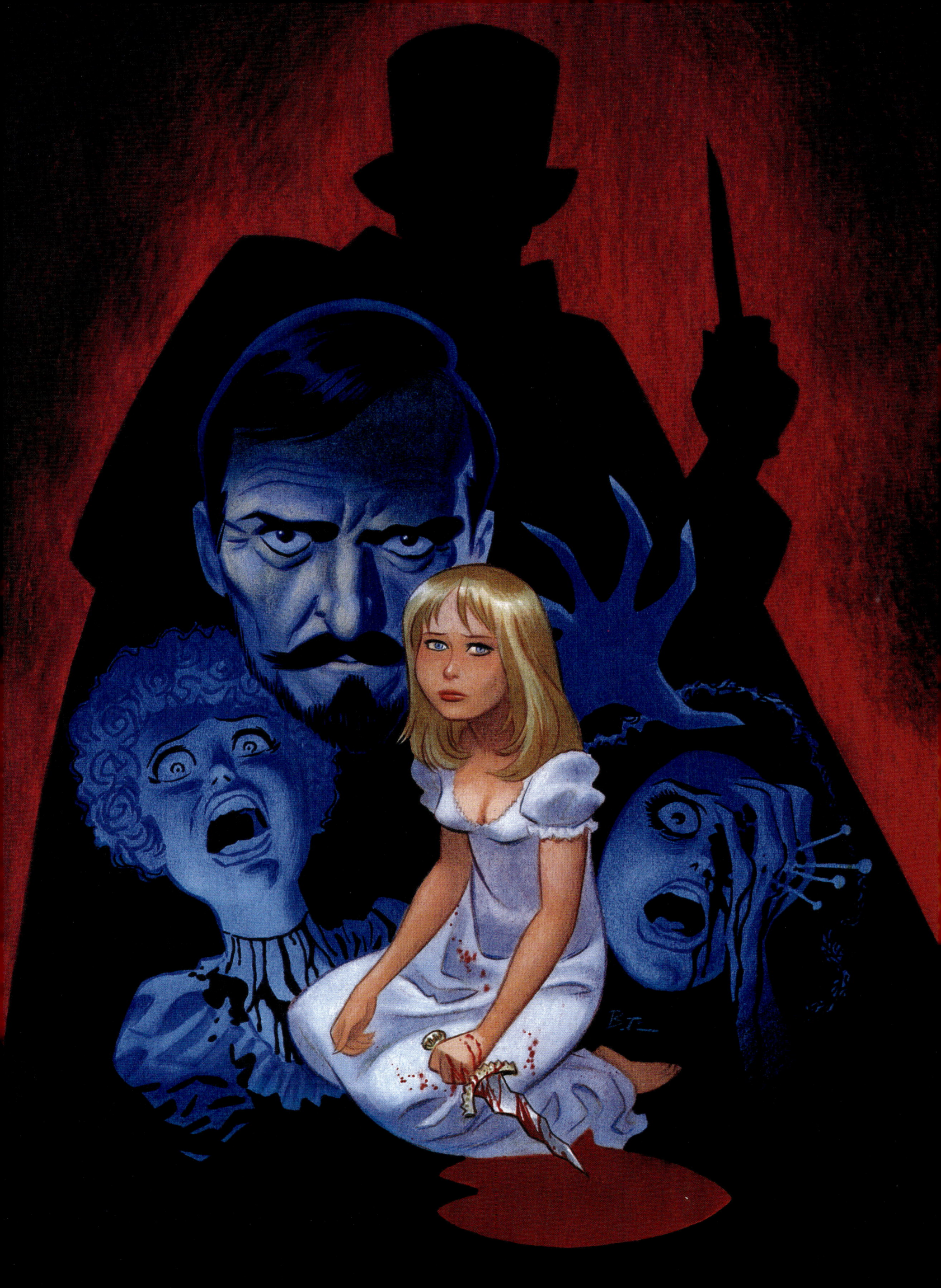

I wouldn't say *Vampire Circus* is necessarily the "best" Hammer movie, but it's my favorite. As I've mentioned before, Hammer had long had a reputation for emphasizing sex and violence in their horror films. In my mind, *Vampire Circus* is the epitome of Hammer's "Boobs and Blood" style. When I first saw it on a Saturday afternoon in the mid-1980s on cable's USA Network, the in-house censors had done their best to trim all the "naughtiest bits," and it *still* packed an incredibly potent, darkly erotic charge. But it's not just the increased nudity and gore that fascinates here. The somewhat tawdry circus setting—with its supernaturally enhanced animal acts, aerialists, illusions and other attractions—adds a layer of nightmarishly dangerous atmosphere. It all feels deliciously, deliriously "wrong."

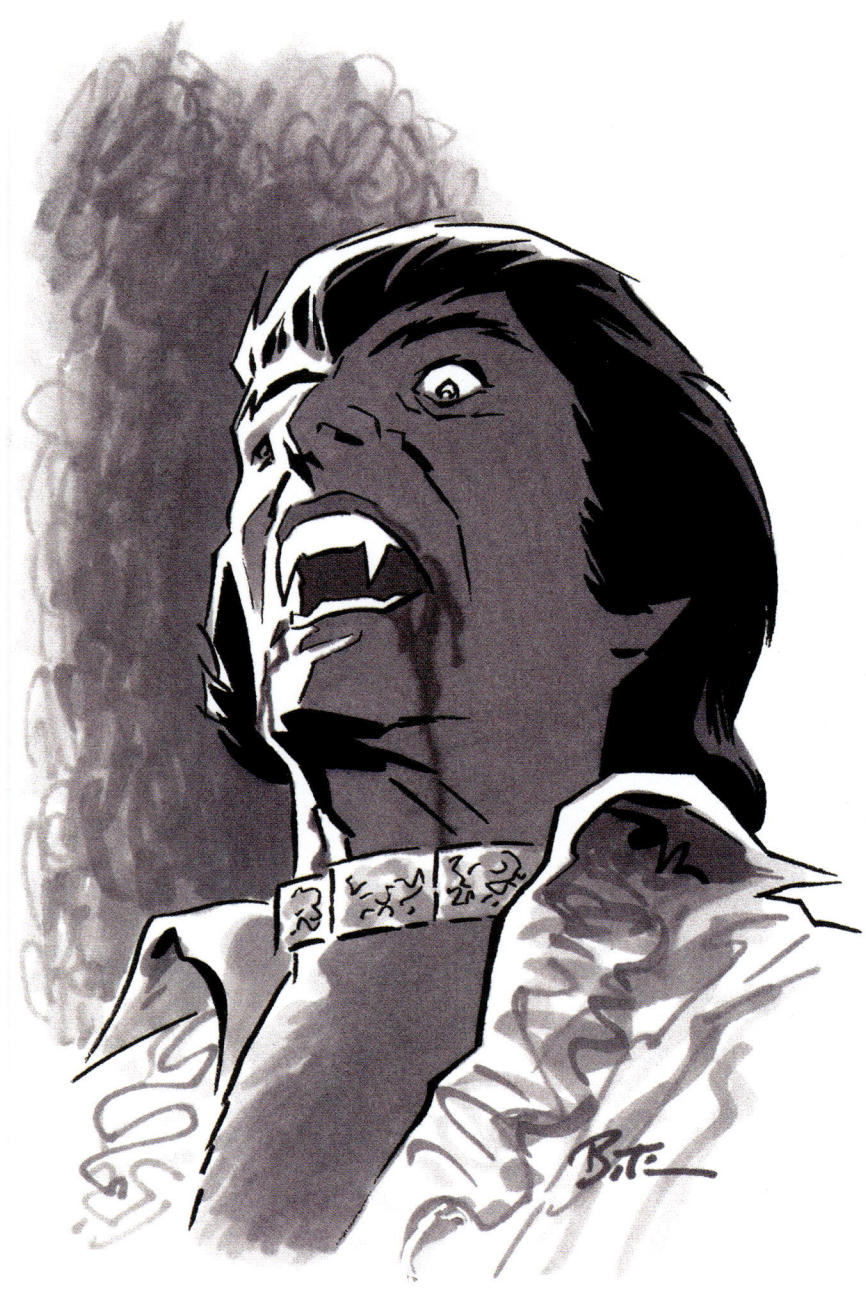

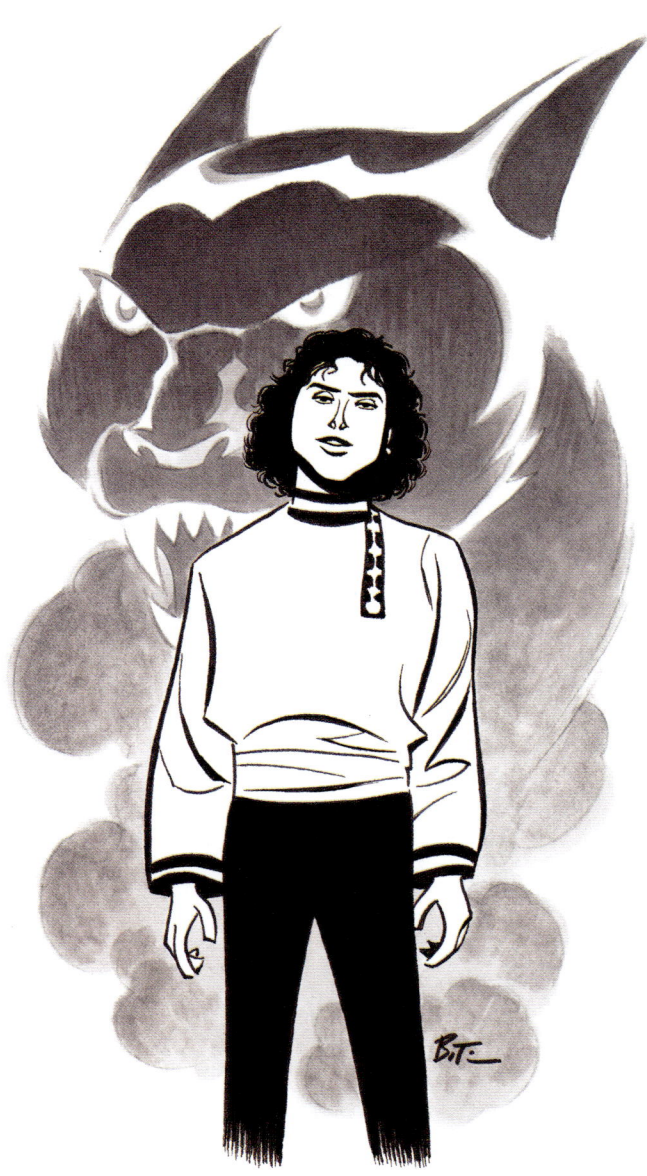

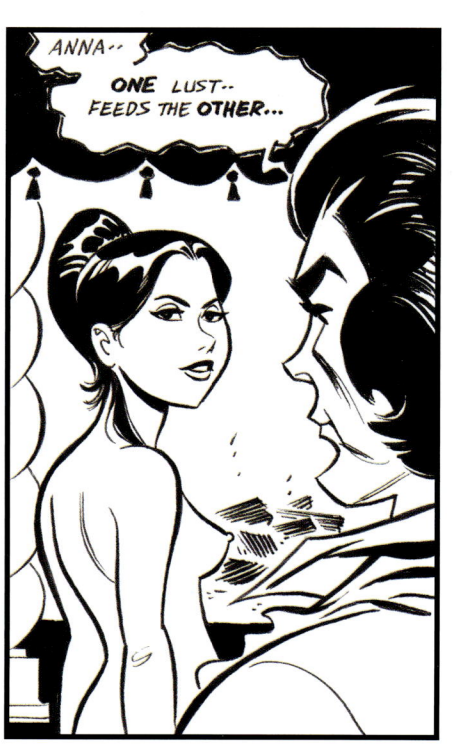

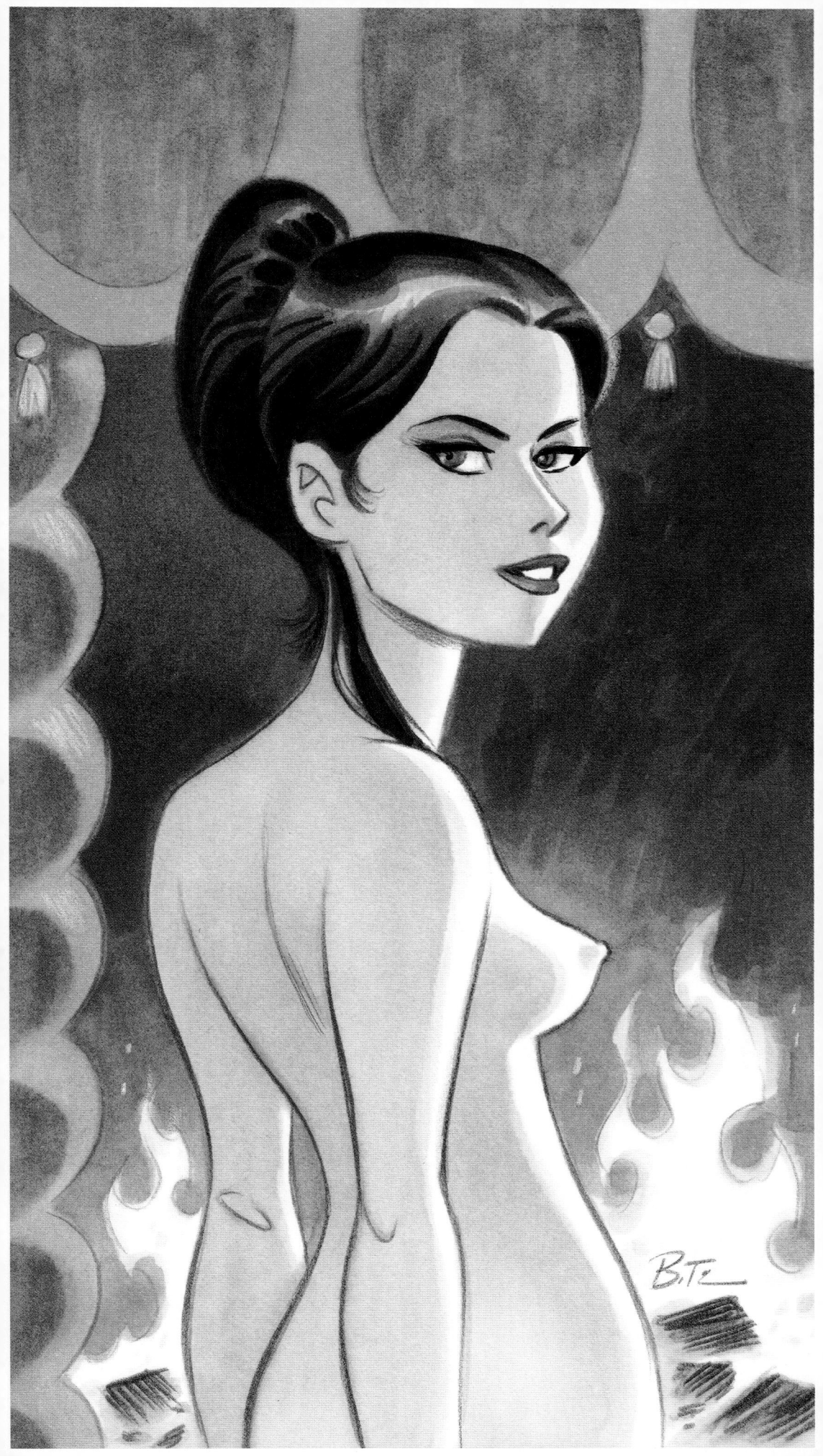

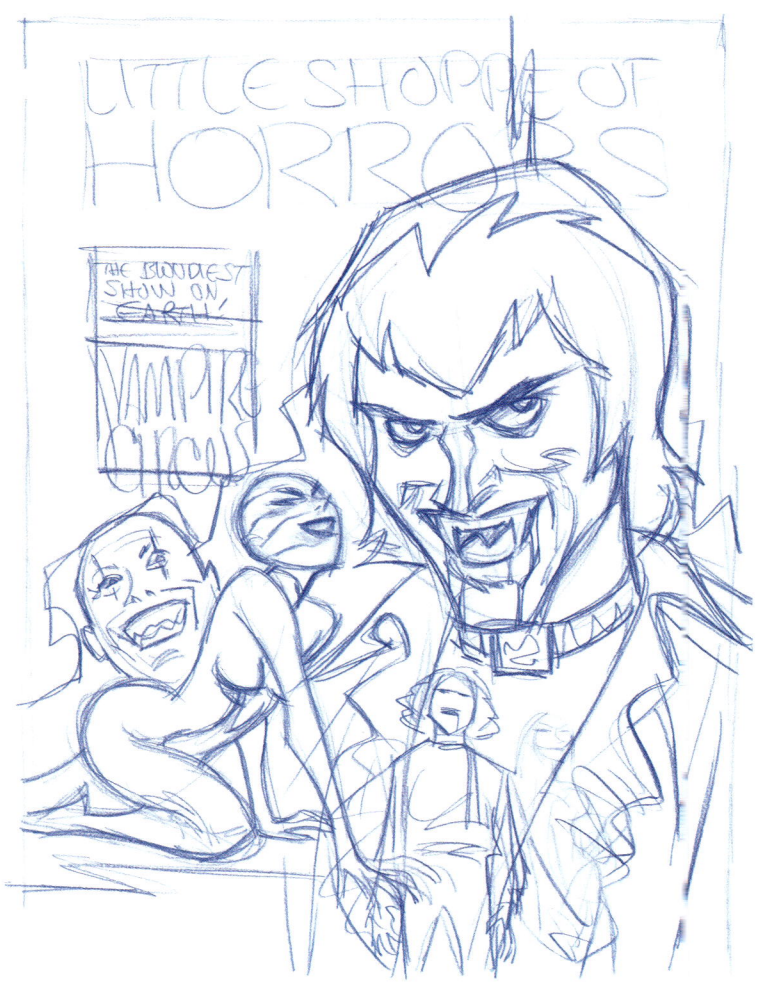

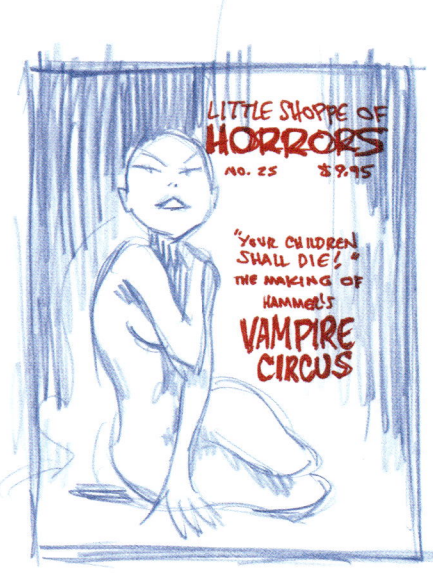

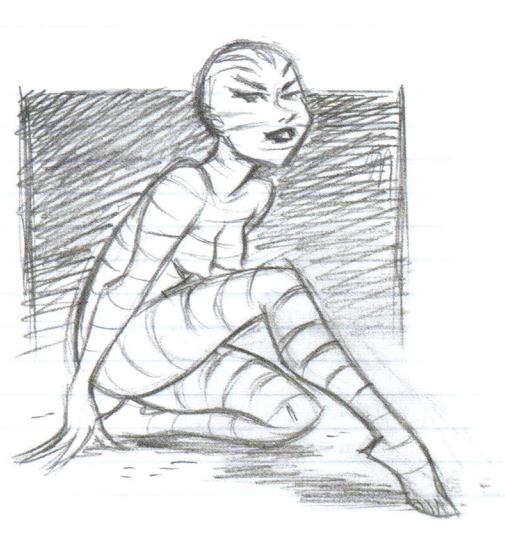

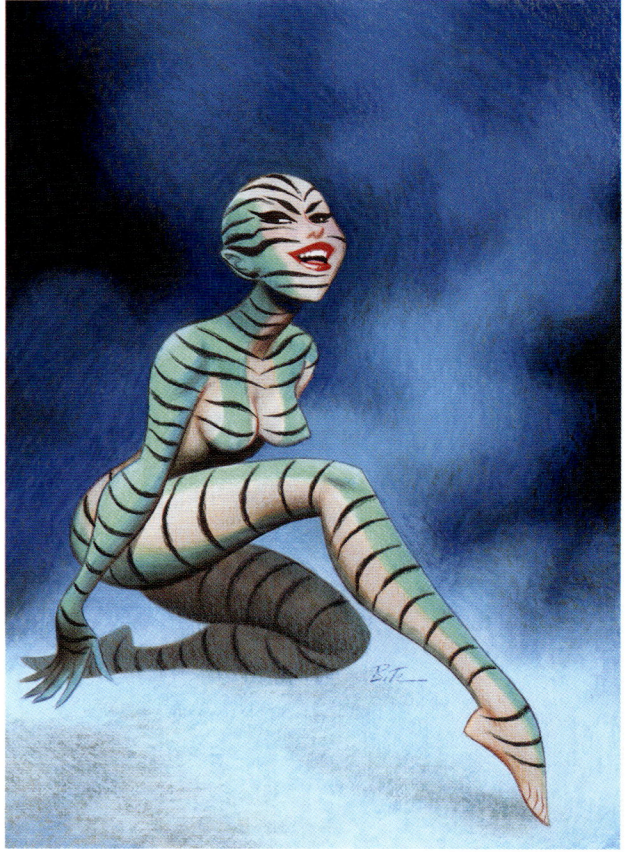

The movie is so full of bizarre imagery that, when I began sketching cover concepts, I greedily tried to cram as much as I could into a single composition. I don't remember how many roughs I did, but it was a *lot*, and I didn't love any of them. Ultimately, I abandoned the montage idea and decided to focus solely on actress/dancer Serena as the Tiger Woman. She's probably the single most memorable key image from the movie, alluring and repellent in equal measure—*Vampire Circus* in a nutshell.

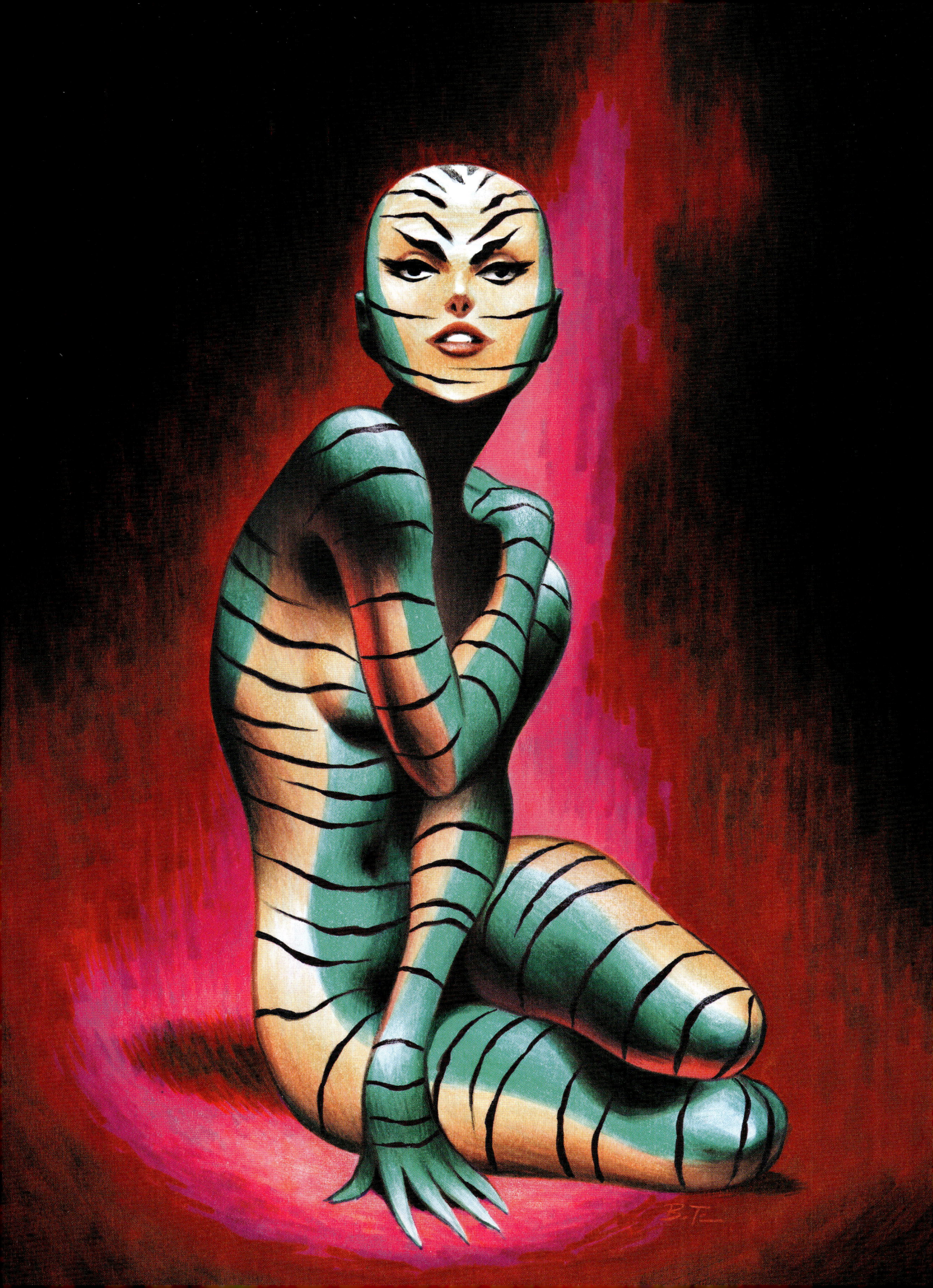

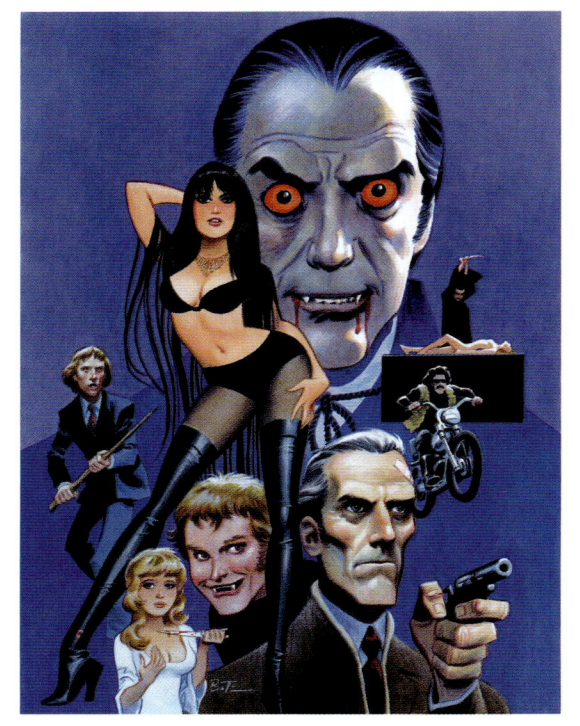

I'd had a blast doing the back cover for *Little Shoppe* # 22, featuring a montage of elements from Hammer's two "Modern Day" Dracula movies, and was fairly pleased with the result. Years later, just for shits and giggles, I started sketching out ideas for a companion piece featuring characters from the later films in the Frankenstein series. This is as far as I got with it. I may get around to doing a full-color version someday. But then again, I may not ....

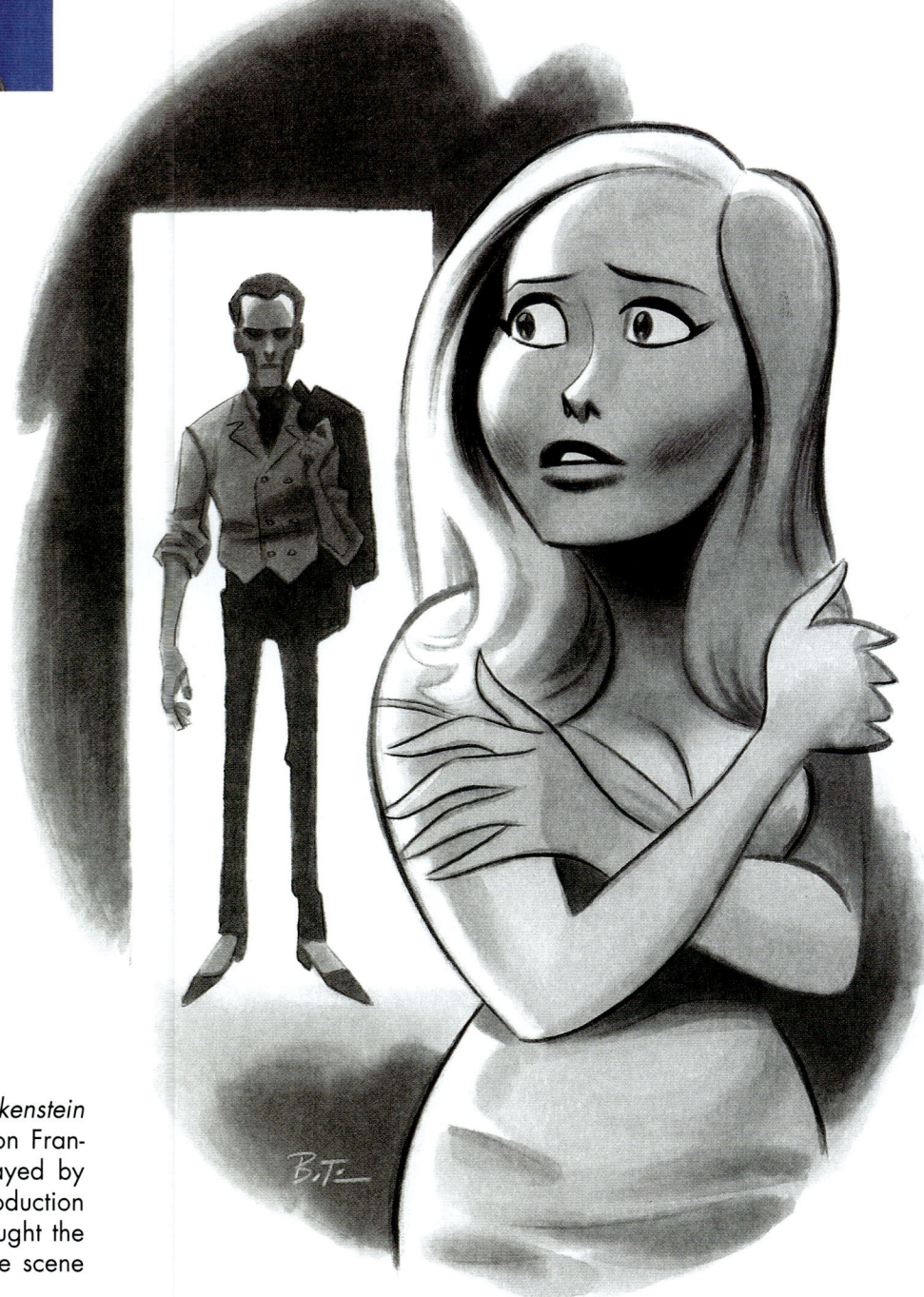

There's a controversial sequence in *Frankenstein Must Be Destroyed* where Cushing's Baron Frankenstein rapes his reluctant assistant, played by Veronica Carlson. It was added in mid-production by studio head James Carreras, who thought the movie needed some sex. The thing is, the scene isn't remotely sexy—not in the least.

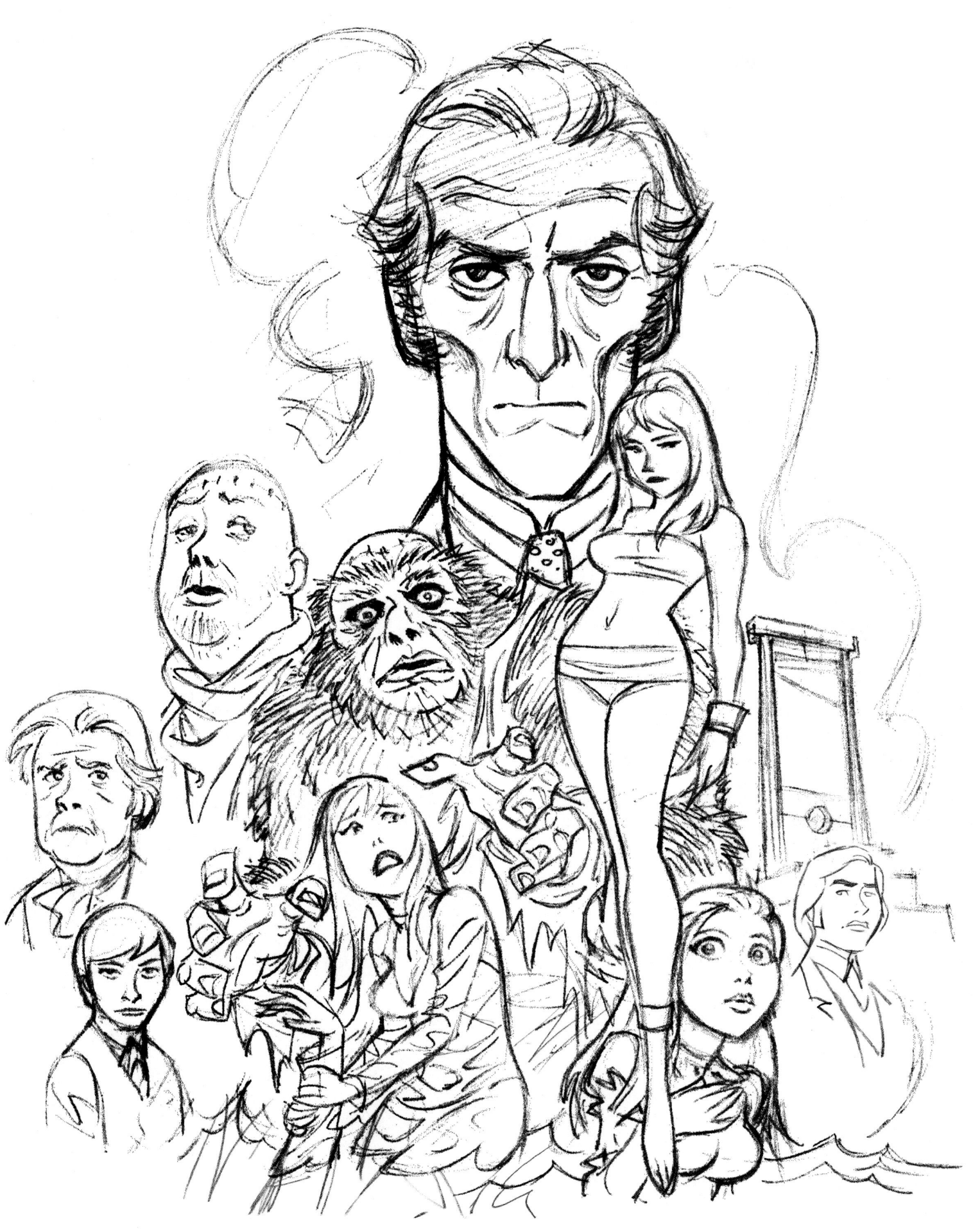

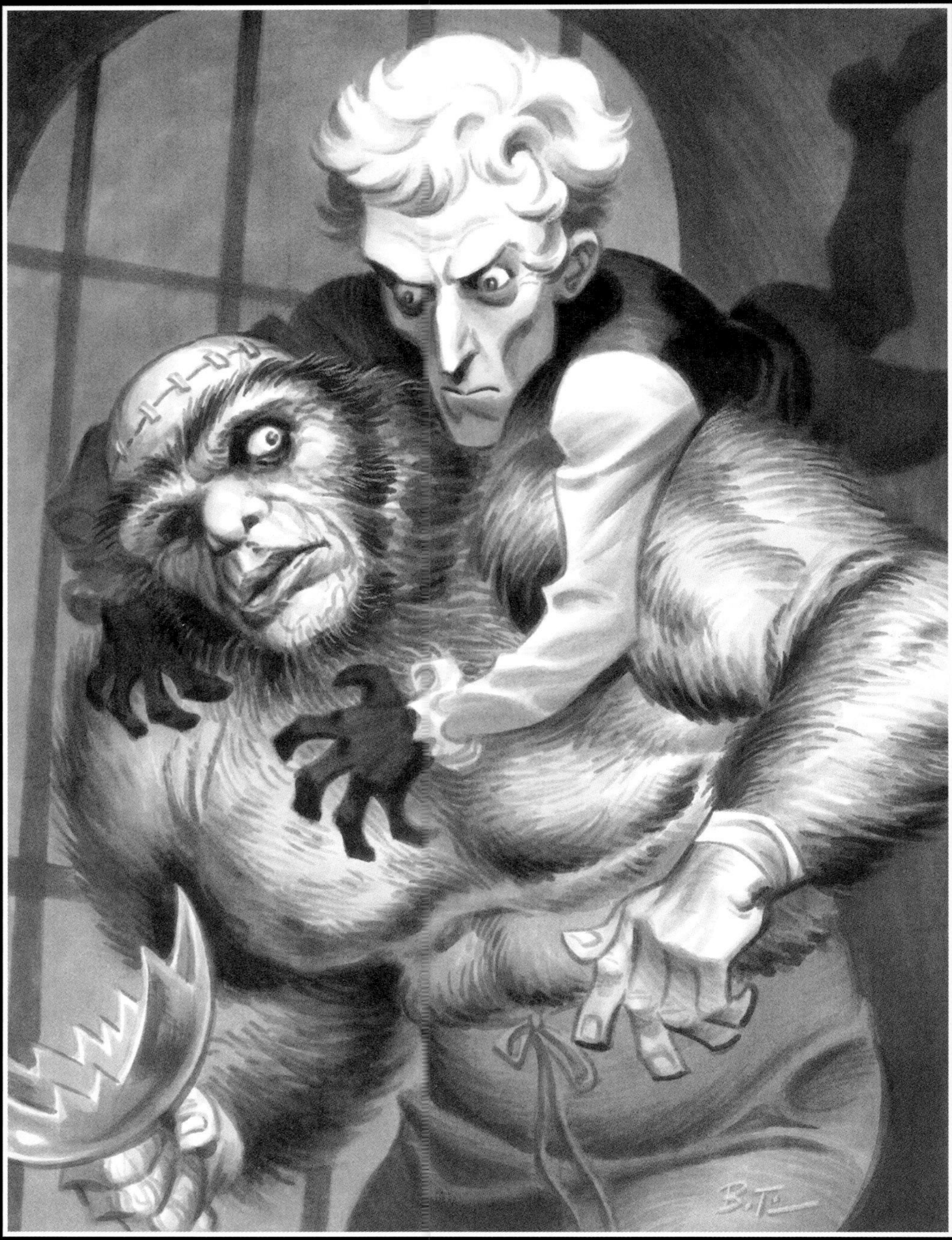

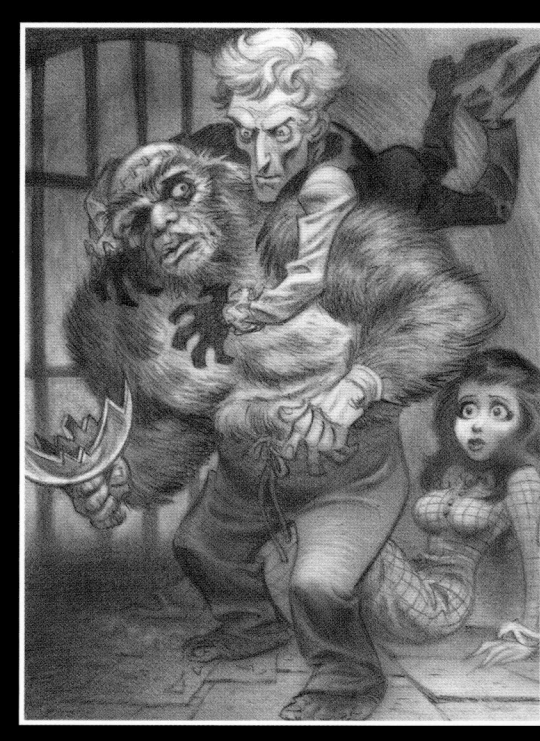

Unlike Universal's Frankenstein films, the Hammer series follows the misadventures of the creator, not his creature. Half of the movies in the sequence don't even have a traditional monster in them. It's certainly a bold creative choice ... but is it a *good* choice? Call me old-fashioned, but I think any movie with the word "Frankenstein" in the title really ought to have a proper monster in it! The last film in the series, *Frankenstein and the Monster From Hell*, does have one. But yeesh .... I'm not crazy about the design. Oh well!

Anyhow, I did the piece in the lower right first, but I wasn't happy with my drawing of Madeline Smith. For my second pass, I cut in tighter on the composition and just cropped her out of the shot. I like the tighter version better overall.

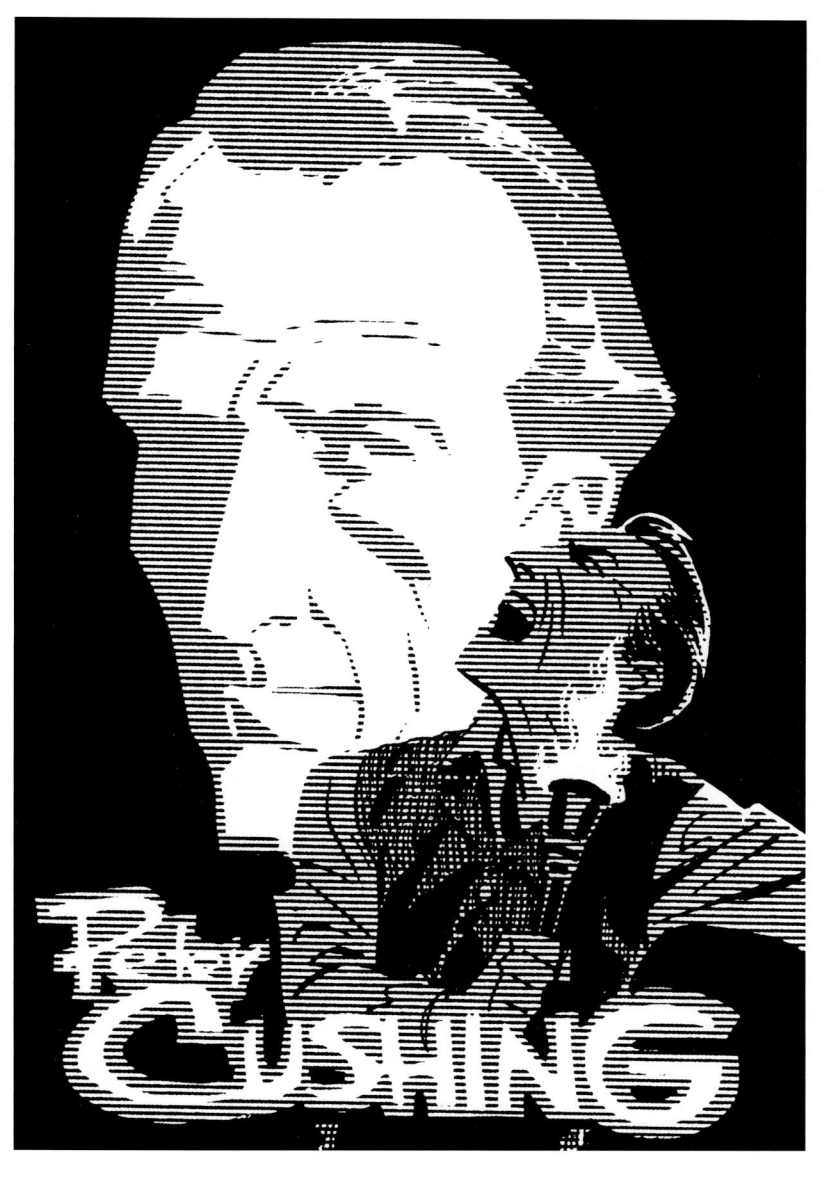

There's a neat "shock scene" in *The Brides of Dracula* where Van Helsing has been bitten by a vampire and burns out the contagion by jamming a small torch into his neck wound. Cushing totally sells the moment. It looks *very* painful!

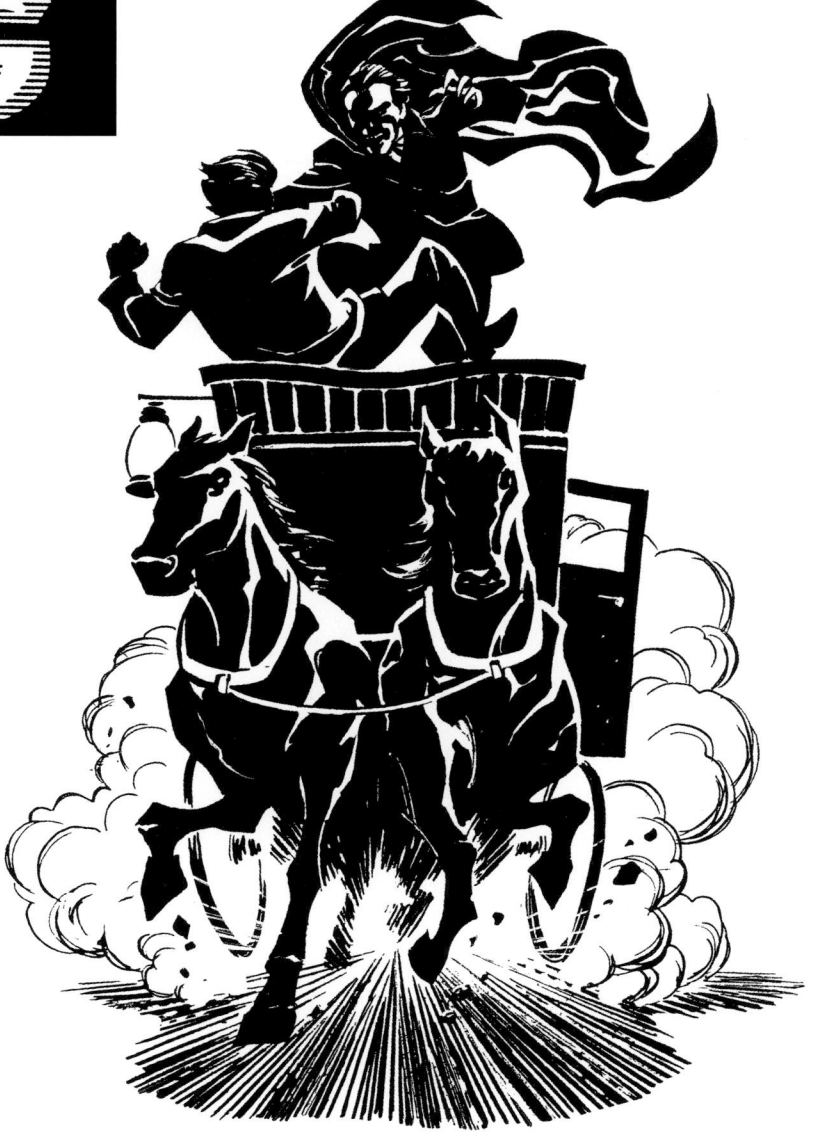

Dracula A.D. 1972 begins with Van Helsing and Dracula having their "final" battle atop a runaway carriage in 1872. The carriage crashes, and they both die. Cut to the "present day," and it's all bell-bottoms and fringed vests and rock music and swingin' chicks and hapless "with-it" dialogue. Many "Hammerheads" consider it the worst of the Hammer Dracula films, but I get a big kick out of it. The pre-title sequence is well-staged and exciting, but I probably shouldn't have chosen that bit to illustrate. Turns out horses are *really* hard to draw.

GO-GO GHOULS

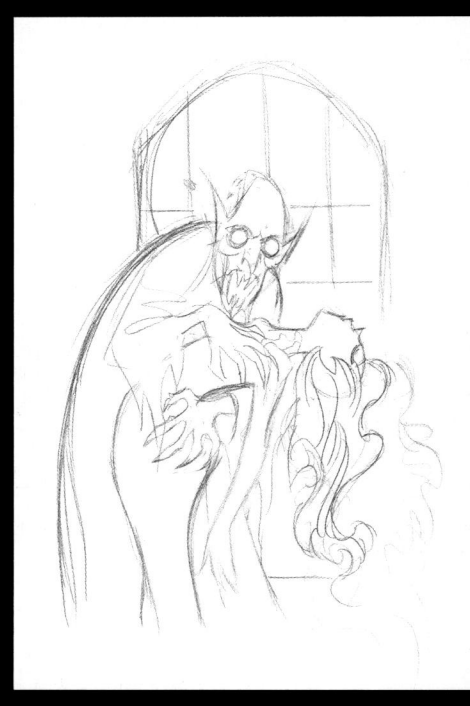

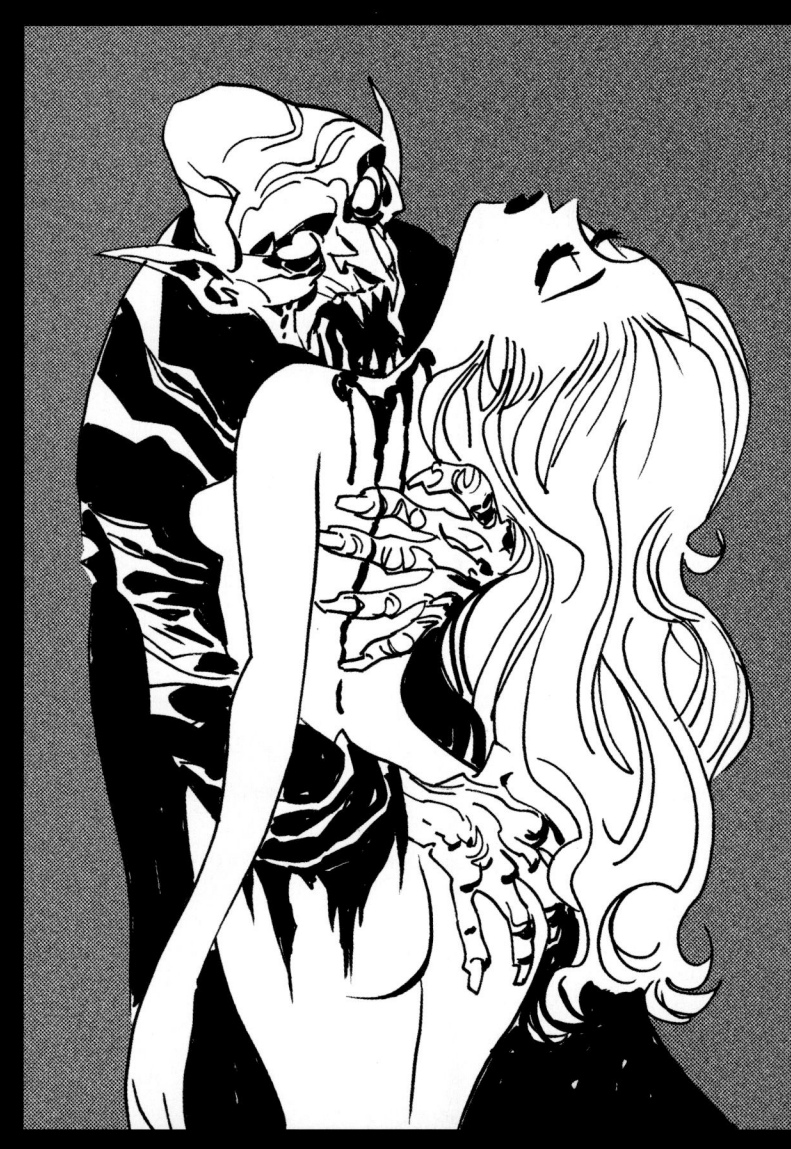

I love drawing monsters, and I love drawing beautiful women, so doing art for the *Monsters and Dames* art books was always fun for me. One year I decided I wanted to do a nasty-looking "Nosferatu-esque" vampire feeding on a pretty lady. As usual, I did a bunch of preliminary sketches before settling on one.

I like the piece on page 61 a lot. The thick, swirly brush-strokes in the background, as well as the languid textures in the lady's hair and the folds of her gown, remind me a bit of the work of Esteban Maroto. I may have been subconsciously trying to channel his style.

Oh, by the way—the color Nosferatu piece on page 1 of this book is the one I ended up sending in for the art book.

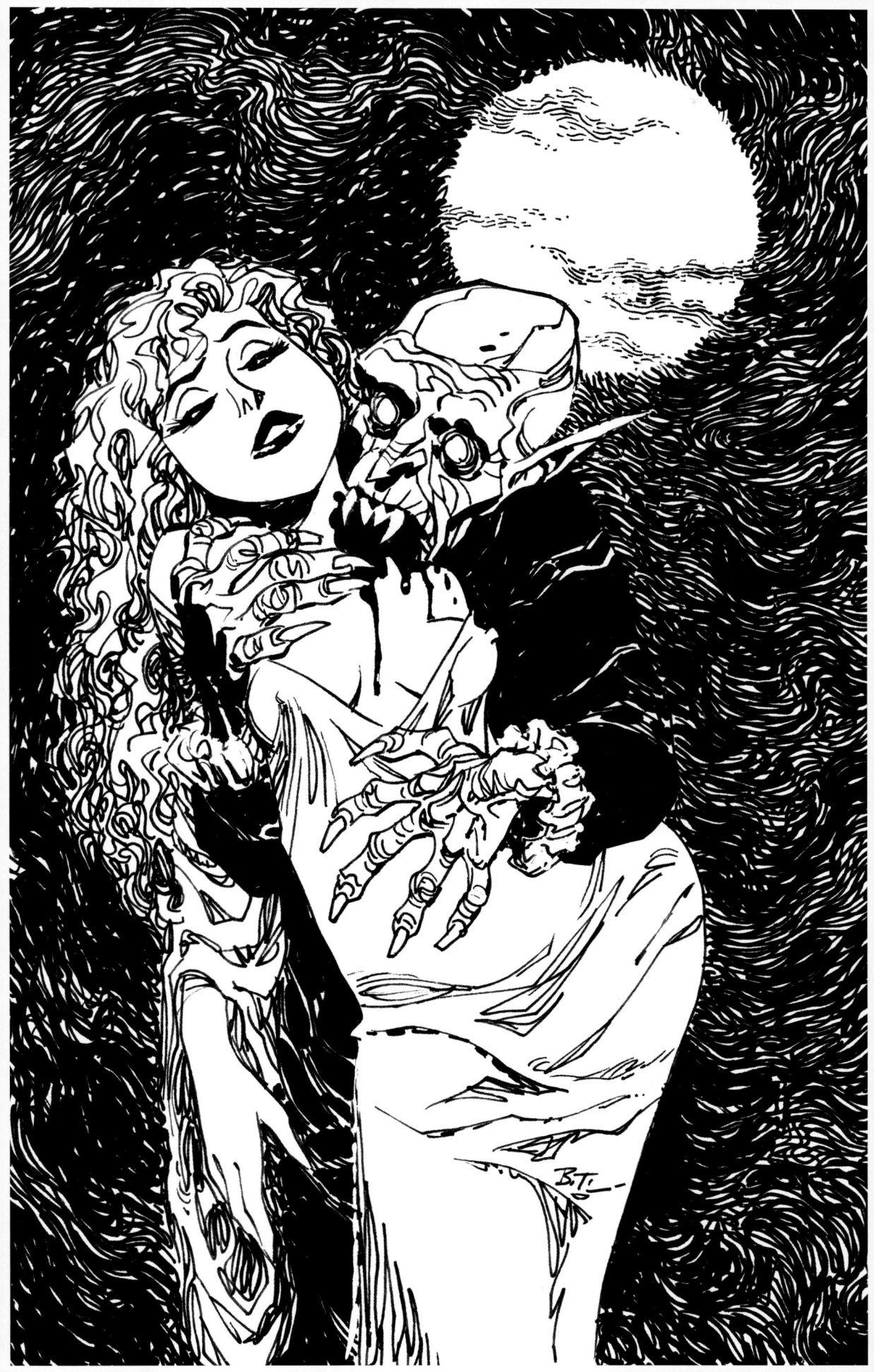

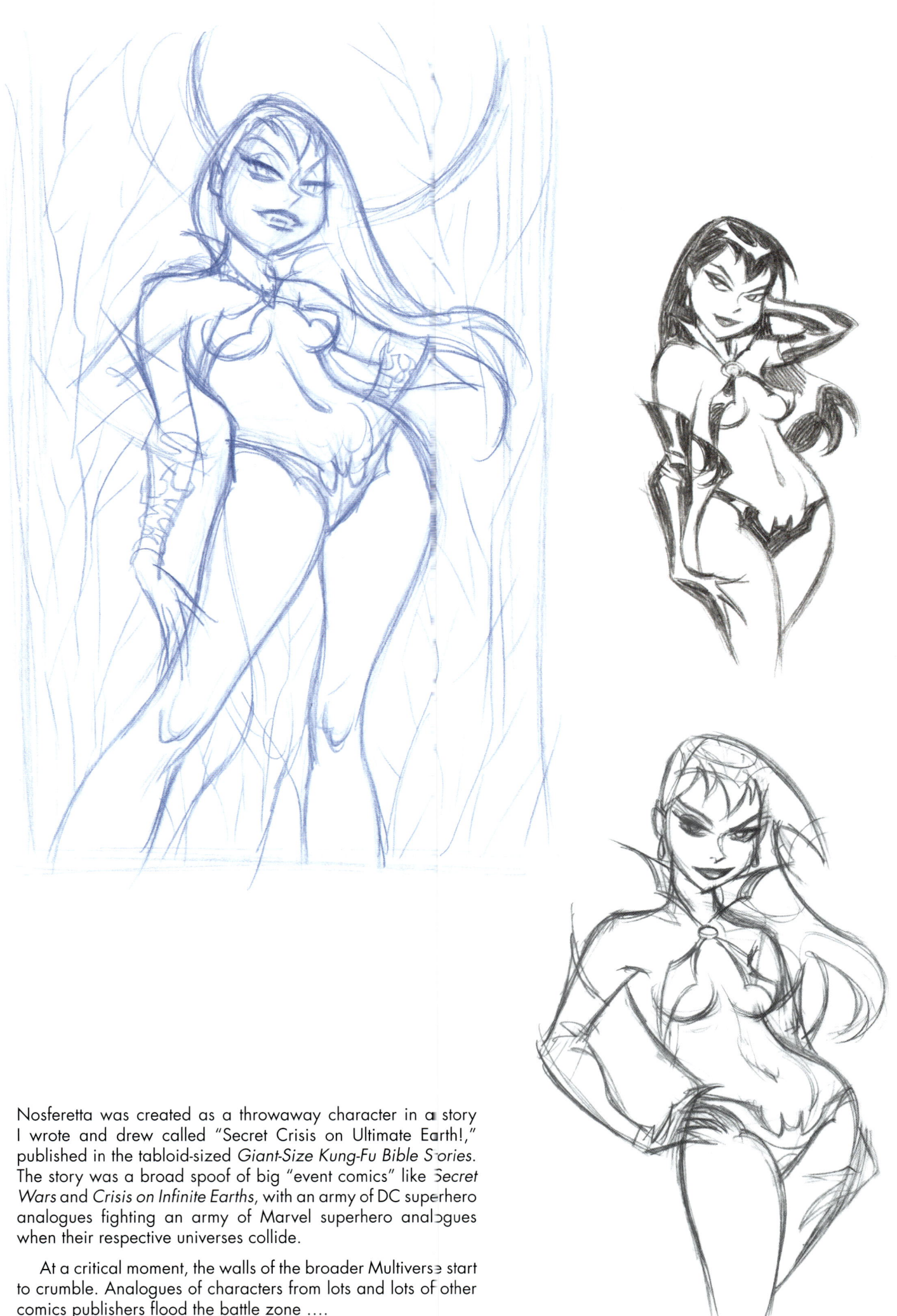

Nosferetta was created as a throwaway character in a story I wrote and drew called "Secret Crisis on Ultimate Earth!," published in the tabloid-sized *Giant-Size Kung-Fu Bible Stories*. The story was a broad spoof of big "event comics" like *Secret Wars* and *Crisis on Infinite Earths*, with an army of DC superhero analogues fighting an army of Marvel superhero analogues when their respective universes collide.

At a critical moment, the walls of the broader Multiverse start to crumble. Analogues of characters from lots and lots of other comics publishers flood the battle zone ….

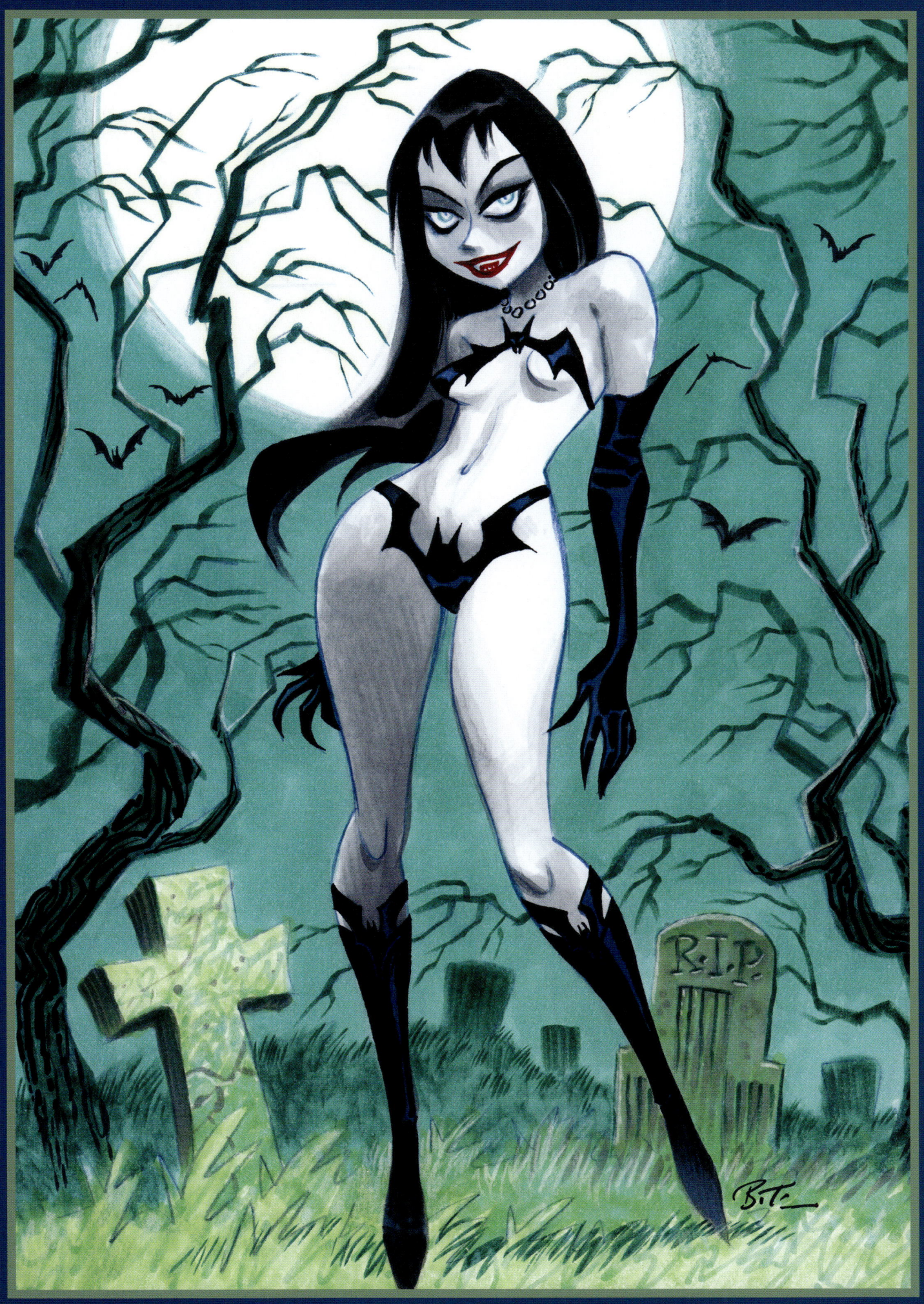

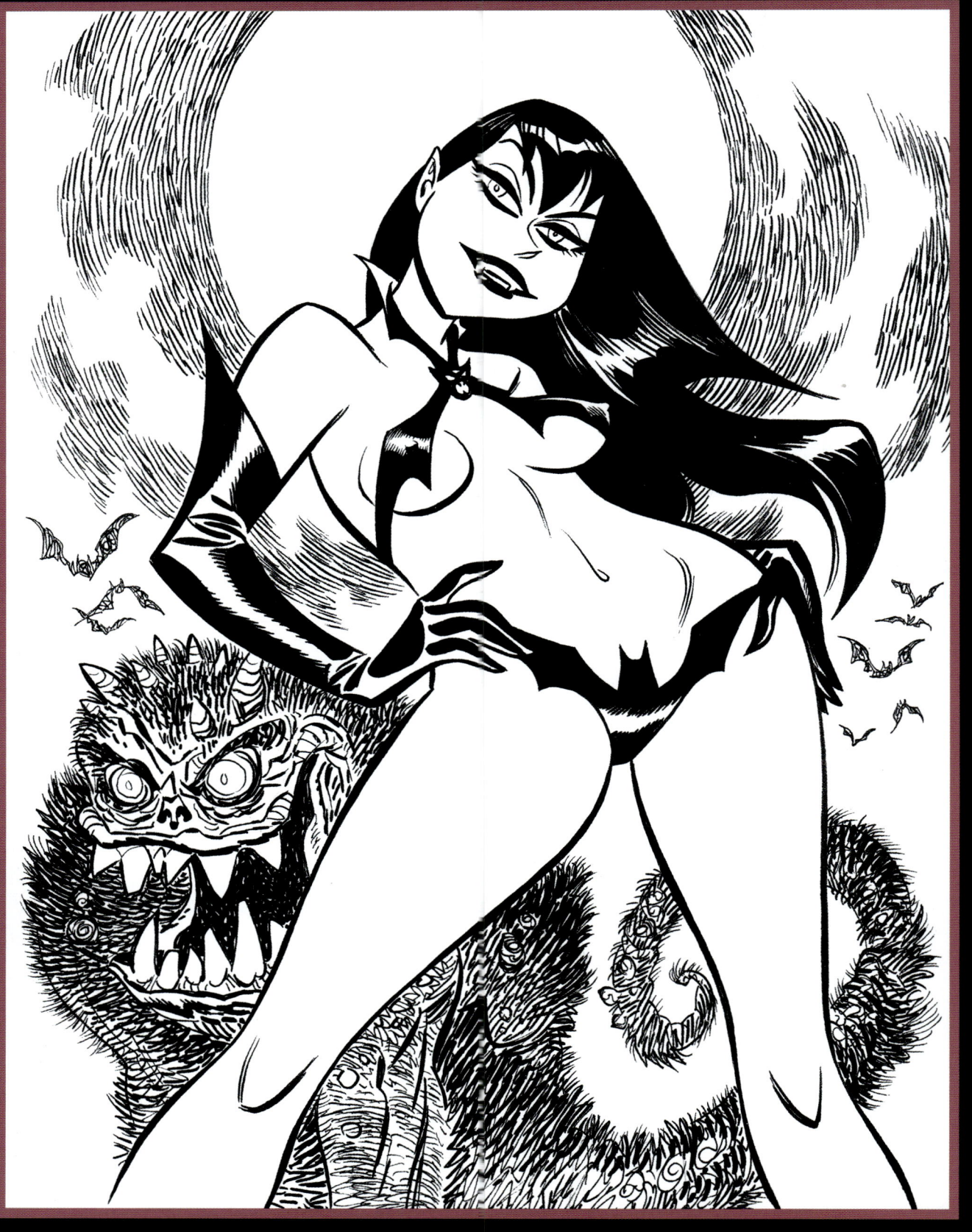

My barely dressed vampire girl appears in just a single panel of "Secret Crisis," but I like her design so much that I occasionally get the urge to draw her—just for my own amusement. A fan bought the above black & white drawing and then commissioned me to do a full-color version of it. Sometimes the qualities that make a successful black-and-white piece get lost in the process of converting the picture to color. Happily, that didn't happen in this case (in my opinion). I actually like them both about equally.

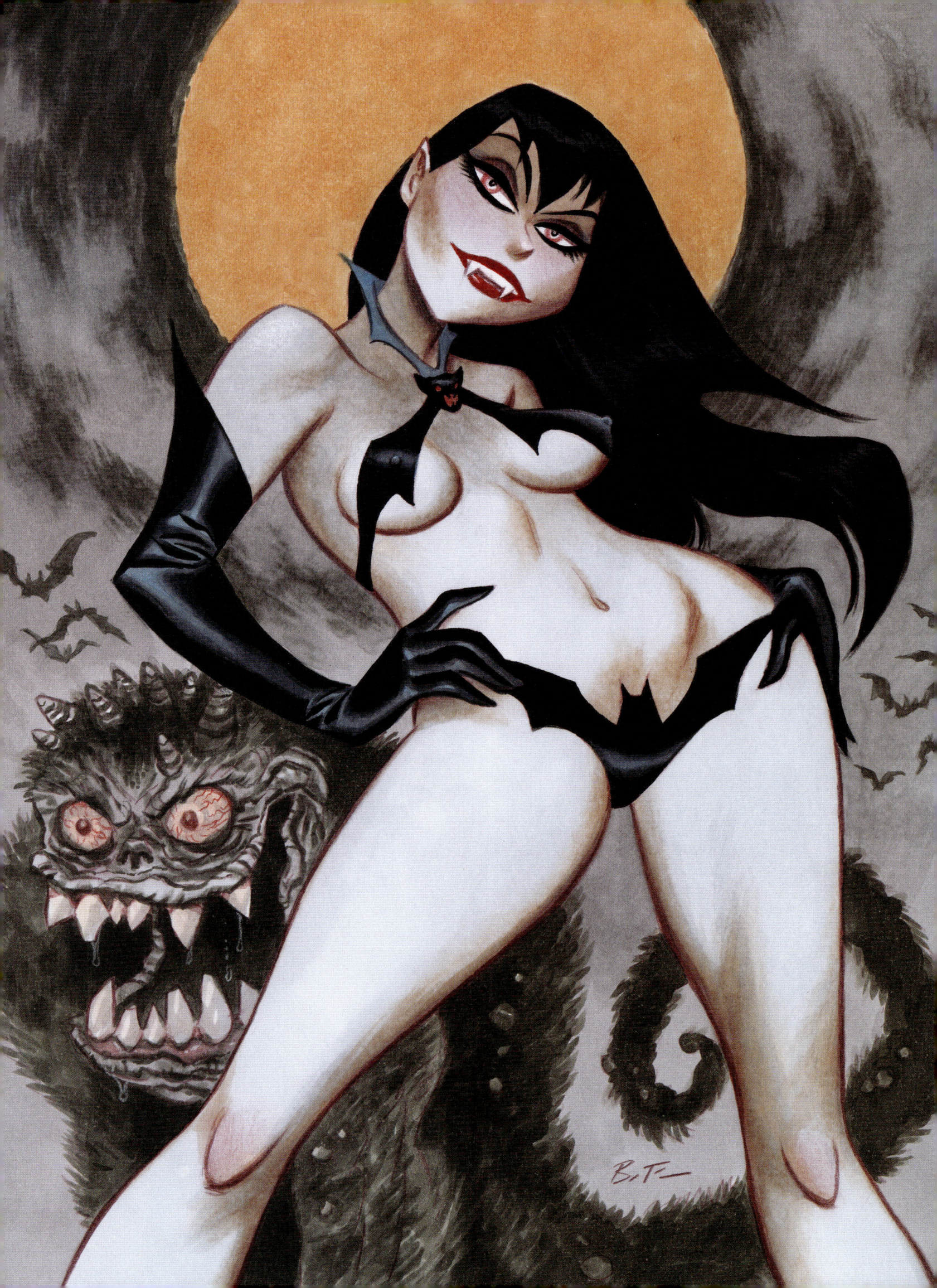

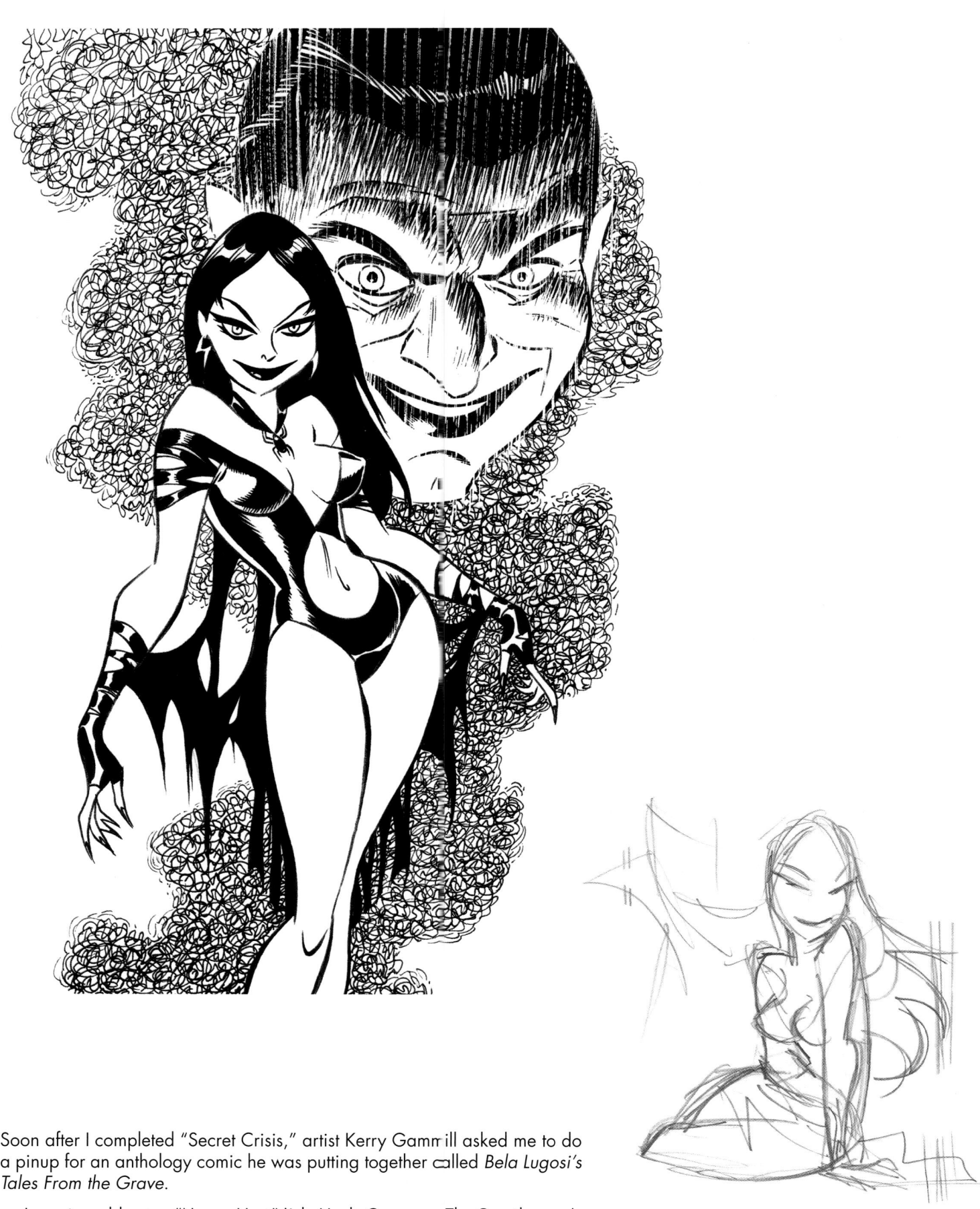

Soon after I completed "Secret Crisis," artist Kerry Gammill asked me to do a pinup for an anthology comic he was putting together called *Bela Lugosi's Tales From the Grave.*

Lugosi would act as "Horror Host" (à la Uncle Creepy or The Cryptkeeper), introducing the individual stories in a somewhat tongue-in-cheek manner. To make things even more interesting, Kerry gave Lugosi a sidekick—a sexy redheaded vampire girl named Nosferella. I laughed when I heard the name and told him, "Full disclosure, I have a sexy vampire girl named Nosferetta appearing in a story coming out soon." Fortunately, the two ladies look nothing alike.

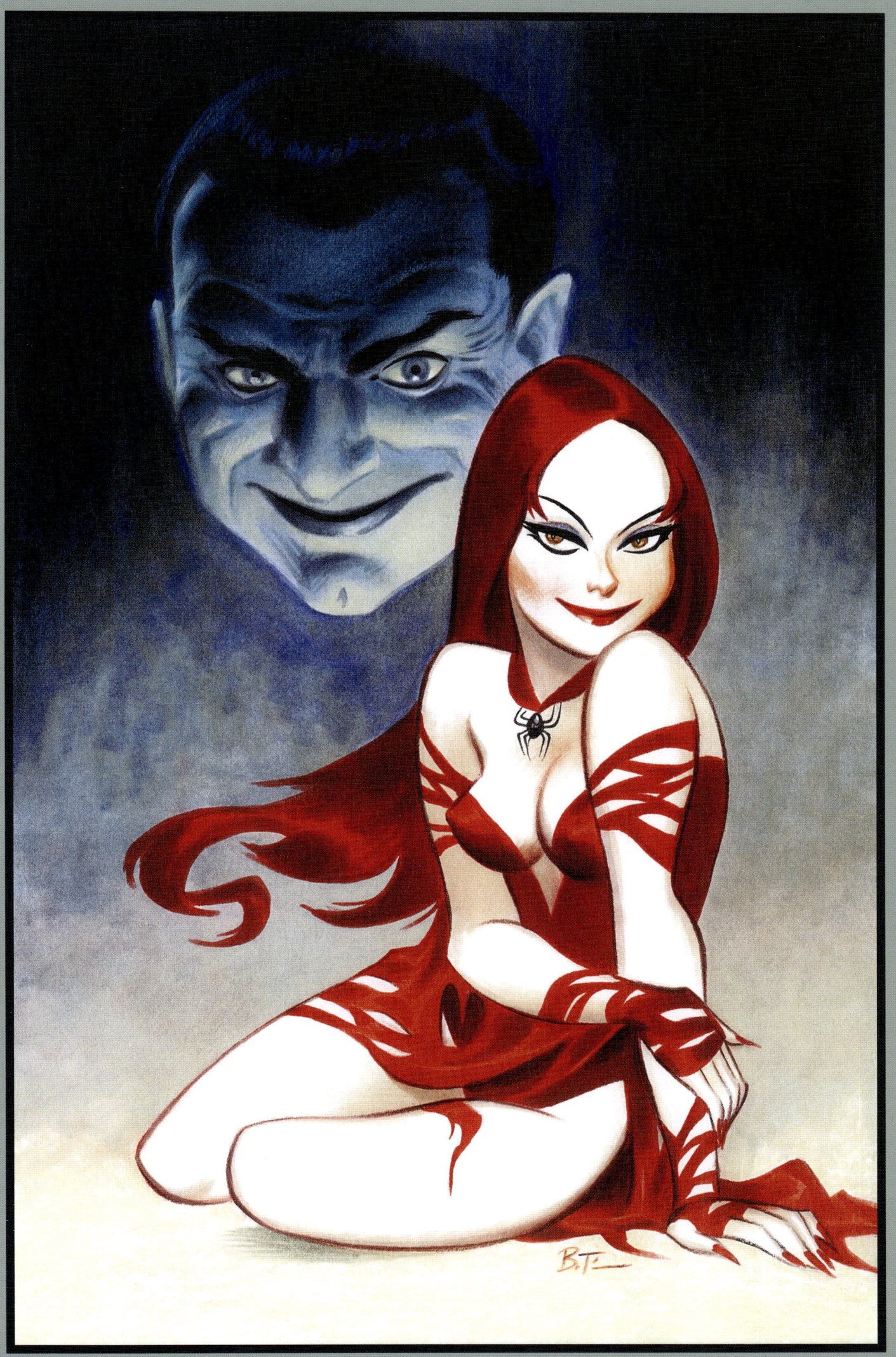

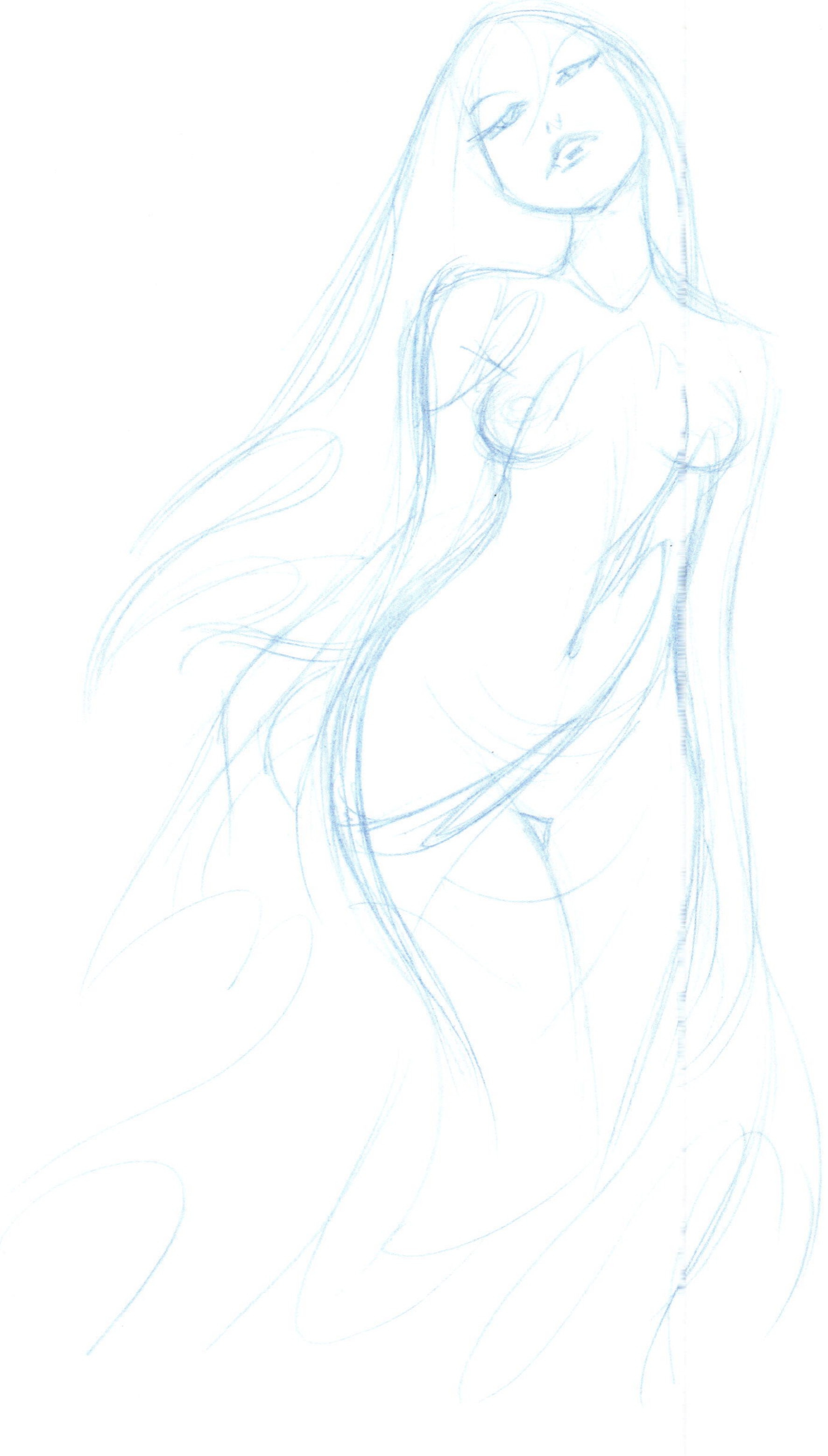

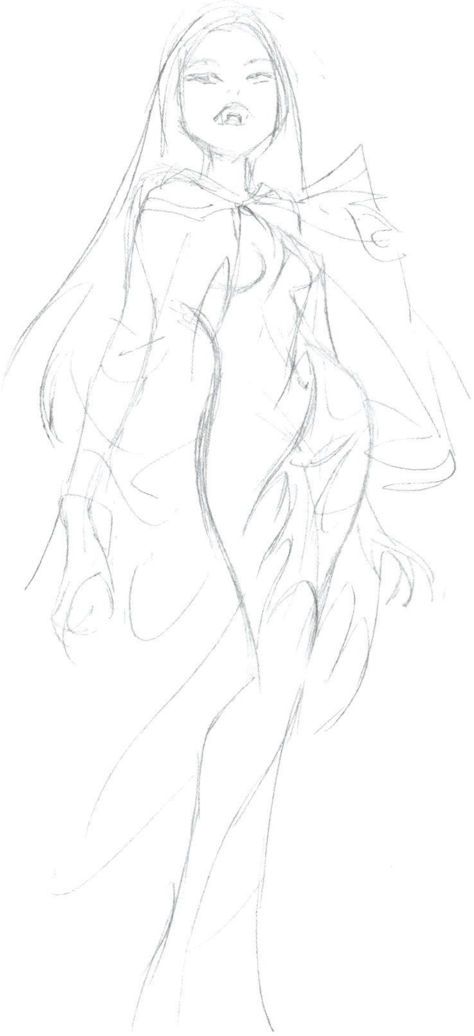

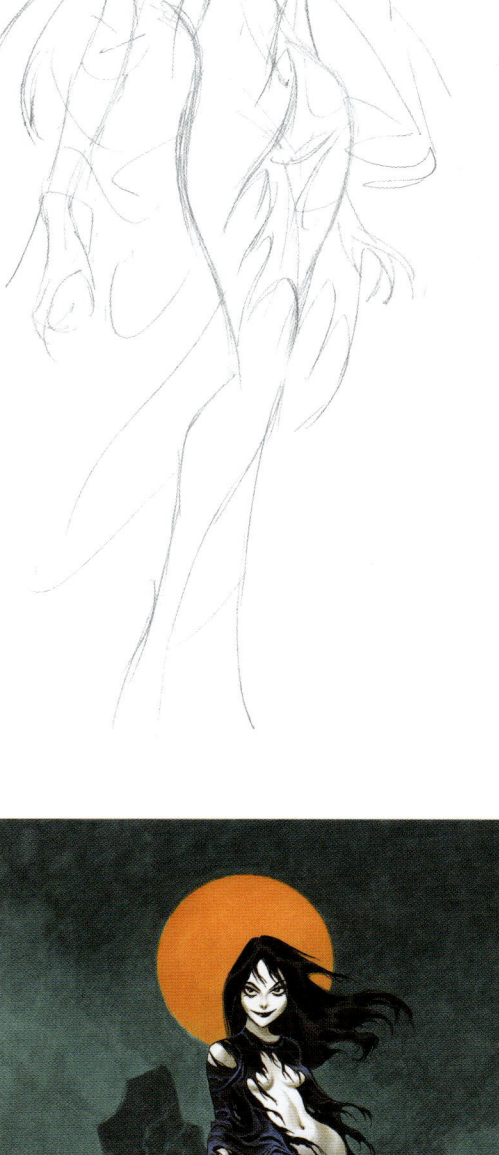

For this *Monsters and Dames* piece, I drew the vampire girl, her pet werewolf and the rocky foreground in black ink, then added the color on a black-and-white Xerox copy of the line art. I thought the result looked pretty sharp. I wanted to use the black & white version in this book, but there was just way too much empty space without the moon and distant rock formations. It would have been easier to add some background elements in marker or soft pencil, but I opted to stay consistent with the line-art aesthetic of the foreground figures and rendered them in ink. My hand was pretty cramped after several hours of vigorous cross-hatching, but I think it was worth it.

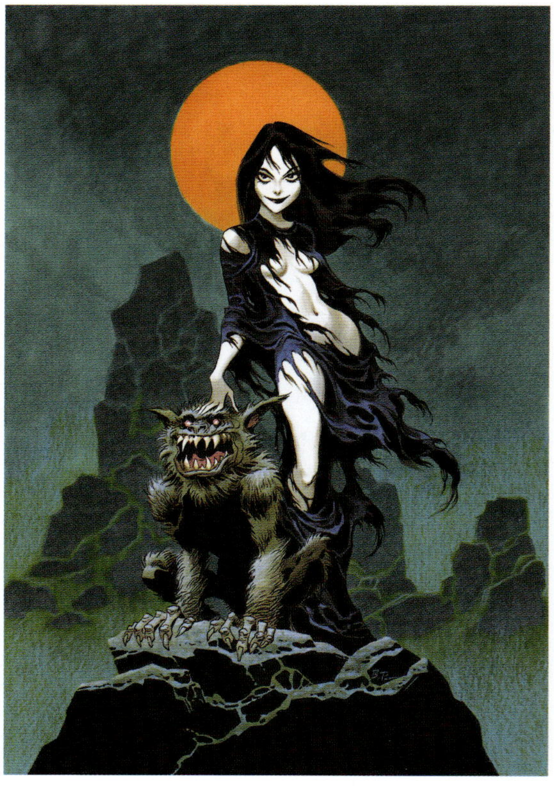

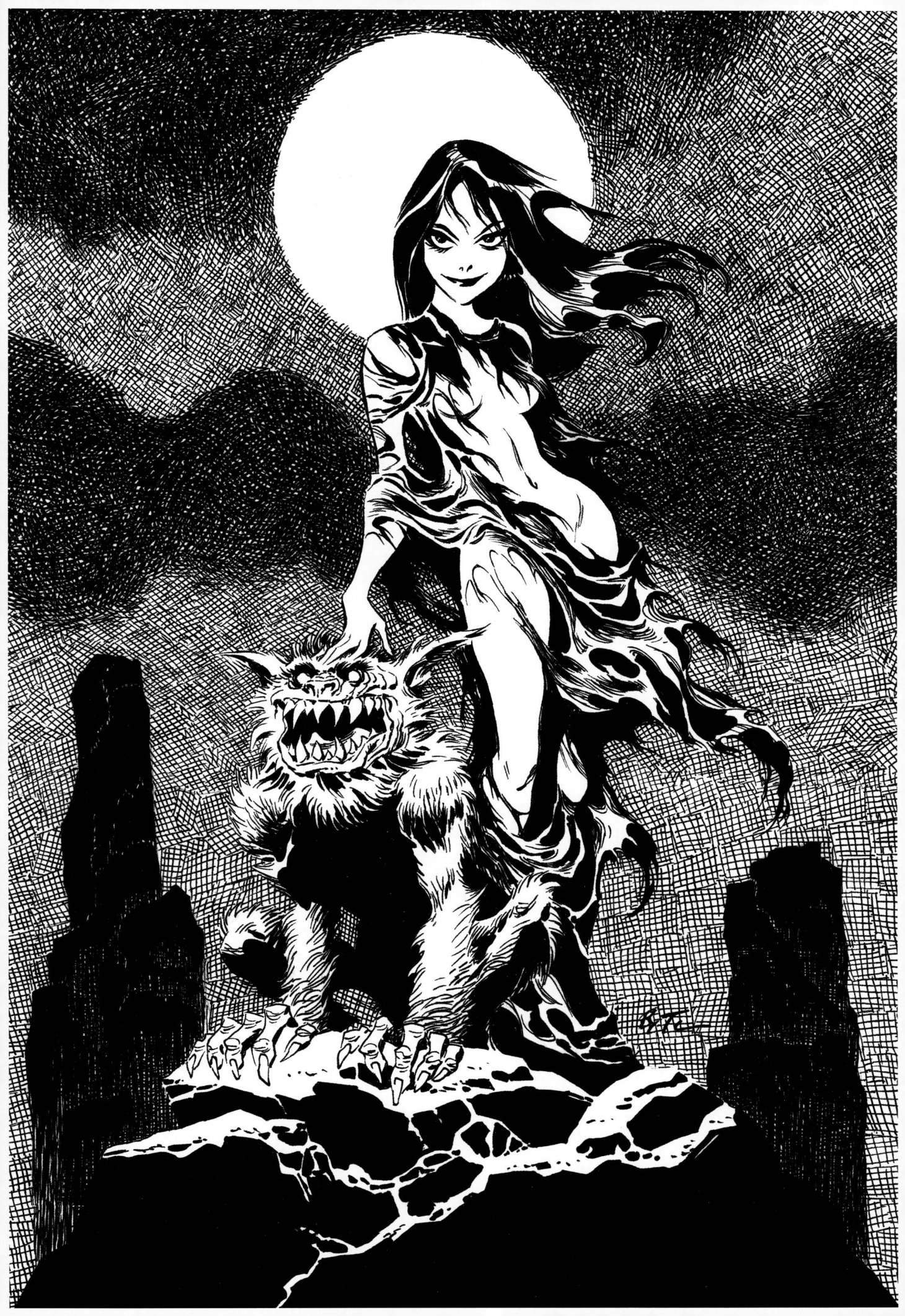

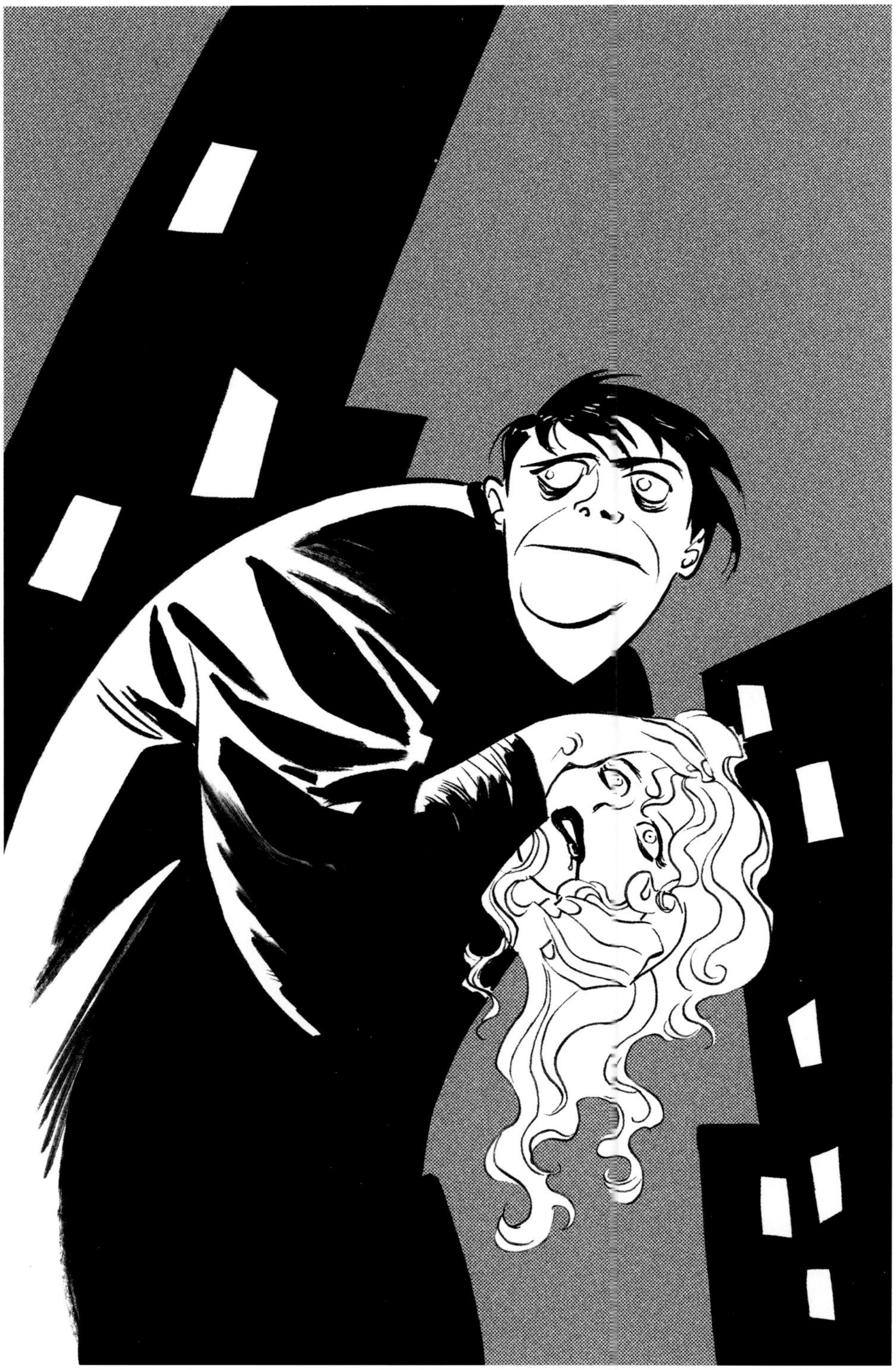

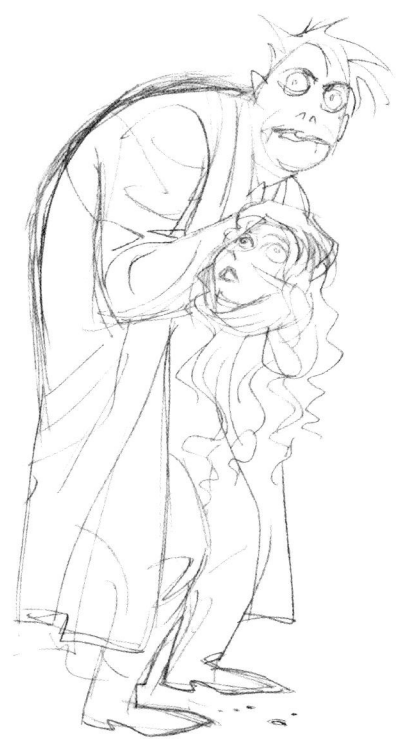

The basic idea behind these creepy images just came to me one day: a vaguely Peter Lorre-ish serial killer and his latest victim in a distorted German Expressionist city. It's just kind of a weird, random idea. I've drawn different versions of it over the years. I like that the lady looks startled but not completely horrified. Who knows, maybe she's not even a real person. She could just be a figure from the wax museum that he became obsessed with.

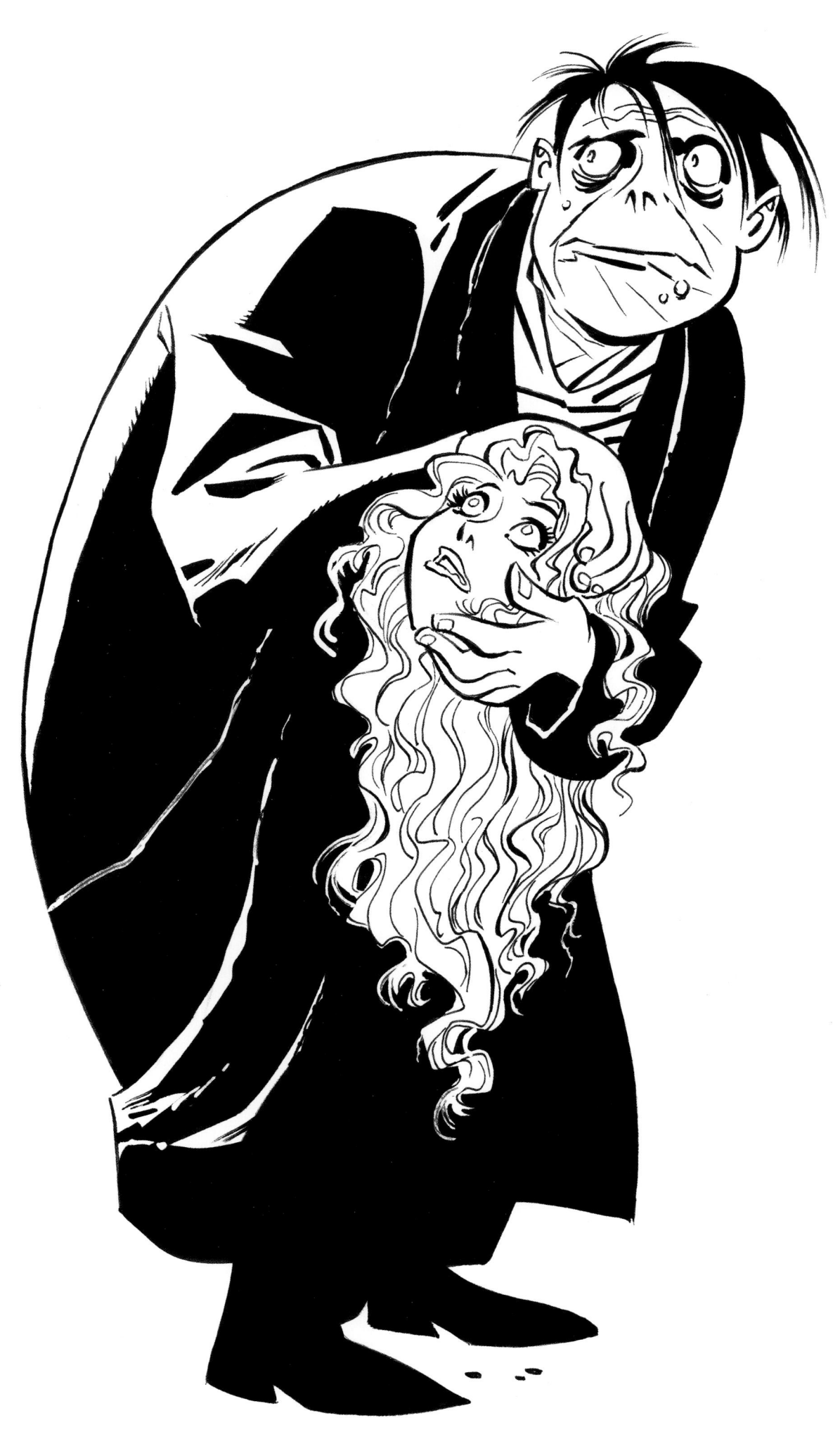

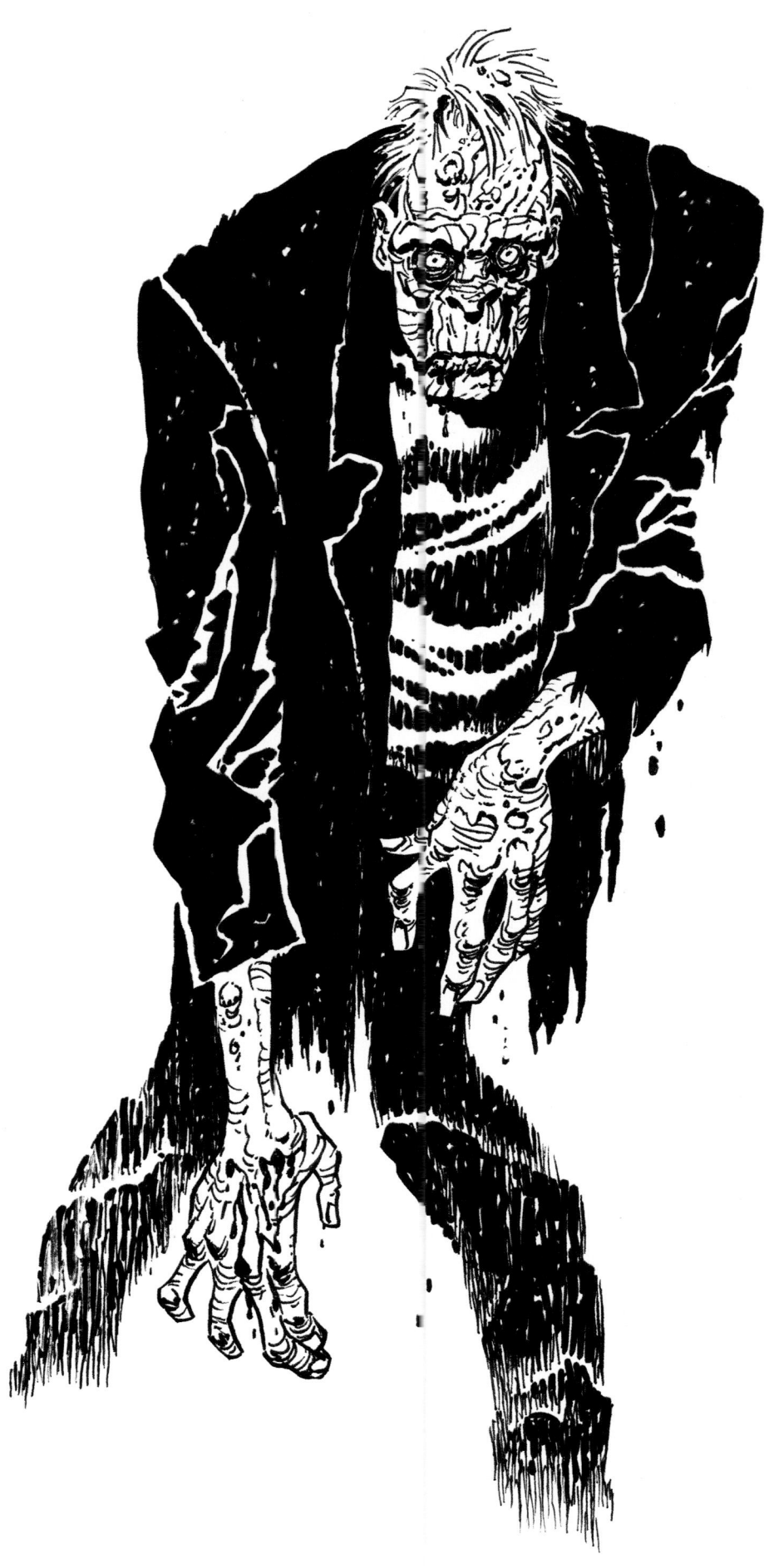

I'm not a huge fan of zombie movies, but I've always loved George Romero's *Night of the Living Dead*. I recently re-watched it and thought it was still creepy as hell. Here's a somewhat *NOTLD*-ish shambler.

The concept for this piece (opposite), which I did for the 2015 *Monsters and Dames* book, popped into my head pretty much fully formed. I don't remember doing a bunch of preliminary sketches for it. As I recall, it took just a few hours, start to finish. Oh, if only it was always that easy!

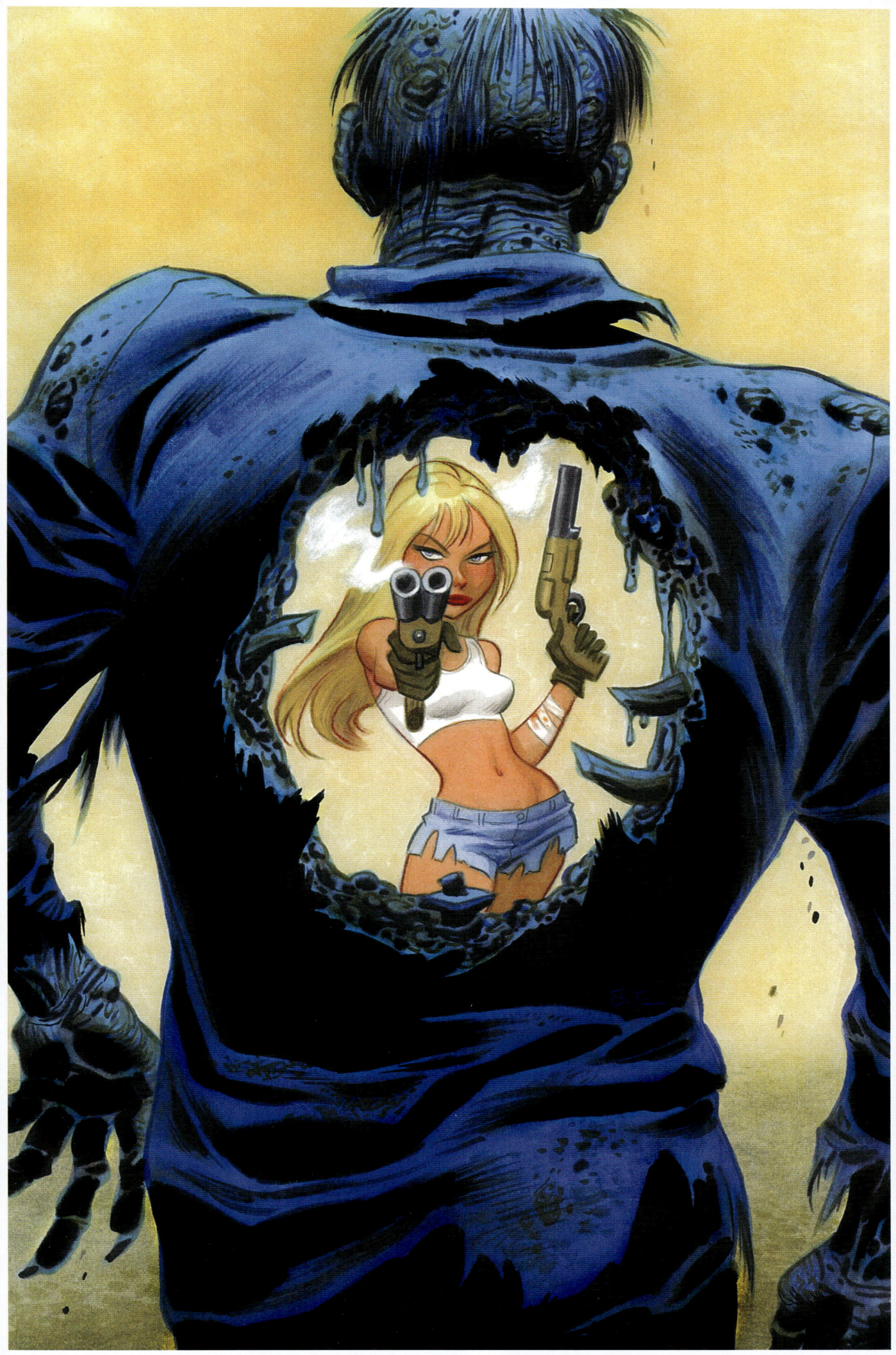

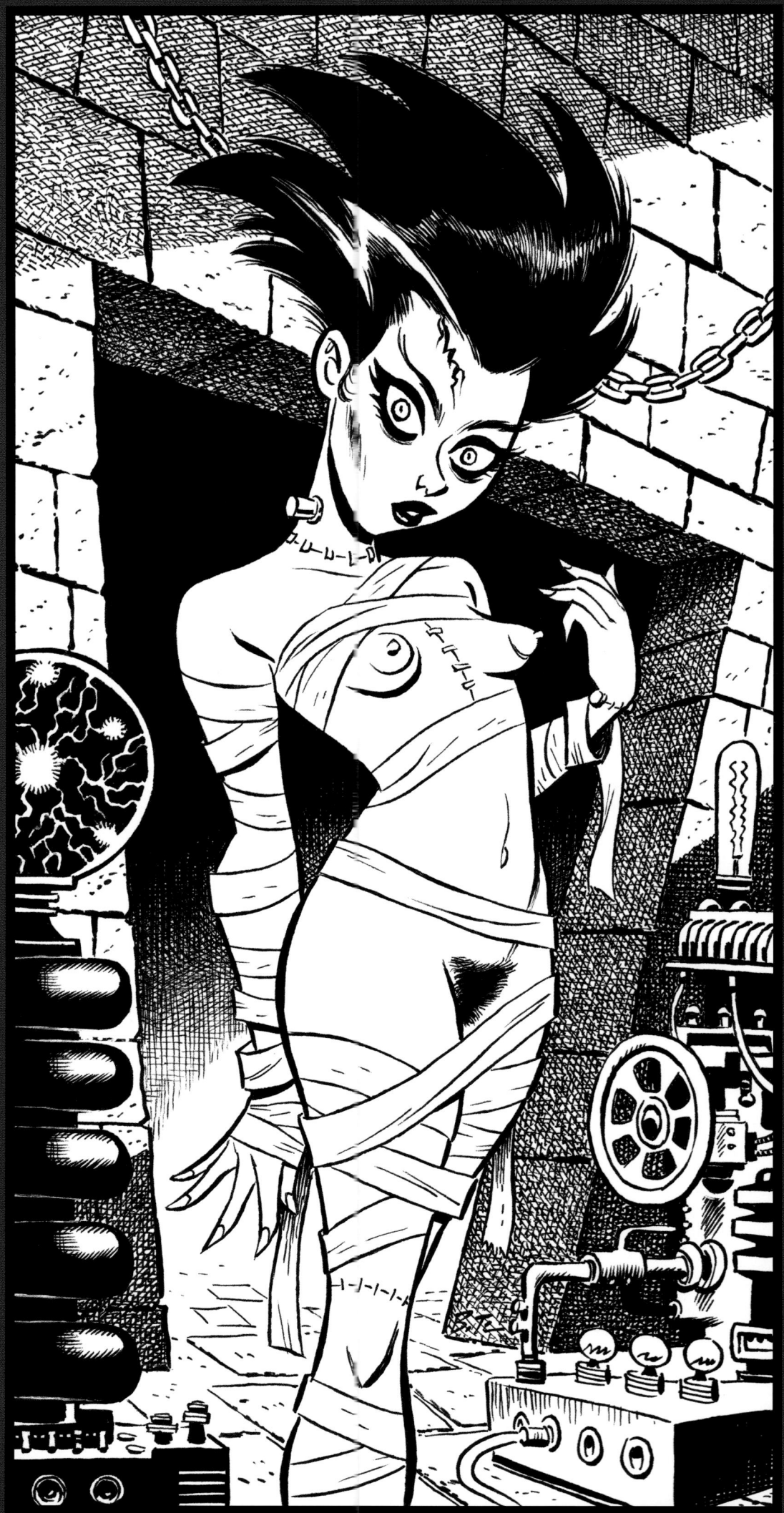

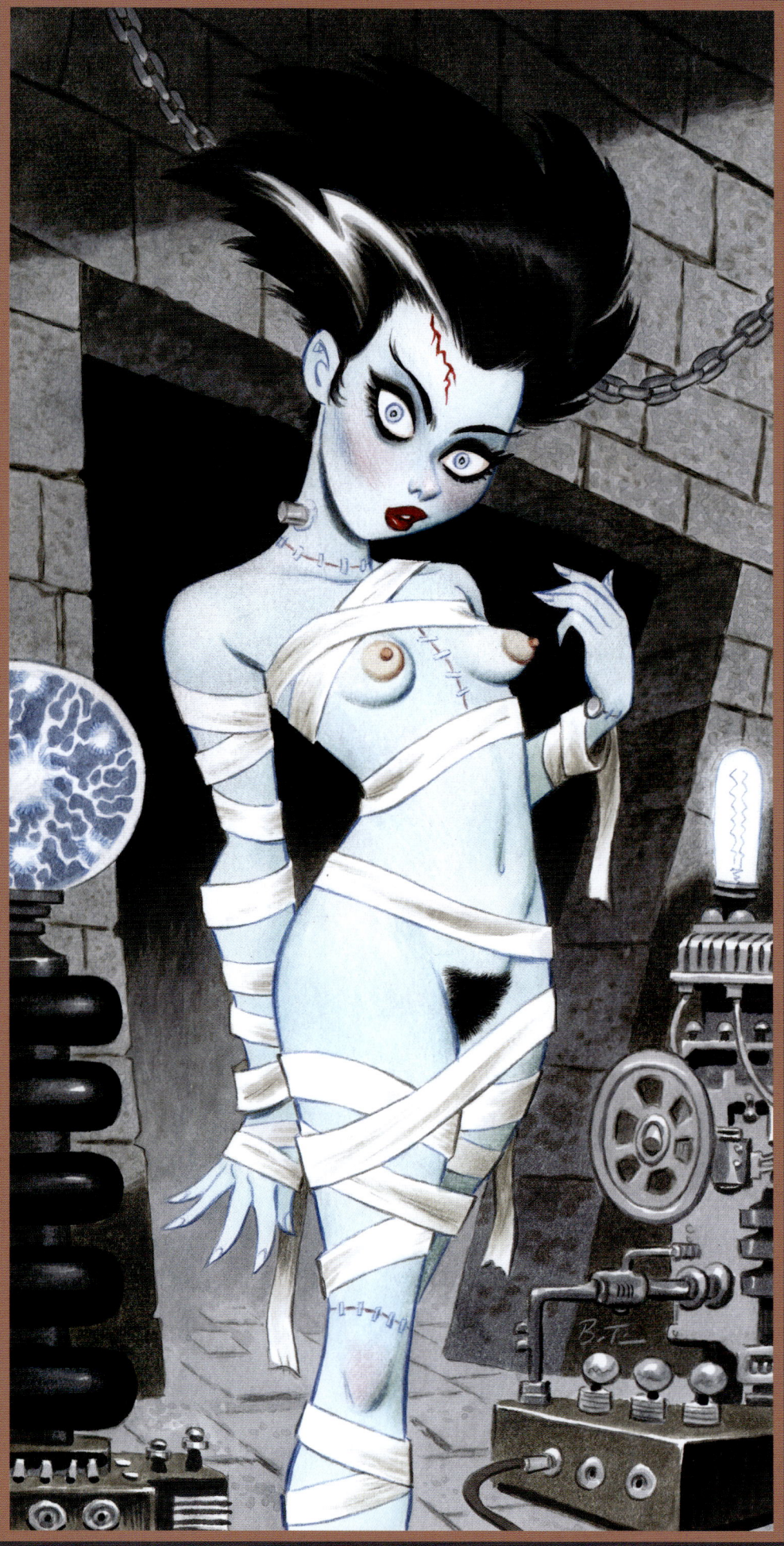

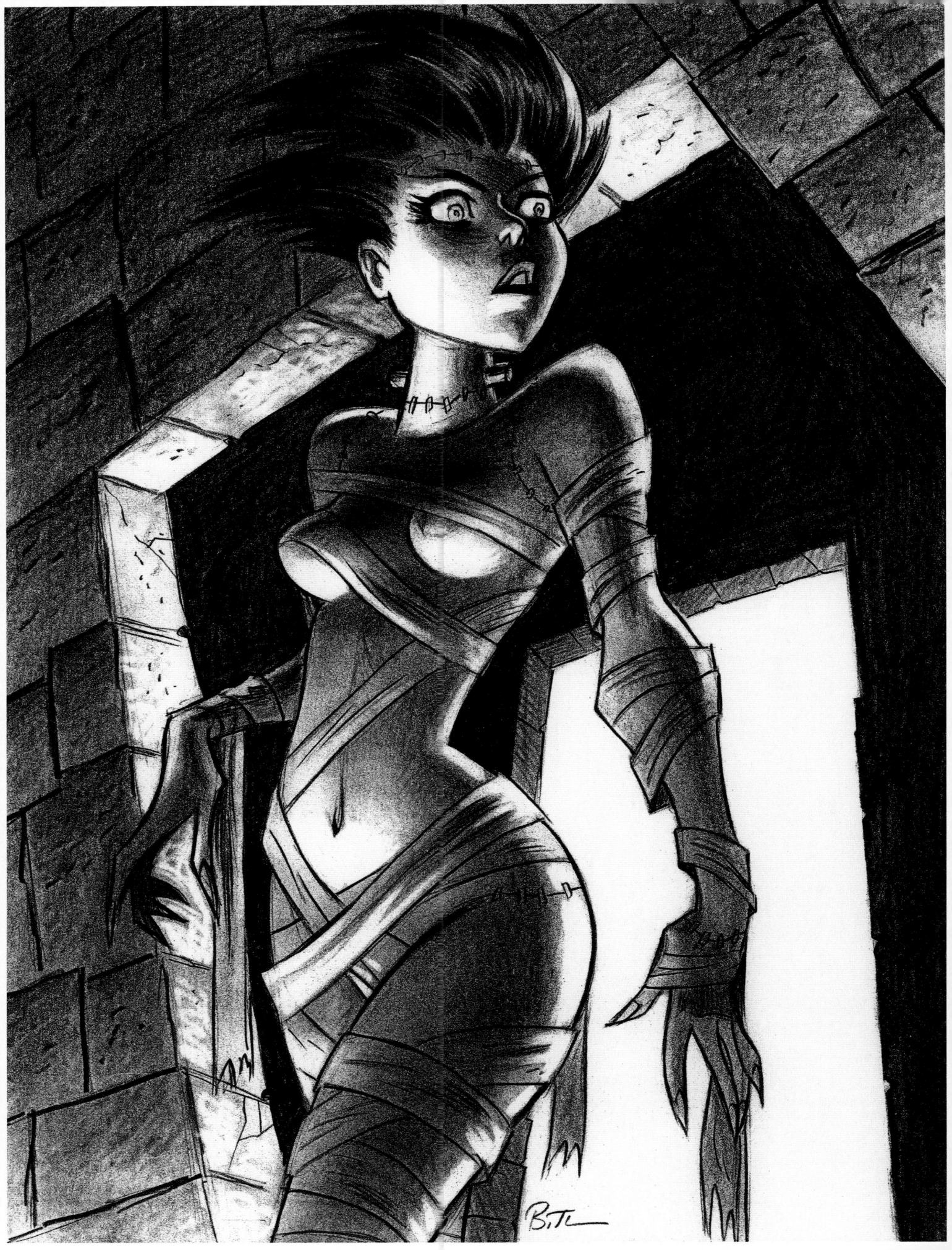

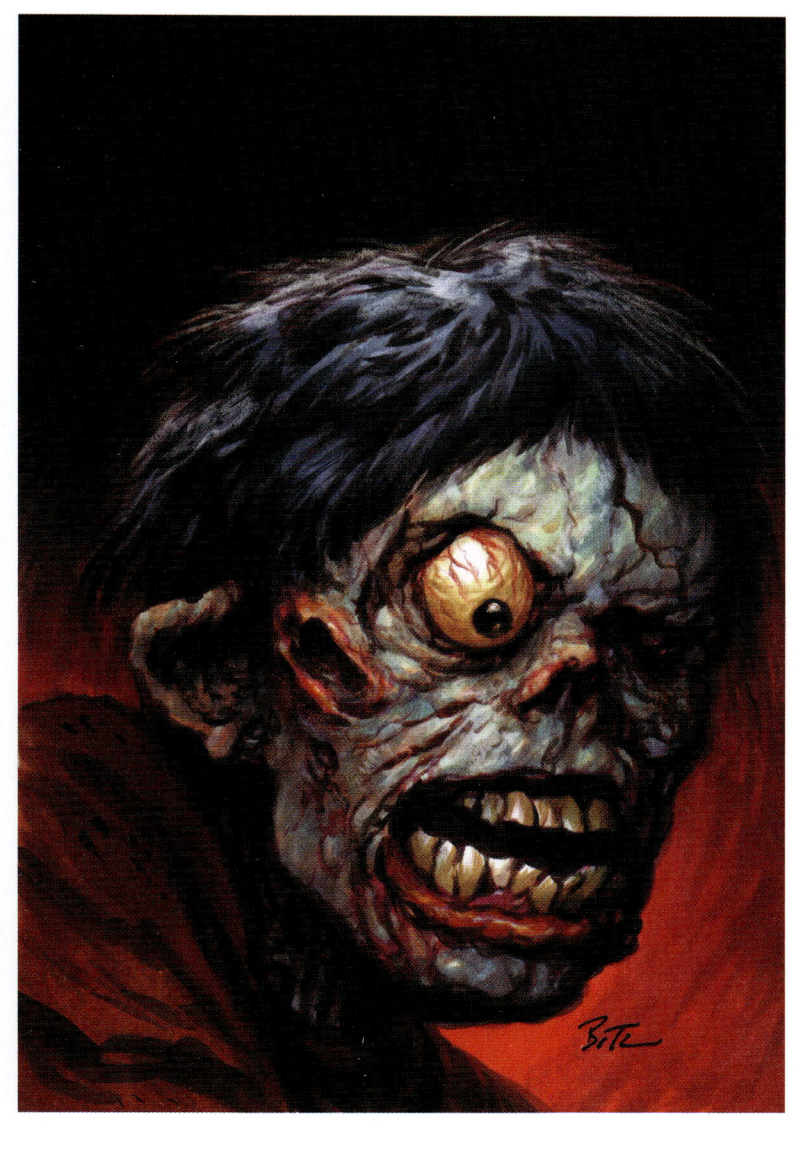

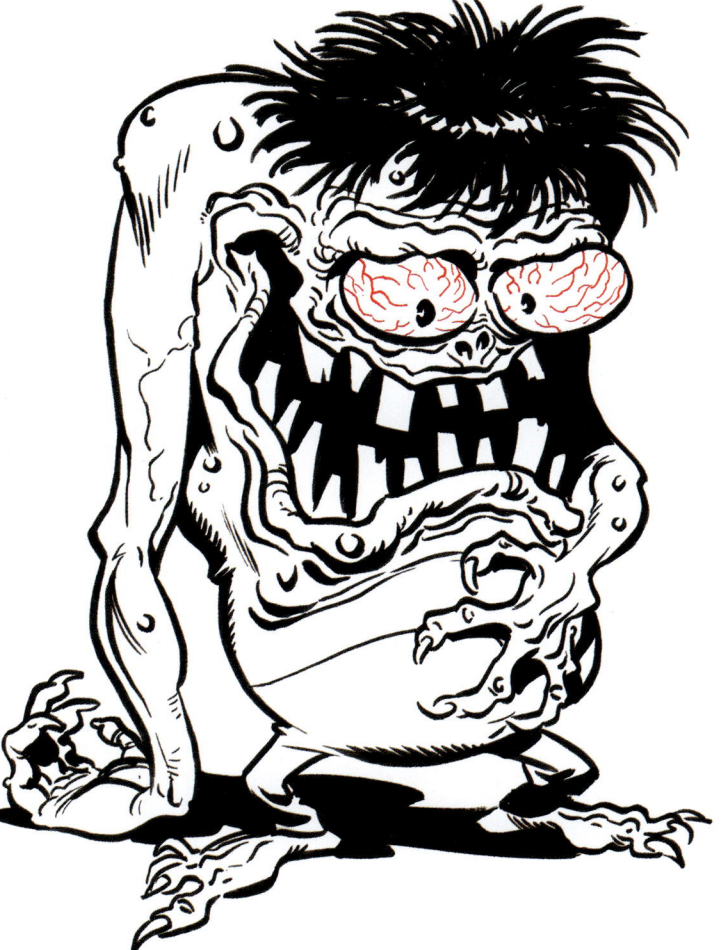

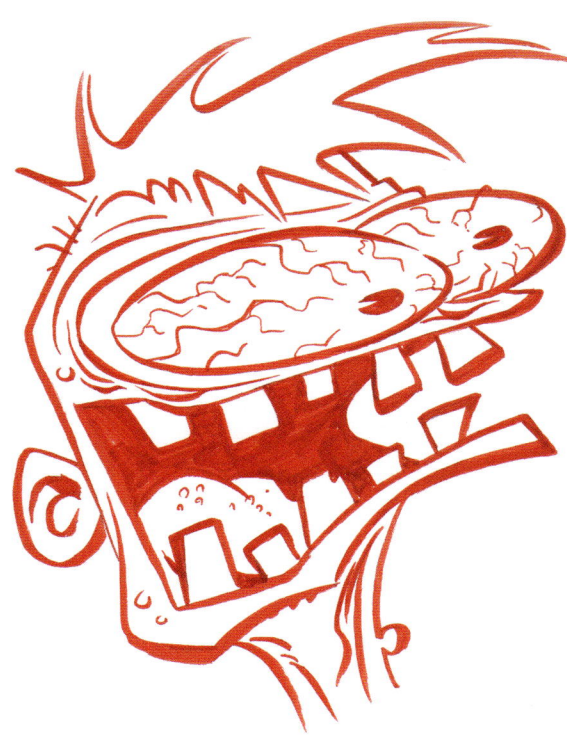

Opposite page and the previous two: Some sexy Brides. 'Nuff said.

Top Left: My attempt at doing a Basil Gogos-ish rendering of the Monster Kid-era icon called the Shock Monster. This guy was *everywhere* in the 1960s. There was a popular inexpensive rubber mask as well as trading cards, T-shirts, stickers … you name it.

Top right and bottom left: These handsome dudes were inspired by the collision of *MAD* magazine, movie monsters and hot rod/car culture that resulted in Big Daddy Roth's Rat Fink, the Weird-Ohs and Nutty Mads T-shirts, toys and model kits.

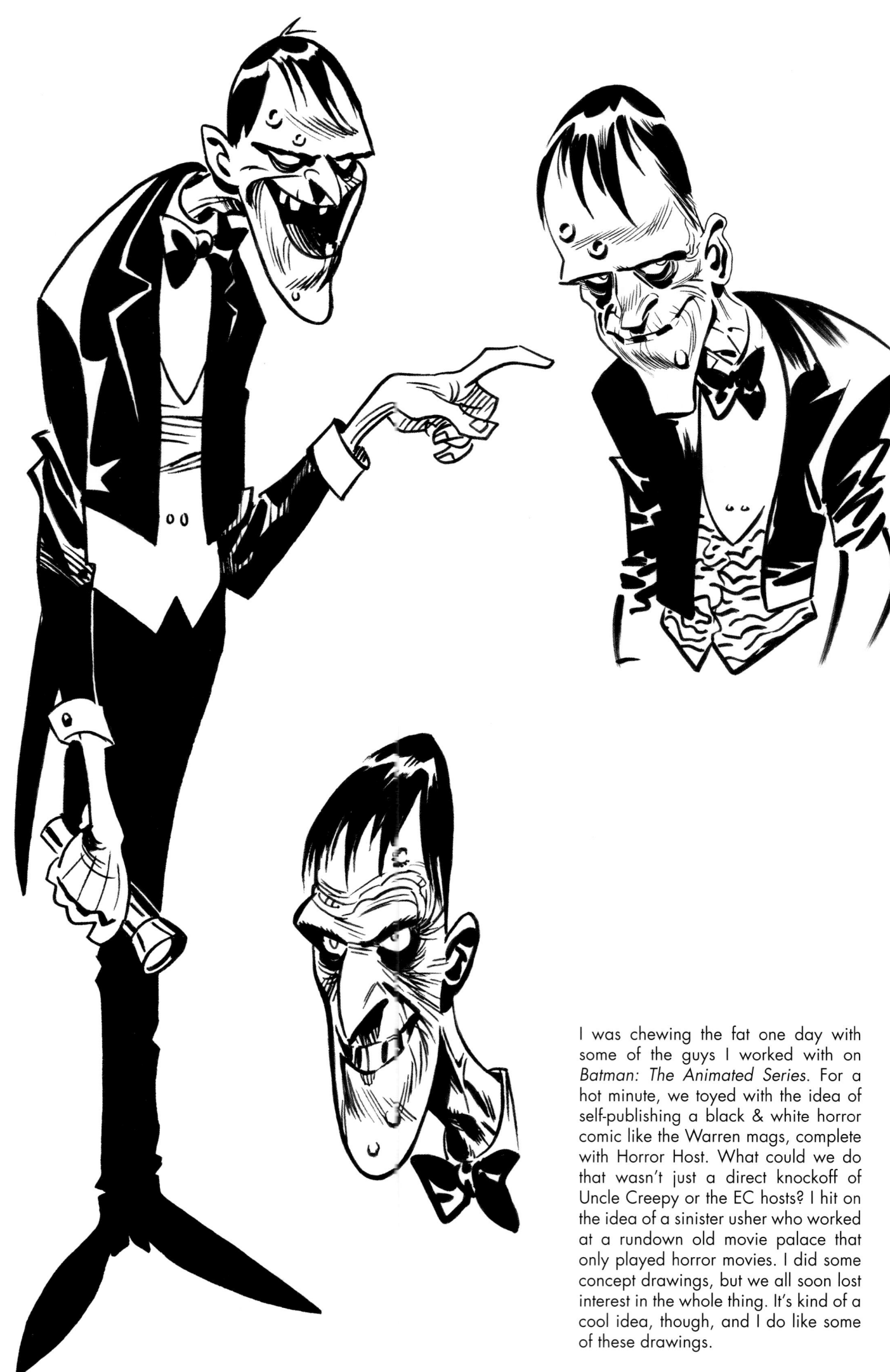

I was chewing the fat one day with some of the guys I worked with on *Batman: The Animated Series*. For a hot minute, we toyed with the idea of self-publishing a black & white horror comic like the Warren mags, complete with Horror Host. What could we do that wasn't just a direct knockoff of Uncle Creepy or the EC hosts? I hit on the idea of a sinister usher who worked at a rundown old movie palace that only played horror movies. I did some concept drawings, but we all soon lost interest in the whole thing. It's kind of a cool idea, though, and I do like some of these drawings.

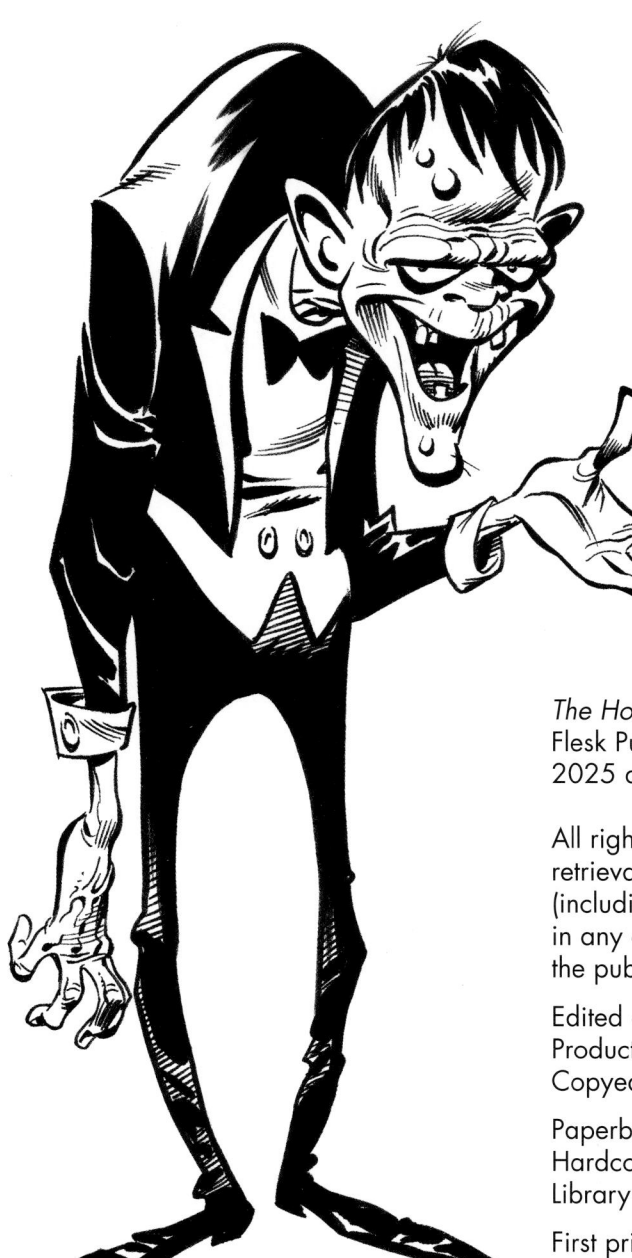

Edited and designed by John Fleskes and Bruce Timm
Production assistance by Vicky Lien
Copyedited by Martin Timins

Paperback edition ISBN: 978-1-64041-100-5
Hardcover edition ISBN: 978-1-64041-099-2
Library of Congress Control Number: 2025942386

First printing
December 2025

Thank you to Steven Bello, John Butler, Jim Demonakos and Wayne Mousseau for art scans on pages 1, 14 (bottom), 26,and 54 (bottom right). Big thanks to Richard "Dick" Klemensen's and his *Little Shoppe of Horrors* magazine, and to Glen Murakami for the pumpkin.
Printed in China
Asia One Printing Limited, Hong Kong

www.fleskpublications.com

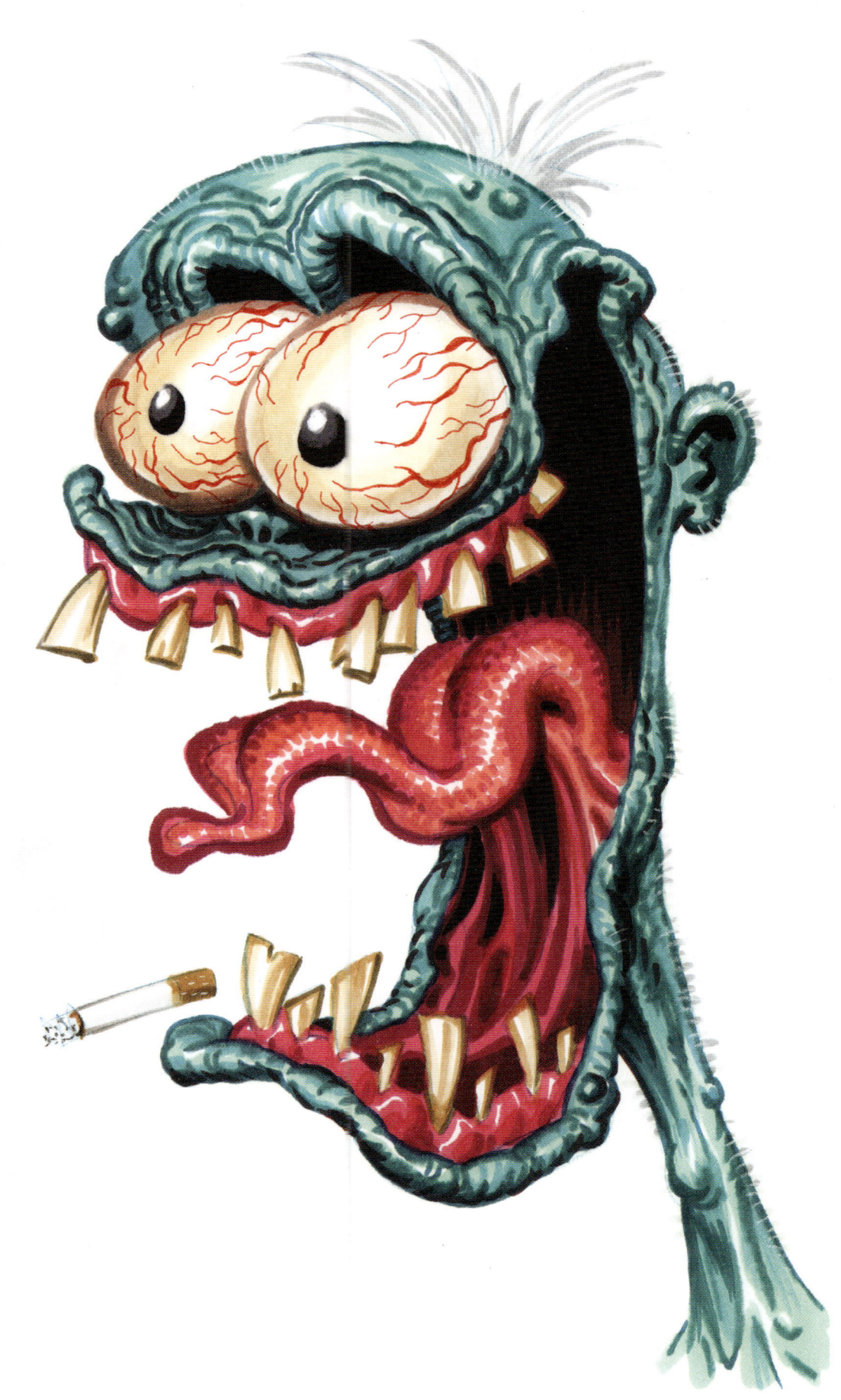